"Enlightenment is not a destination, it is a way of traveling."

- Wayne Dyer

"Enlightenment is the ability to see peace in any situation."

- Nisargadatta Maharaj

Onami House Media

Box 768

Santa Fe, NM

87321

Printed in the United States of America

Any quotes from *A Course in Miracles* are from the first, original edition also known as the UrText, copyright free.

Publisher's Cataloging-in-Publication data

Onami House

A title of a book: a subtitle of the same book / Onami House

ISBN 9798369699713

The main category of the book —Self Help —Other category. 2. Another subject category —Education. 3. More categories —And their modifiers. I. Onami House. II. Title. HF0000.A0 A00 2030

299.000 00–dc22 2010989999

Second Edition

1413128110/10987654321

Introduction:

I started writing this book on December 31, 2016, because I knew 99% of my mom's drama would go away if she read *A Course in Miracles* and practiced a bit of magic. *A Course in Miracles* taught me how to forgive, low and slow with a lot of repetition over the course of a year. I felt like that book was a great starting place, but she (like me) felt ACIM was too difficult to understand and too long as well. No one in our family has that kind of time, or patience. I translated *A Course in Miracles* into terms she could understand, one page a day and add whatever I felt would round out the practice perfectly. She loves Chicken Soup for the Soul and other daily bites of spirituality. She needed something she could leave on her bedside table, throw in her purse, or, best: leave in the bathroom.

It was about 6 pm on the 31st of December when I got bored of watching Narcos on my mom's couch, where I had been posted for a few months. I decided to translate all 365 lessons of *A Course in Miracles* for her. I had read it a couple of times but was ready to move on, and a law of teachings says that you can't reach the next step until you put someone else on the step you're leaving. When you teach something in your own words, you master it.

I decided I would sell a lesson per day as an automated email series. By the end of the year, I would have 365 pages, which was basically a book. I wasn't sure if I could legally translate ACIM (first edition, A OKAY!), and I also knew that once you start writing, the whole concept of the book can change, so I didn't want to commit. It's a lot easier to talk about writing a book than it is to write one, and I basically only get shit done if there's a deadline attached to it. There's also the first draft, the second draft, and the final edit, which need to be done. This has taken me four years to complete, but I got paid the whole time while retaining all rights to whatever it was and whatever it would morph into. If I can do it with 24-hour notice, you can do it too.

I posted on my Instagram that I had a 365-day course available for $28, so you could work with me for a whole year for just $28. I sold about 15 subscriptions, and I was stoked! I also remembered something very valuable I was bringing to this course.

I had bought *A Course in Miracles* and threw it away twice before I was desperate enough to get through the salvation sludge. I had SUCH a hard time with the Jesus language. Words like "sonship" and "atonement" sent my recovering inner agnostic into religious PTSD. You know Jesus is like spinach, right? If you're forced to have it as a kid, you'll hate it as an adult.

Studying the Course is like getting your first coaching degree. I taught almost exclusively what I had learned in ACIM from 2015-17, so this education wasn't just helping me, it was helping me support myself. $28 (the price of ACIM on Amazon) was not a lot to put down on spiritual tuition. The hidden price is that ACIM is hard as hell to understand. It's long and occasionally rambling. It's a thick book, to begin with, then when you crack it open, you realize, "oh shit, these are Bible pages. You could roll a joint with these things! This is a long-ass book!"

Another hidden cost is that *A Course in Miracles* never addresses the concept of the shadow self, which is 50% of the work and marks a serious transition from Level One spirituality (exoteric teachings describing many different Gods) towards Level Two (mesoteric teachings explaining how it's all one God).

A year of your time is a lot, and a shiny new ACIM teacher is a pain in the ass with their "love and light will save the day" attitude. If you only study ACIM, you stay blissfully unaware of the impending Dark Night Of The Soul, which is where the real work begins. Because of this, I wanted to incorporate more advanced teachings and caveats into your first year of study with me. ACIM is a lot, a lot, a lot of repetition. By putting it into simpler terms, I had the space to incorporate and explain some supplemental teachings so you really see results.

Here's something they don't tell you about writing spiritual books:

By the time your book is done, you'll feel like it was a million years ago that this topic was doing it for you. You'll want to scrap the whole thing (many times) because you're a different person now! Don't.

I learned as a yoga teacher that even if visvamitrasana (side plank meets split meets bind meets leg behind the head) is what your daily practice is made of, you need to teach a beginner's class regularly. People want to study with you, and they want to study with you for a long time. Your customers have signed a spiritual contract to not ever understand these lessons until you teach them and in a language they understand. You have to keep a beginner's class somewhere for people just arriving into your world. Your spiritual contract requires it, and your people need you.

The main premise of ACIM is forgiveness and understanding how judgments force you to live in a sub-par world. With forgiveness, to make it stick, you have to keep hearing it repeatedly. Like a Tony Robbins book and *A Course in Miracles*, this has a lot of repetition. I repeat myself, on purpose, a lot!

As the daily repetitions of the Ashtanga primary series prepare you for defying gravity in the second series, a thorough understanding and application of forgiveness (Level One) is the only way you'll ever be able to surrender at Level Two. There's no way you will hand God the keys to the next decades of your life if you felt like you'd been done dirty for the last ones. You cannot skip this lesson, and after editing three drafts of this, I'm so proud of this work and the many lineages and levels it weaves into one beginner's manual.

The original title of this book was Entelechies (intelli-keys), a word I love that means "the realizations of potential." While it is the exact word for the exact thing that this book is, I couldn't release a book that swears to make difficult spiritual texts easy to understand and give it an unpronounceable name. I know it's unpronounceable because I've sold this book for three years under that title before sending it to print.

My first chef boss, Liza Queen, also had it tattooed on the back of her forearm, which I saw a lot of because I stood behind her for 12 hours at a time in the kitchen. During this time, I heard so many people trying to pronounce her tattoo and completely bungling it. Yes, it's my favorite word and would have been a great book title, but my #1 priority as a teacher is to keep it simple for you and not let a bunch of curlicued language and darling, poetic sentences stand in the way of simple, ancient truths.

I polled a few hundred people who had read the book on their opinions while I was changing the name, and while about 65% said "YES, DO IT!" 35% said some variation of "You're not doing your book justice naming it that." More significant was the three or four emails I got from the vegans informing me that if you have time to read in the bathroom - you're constipated.

For 15 years of my life, I never farted in front of anyone. I farted in a yoga class one time and never went back. I was so embarrassed. I kept the fact that I'm human and take shits a secret from basically everyone I knew and was horrified if anyone ever discussed having a shit.

Shortly before I met Magic, my husband, I spoke to a woman who had been married for decades and had never farted in front of her husband, and every time she used the bathroom, she went to the opposite end of the house armed with matches and a four-minute time limit. She reminded me of myself for most of my life.

"Perfect."

No one sees my bad side, no one sees my human side. I made a note on my mental vision board: "A relationship I'm TOTALLY comfortable in."

I definitely got it. The first timemy husband stayed the night at my house we had coffee in the morning, and he excused himself with his phone to go to the bathroom. A full forty minutes later, he returned like he hadn't just been gone forever. There was no problem, he wasn't constipated. The man simply has always been THE most secure person in the world and has always thoroughly enjoyed his morning shit AND talking about it for the better part of the morning.

Maybe this was normal behavior where you come from, but it wasn't for me! Me and every other woman I knew would straight up leave our boyfriend's house right when things were getting fun to go have a shit. Sometimes you'd love to spend all day with someone, but it's 9 AM and nature calls, and he has roommates. You can either book it home or go to the nearest coffee shop or crank the shower and give yourself 5 mins with the water running to take care of everything. It ain't easy being a woman, I'll tell you that!

I've always loved going to people's houses and seeing a comfortable bathroom. Reading material, a squatty potty and a candle? My kind of person! The most relaxed people I knew had the kind of bathrooms that said, "I enjoy my morning shit." Not "Nobody uses this room."

Once I became a mom, I valued that bathroom time even more; any mom will tell you sometimes that's the only free moment you get in a day. Milk it! ENJOY it.

Put this book in your bathroom, read it when you're in there, and you'll become enlightened in a year. Glamorous? No. Oxford approved? No. Totally fucking understandable and delivers exactly what it says it does? Yes. And remember:

Enlightenment is not a destination, it's a way of traveling.

This book was designed to be passed along to a friend or family member because your friends and family don't want to learn from you. Jesus even said, "a prophet is without power only in his hometown.." That means when Jesus went home to see his family, they were like, "OMG, Jesus, stop coaching me. You'll always be Jesus to us. I know you're like, the Son of God now but let's talk about farming and livestock. We don't want your help."

Receiving a self-help book isn't much more appealing.. Because of that, this book is designed to be morning bathroom friendly! With no fuss, these simple, repetitive lessons will break down the judgments, resentments, and jealousies that hold us and our loved ones hostage until we learn, low and slow, how to release them. In addition to that, essential life skills like following joy, observing our thoughts, and releasing control are snuck in as well. This book will casually change your life in one year, one page a day. You're not allowed to skip ahead or try to be the best student in the course. Relax. You're not a basket case. You only need the teensiest bit of help to get everything in your life the way you like it.

I wanted to make sure you had as many resources as possible to help you complete this book. If you go to mamionami.com/365bookbonus , you'll see multiple treasures with your name on them.

First of all, access to this book in my app, where you'll be able to continue your studies when you're traveling without having to tote a book around. All of the lessons are there for you.

We also have a virtual book club, with live calls you can access, and a chat room where you can meet other people waking up on your same timeline. It's also a great place to start to flex your spiritual muscles privately. You master things when you talk about them, but it can be really hard to start talking about this kind of stuff in a friend circle that has only ever known you as a Muggle.

I made this especially for you, and all of these little bonuses are here to make your experience easier and more fun. I hope you enjoy it.

My purpose as a teacher is to remind you of the choices you forgot existed for your life (a.k.a. Entelechies), and GENTLY, with a laugh, question everything you know to be true.

Thanks for buying the ticket, I hope you enjoy the ride :)

xx

Onami

11/20/2020

One lesson a day. No need to skip ahead.

Lesson 1:

Everything I see is neutral.

We're getting straight to work. The next few days are walking meditation instructions designed to challenge what you see. It'll seem a little weird, go with it. Once this seed has sprouted we'll talk :)

Everything that you can see is neutral. Even though some things may seem more special than others because of sentimental or monetary value, everything you see is neutral. These first lessons are meant to challenge you, so if you're scratching your head - go with it. Scan the room from where you are. You'll select ten objects from your surroundings to look at and try to make them a mix of "special" things and "ordinary" things. Bring your focus onto an object one at a time and say: "This _____ is neutral."

Lesson 2:

Everything I see is neutral until I give it meaning.

Regardless of how meaningful certain things may seem to you, understand that you give everything that you see all the meaning it has. It's not about what someone has appraised it as or what the history of an object is; you decide how it makes you feel. You decide its value. Think about how a $2 Hanes T-Shirt becomes a prized possession when it belonged to someone no longer here. Or maybe a matchbook of basically no value becoming valuable when it was the matchbook from the place you went on the first date with your soul mate. What we see is a collection of our thoughts and feelings, more so than what actually exists. Select ten objects from your surroundings again and notice as you observe each one the meaning that you have assigned to it.

Lesson 3:

I don't understand what I'm seeing.

Until you've mastered your thoughts and the individual value that you've assigned to all these neutral objects and the subsequent thoughts they trigger - you're seeing a big mumble-jumble. We're taking in so many things. A nice car goes by, and our thoughts start firing off: "STATUS! RELEVANCE! SUCCESS! REWARD!" and then the little offshoot thoughts start in: "I'm probably never going to have a car like that, whatever, only assholes need big flashy cars anyway...." This from a neutral object. If we were seeing it for what it is, we might understand it. But until we do, let's be okay with admitting to ourselves that we understand none of it.

Pick ten objects throughout the day, and as you observe each say: "I do not understand this."

Lesson 4:

None of these thoughts mean anything, they're just noise.

Here's where things start getting pretty interesting. During this practice, you will realize how many thoughts are in your head. There's a running commentary in your head, pushing you one way and pulling you another. Don't judge the thoughts, they're not "right" or "wrong." They're just noise.

With practice (and we'll practice a lot this year), we can select our thoughts. We will consciously choose thoughts that lift us up over thoughts that pull us down. The best way to watch your thoughts is one at a time, and the best way to see thoughts one at a time is to practice being without thought, and that's what meditation is.

Here's a breathing exercise I love that helps me empty my mind. I use it all the time. Inhale for the count of four, hold for the count of four, exhale for four, and then hold on empty for four.

Lesson 5:

I'm never angry about what I think I'm angry about.

In AA, we learn that anger is just sadness down the road.

Anger might be what we're sure we're feeling, but sadness is the true emotion beneath it.

This is such a valuable tool! When someone is flipping their lid at you, *listen*.

*"I'm pissed because I've been working my ass off, and you're not even paying attention, and **nobody ever pays attention to me.**"*

That sounds sad, right?

I'll give you a little spoiler alert. All sadness, all discomfort, and any other crappy feeling come from one root, and that root is a sense of separation. Feeling like we're alone in the world. That we've been abandoned by our friends, our family, ourselves, and ultimately - God.

There is no greater suffering than feeling like you're suffering alone.

*"I'm pissed because I've been working my ass off, and you're not even paying attention, and nobody ever pays attention to me *and I feel like I'm all alone and that nobody loves me*."*

If this sense of separation is the one root of all suffering in all beings, what would be the cure for it?

The answer is love. Presence. Taking a moment to let someone feel that exactly as they are is enough, and they're not alone.

If this is the Universal solution to anyone's upset, how does this make you want to behave towards the world? Think about it…

Journal:

What am I most angry about?

_____

_____

_____

_____

_____

_____

What needs to be forgiven for this to go away?

_____

_____

_____

_____

_____

_____

Lesson 6:

I'm upset because I believe an assumption.

The stress you are under is voluntary.

This lesson works well with the second and third of the Four Agreements by Don Miguel Ruiz Jr.

2.) Don't take ANYTHING personally.

3.) Don't make assumptions.

Is there really a conflict here? Do you feel judged? Do you have proof? Did someone say something out loud? Or is it in your head? Are you *assuming* they feel a certain way about you? What has actually happened that is upsetting you? How much of this painful experience is from how this incident made you feel? Dr. Maya Angelou said, "People don't remember what you tell them, they remember how you made them feel." Our thoughts and feelings comprise our reality, not so much the facts.

Sometimes there is actual proof. I've had people so close say some insanely hurtful things right to my face. I wasn't assuming this was happening; it was happening in real-time.

Agreement Two: Don't take anything personally. They're not upset for the reason they think, either. Inside they're hurt, like you. Feel alone, like you. There's only ONE problem, and that's a sense of separation.

While you might be physically seeing a problem, and it's making you upset, if you could see this discomfort as the opportunity for healing it is, you would be so grateful (I mean it), that it wouldn't upset you. You would just get right to work! Keep an open mind. You can do it.

Lesson 7:

All I see is what's behind me.

This is an insanely hard thing to wrap your mind around, and we'll talk about it much more this year. I'm literally telling you that everything you see is the past. You see the history of things, and because of the shadow your memories cast, you're unable to see anyone or anything in the light of the present moment. It holds you back like you wouldn't believe.

When we understood the first three dimensions that made up our 3D world (length, height, depth) our brains could handle the concept of a fourth dimension - time. When we master the fourth dimension by opening up to space-time, where all possible realities exist simultaneously, we can process the fifth dimension. The fifth dimension is a parallel Universe with a start date like the one you live in, with a character in it identical to you. This is like the movie Sliding Doors. In a parallel universe, miracles are natural. Anything you want can come to you, and your wishes manifest instantly. In this parallel universe, you are unlimited.

Open up to a new idea of time. Everything you think you know about what is possible today is based on the past, your history, and experiences with people, places, and things. You know much less about time than you thought you did. You cannot appreciate the present or see the future if all you see is the past. All worry is the fears from the past casting a fog over the possibilities in the present and future.

Lesson 8:

I'm always thinking about the past.

We all know that we don't know what tomorrow brings and that yesterday is never coming back. The only point in which the illusion of time intersects true time is in the present moment. Right now. Right here.

Because we see only the past until we train ourselves to see differently, all thoughts are thoughts of the past. All we can assume of the future is based on what we have learned from the past, so even future thoughts are past thoughts. Look, I never said this would be easy...

Close your eyes and watch your thoughts. No need to do anything fancy; observe your breath until you notice that you're thinking a thought. Now, look at this thought. Is it a memory? Is it a future trip? If it's a trip to the future, where did you get this storyboard from? A movie you saw? An interaction you witnessed in the third person or first person? Where in the past is it coming from?

Forgiveness (the axis of this book) frees us from the pain of the past, which creates anxiety for the future. When the threat of a terrible history repeating itself is lifted, we can experience our present moment fully. We can enjoy it, for once.

Lesson 9:

I'm not seeing the real story.

So, the last couple of days, you've experienced a bit of a brain skip. You've been looking at your thoughts and looking at your things and telling yourself that you aren't seeing anything but the past in it, which is challenging for sure.

I realize these lessons are a little repetitive, but that's what practice is about. A belief is a thought you keep thinking. To believe something different, you will have to keep thinking different thoughts, and this is how you do it.

Today, we accept: "I'm not seeing the real story."

To make it simpler:

Imagine if we had a dinner party, and a few minutes before Guest X arrives, I lie and tell you he's on some very strong LSD. This backstory means that every move he makes, everything he does, will seem weird to you because you see the past story in him, and he cannot show up differently. Even if I were to recant my story and say, "I was just kidding; he's stone-cold sober." the impression was still made. You might even amplify the story, convinced he is on LSD and that I'm now lying about it to cover his ass.

How much of what we see is based on past stories, assumptions, judgments, and worry? If we weren't seeing this, what would we be seeing?

Journal:

Who is someone you have judgments about because of a backstory someone gave you about them?

_____

_____

_____

_____

_____

_____

Can you know that this story is true?

_____

_____

_____

_____

_____

_____

How do you feel about this person because of this backstory?

_____

_____

_____

_____

_____

_____

How would you feel about this person without the backstory?

Lesson 10:

I am not my thoughts.

If you have ever meditated, you know how difficult it can be to keep your mind thoughtless. You'll be sitting there all Zen, and then you catch yourself thinking about something and get upset. "Why am I thinking about this right now?" But isn't it amazing that you can *catch yourself thinking*? So, *who* is it that is behind the thoughts? And how can you spend more time with *that*? The Yoga Sutras of Patanjali refer to this consciousness as the Seer. In Norse mythology, the god Odin has two ravens on his shoulder, Hugin and Munin, translated as Thought and Mind. They are two things with Odin (supreme consciousness) ruling over them. Odin gave his eye for wisdom, and it arrived in the form of the ravens. The symbolism here says that the wisdom of the Allfather comes from seeing the two as separate. When you can differentiate the thought waves on the surface from the depths of the ocean, that's when you gain vision. You become the Seer. You can observe your thoughts without falling prey to them.

If all we know is the past and all we see is the past, and we want to see differently so we can work all kinds of amazing miracles in our lives - we want to start with a blank canvas.

Notice that we're not saying thoughts are "good" or "bad"; we're acknowledging that we're not our thoughts.

Sit still and relax, allowing your breath to create a blank screen in your head. Try to clear the mind completely so that when the first thought arrives, you can observe it. Something inside of you will realize, "I am thinking right now." Take this as a sign that you're good at meditating, not bad at it. Gently push the thought aside by saying aloud - "I am not my thoughts. I am not even my mind."

Lesson 11:

Each thought I believe creates a world I see.

When we see anything but miracles, we're not seeing. This is not spiritual bypassing or some slick metaphysical avoidance routine. It's only that our thoughts create our reality. It's not like the discomfort of the present situation you see is "bad" or "wrong," it's just that it isn't accurate.

Let's say our eyes witness something, two people fighting, for example. Judgment kicks in: "This shouldn't be happening!" Thought One rushes to support Judgment: "People are monsters." Thought Two and Three chime in, "It's like that headline we just read about the serial killer!," "And that incident from ancient history! It's always been like this; we're doomed!" You, under the influence of your thoughts, carry on with heavy boots. Because you see through the lens of these thoughts you believe, everything seems to fall into this category. As you carry on through the day, everything you see seems to reinforce this thought. All you see is conflict.

An alternate perspective could be that the two people fighting are exactly where they are supposed to be. That both parties need this situation to finally assert their boundaries and step away from a mutually abusive situation and permanently raise their standards from here on out. Thought One says: "It's remarkable how things work themselves out when I don't get involved." Thought Two and Three chime in: "There's a perfect flow to everything.," "All is well!" You, under the influence of your thoughts, float on. All you see is peace.

You can choose your thoughts; did you know that?

Write down a situation you recently observed that bothered you.

What is an alternate perspective of the same story?

How is it perfect?

Lesson 12:

I am upset because I believe a thought that isn't true.

Affirming that a thought isn't true is important because we are not using "right," "wrong," "negative" or "positive" to describe our thoughts. It's not that it's bad; it's just not accurate. Why isn't it accurate? Because we're preoccupied with the past, which makes us unable to see the present situation clearly. So, it's not that the thoughts we have about the world are bad; they're just not accurate. We'll observe a situation through a past-based lens, create a thought story about it, believe it to be true without checking, and then get upset at the dismal world we believe is real.

Usually, when I'm speaking to someone who is in great denial about wanting children, they'll tell me that it's such a messed-up world to bring a child into. The world has always been messed up if you see it that way. If you see the beauty of history versus the horrors, you could easily come to believe that the world always has been and always will be a beautiful place to bring children into.

A spoiler alert for this book is that peace is the reality, and everything else is your thoughts. You don't have to believe this right now, but your life will get profoundly easier as you start to. Until then, are you willing to entertain that you are only upset when you believe the story you have written about the incidents you see?

Repeat after me:

Miracles start with me. I am determined to see this differently.

Lesson 13:

My unchecked thoughts empower fear.

The majority of what we see is "empty" space. Only 4.6% of the Universe we observe comprises atoms, and 99.99% of your body comprises empty space. If we took the matter (what's left outside of the "empty space") of **the entire human species**, it would fit into the size of a sugar cube. It's important to note that all of Western medicine as we know it is only based on what we can figure out of that .01%. According to science, it's matter over mind. Because this .01% is all we can prove exists, and the rest is "empty space," it must not be real.

Empty space is what peace feels like. Stillness. Quiet. The absence of agenda. Presence.

Ease.

The ego has a hard time with this because there is no place for fear in presence; it requires focusing on the past or future. Ego rushes in to fill the quiet with all kinds of chatter to keep itself in existence. Its life depends on it.

We aren't accepting that we will live in a meaningless world from here on out. We're becoming conscious of what we think we've been seeing up until this point, so we can create space for a new paradigm to appear.

The ego is competing with God (the Universe, your Innate Self, your subconscious mind, Source, Dark Matter) for control of these quiet spaces. As you do your exercises for today, looking around you 4-5 times and saying, "I am looking at a meaningless world," ask yourself do I want to compete with God? I don't.

Journal:

This is a 10–15-minute stream of conscious writing exercise designed to get you in touch with what you believe in. Whether you do spiritual work or not, knowing what you believe in is vital. I use God now because it's the shortest word, and I talk about this a lot, but before then, I used Dark Matter/energy, which I recommend if you can't think of one. A force you can't see that makes up 95% of the mass and energy of the observable universe, keeping you alive and safe? Sounds about right...

Now, grab a pen and paper, Voice Memos, or Notes, and discover what your higher power can do for you. You're going to give yourself only about 15 seconds to answer each question, don't overthink it.

I loved the exact way Gabby Bernstein taught this in Spirit Junkie Masterclass, so I've included it exactly as she taught it in 2015.

What does a higher power mean to you?

_____

_____

_____

_____

What does it mean to rely on a higher power?

_____

_____   _____

_____

_____

What does it feel like when connected to a higher power?

_____

_____

_____

_____

How do you experience your connection to a higher power? Smells?
Sound? Synchronicity?

_____

_____

_____

_____

11:11?

_____

_____

_____

_____

Imagine a world where you're in constant contact with your higher
power. What does it feel like?

_____

_____

_____

_____

What blocks you from this connection?

_____

_____

_____

_____

When do you feel most connected?

_____

_____

_____

_____

When things are not flowing, and difficult - what is your higher power trying to tell you?

_____

_____

_____

_____

Compose a higher power statement that starts with the words: "I believe"

_____

_____

_____

_____

Lesson 14:
Fear is not the natural state of things.

Put everything you're doing down for a few minutes and do a little exercise with me.

Stop for a moment and put your feet on the ground. Feel the four corners of each foot and press them into the ground. Wiggle your toes, even if they're in shoes. Flex and point the feet. Now scan through your body and feel all the parts of your body that are soft. Your thighs, wherever they rest, your butt wherever it rests, feel the soft pads of your hand with your soft fingertips, press your lips with your tongue. Now scan through the body and feel for all the parts that are hard. The back of your head, your elbows and knees, your teeth, your knuckles. Imagine the shape of an upside-down triangle on your torso, with the low point below the navel, the sides along your ribs, and the two top corners at your shoulders. Breathe in through your nose in three luxurious parts. The first breath to the bottom of the triangle, beneath the navel, filling one-third of the way up. The second third of the inhale expands into the sides of your triangle, the ribs. Ahh. The third sniff brings you to capacity, and the inhale reaches its peak all the way up into your shoulders. Exhale with a big sigh out of the mouth.

Do that again twice, please. Inhaling to the navel, to the ribs, to the shoulders, and out through the mouth. Through the nose to the navel, the ribs, and the shoulders, and out with a big sigh through the mouth.

Through a few short minutes of focusing on the present state of the body and connecting with our breath, we escaped fear. We dropped the cords tethering our minds to anxiety about the past or future and allowed ourselves to appreciate what is right now.

When you bring yourself fully into the present moment, there is no fear. The natural state of the Universe is and has always been peaceful. If you ever stop to appreciate and examine all that you have in this moment, you learn you have everything you need in this moment right now. Even if there's a little voice trying to chime in and say, "Well, you haven't paid your rent yet!" or "You're tragically single!" - just brush it away. Fear only exists when we do not appreciate the present. It may seem like a longshot here on Day 14, but good job for today! Every time you release fear, even for a minute, you get stronger. The important takeaway for today is that you understand that fear is the stranger and peace is home. No matter how deep into a fear you've gotten, you can always stop, breathe, and come home to yourself. Always.

Lesson 15:

The thoughts I choose determine the experiences I have.

We have confused most of the software in our bodies with hardware. We think that seeing is hardware, not changeable, but only the eyes are hardware. Seeing is software. It is programmable. Ears are hardware, and hearing is software. The mouth is hardware, and tasting is software.

Through the hardware of our sensory organs, we believe we take in a fixed impression of the world and that it's "just how it is," however, we attach thoughts to every experience and give it a meaning on which we base our lives, our connected thoughts, and our emotions. It changes the way you view the object.

For example, the hardware of the mouth takes in a bite of chocolate. The tongue tastes it. That's it as far as hardware goes, but then the ever-updating software comes in with a slew of pop-up ads.

"OMG, this is heaven."

"OMG, this is off-limits; I must stop."

"Remember that study that said chocolate was good for you?"

"Remember someone telling you in grade school that chocolate gives you acne?"

"That lady you look up to doesn't eat chocolate."

"This is the last time you're ever eating chocolate again, ever. Better finish it off."

Depending on what thought you're choosing, the software of the tasting experience can be programmed from decadent and luxurious to guilt-ridden and frantic. The mouth still chews, the tongue still tastes, and the chocolate is still chocolate - but the thoughts you choose can change the way you perceive it all. Guilty chocolate tastes bad (but you'll eat the whole thing anyway).

Pick a thought, right now. Close your eyes, see all the thoughts swirling and pick one, just one to look at. Is it a helpful thought or a hurtful thought? Did you know you could pick a thought?

Can you pick a better one? When you do, focus on it for just twenty seconds, and notice how similar thoughts show up to meet it.

The thoughts you choose determine the experience that you'll have. If you're choosing negative thoughts because you didn't know you could choose better, you'll have consistently negative experiences. If you have consistently negative experiences, you will have a life you're always trying to escape.

During this year, we'll practice choosing better thoughts. You're not expected to master it today, but as Lao Tzu says, the journey of a thousand miles begins with a single step, and you took it.

Great job.

Lesson 16:

The world is neutral; my thoughts are absolutely not.

You're about to realize how many thoughts you actually have flying around in that mind of yours.

Sometimes we can easily identify a thought as being helpful, e.g.

"I really like the way I look in this dress."

Other times they're obviously hurtful:

"I look horrible in this dress."

Sometimes they SEEM neutral:

"This dress is weird."

But if there's no neutrality, what side is this thought on?

In this hypothetical situation, I might say this dress is weird because it looks like something Person X would wear. I won't wear it because I don't want to be associated with any kind of X Person or X People, and I don't know who in their right mind would. And for that price? PASS.

This neutral thought is a judgment of myself and Person X, the designer's creativity, and how other people spend their money. It is hurtful and not neutral.

At this point in your practice, don't worry about following every thought back to the beginning to determine if it is helpful or hurtful; let's acknowledge that it's not neutral. From here on out, you have this key bit of information: **there are no neutral thoughts**.

Lesson 17:

I see nothing as neutral.

Everything we see is processed by thoughts. It takes a thought to register something as Seen; otherwise, it's just part of the background. If you've ever parked your car in a busy parking lot while you were too busy thinking non-neutral thoughts to *take in* (a.k.a. have non-neutral thoughts about) your surroundings, you know what I'm talking about. You'll have no idea where your car is parked! Whereas if you put thoughts onto your surroundings, like *"that's one scraggly looking tree with a Chernobyl-grade pigeon in it."* you can piece your way back to your vehicle.

If we have no neutral thoughts, we can see no neutral things. Whatever we're thinking becomes the experience we have and determines what we'll see more of.

The majority of the world has this backward. We have lived our lives believing we **see** things first, and then we cook up a thought about it, and **this is not true**.

The order of this Universe is: thought first, object second. If you think about anything enough, consciously or unconsciously, you will start seeing it. A lot.

Again, you don't have to master this today; I certainly didn't. We will start here, though.

The thoughts you choose transform every single neutral thing you see into something that either supports a friendly Universe or supports a hostile Universe. As long as you have thoughts, they'll tint what you see.

Lesson 18:

How I see impacts what others will see.

We're not even going to go into the "we're all connected" part yet, but *spoiler alert* we **are** all connected. Let's just put this in real 3D terms.

Someone you didn't know went out with a guy that cheated on her, and everyone was talking about it. You now perceive this guy as a cheater every time you see him. A new friend of yours met him, years later. She tells you she thinks he's cute. You tell her, "Um, I wouldn't go there. He's a cheater, and cheaters don't change."

You got the thought, and you gave it to someone else. Now your thought is how someone else is seeing things.

Here's another solid example if you're an entrepreneur. You make something you're proud of and assign a value to it. Someone else comes along, wants to buy it, and asks, "How much?" You tell them, and their thoughts go haywire. *"I can't believe she's charging that much.," "I really want it.," "I'll never be able to afford that, and if I did, I wouldn't buy it anyway out of principle."*

They tell you, "It's too expensive."

Now you're looking at your value through the tinted lens of someone else's non-neutral thoughts based on their beliefs and blocks about value, abundance, and the friendliness of the Universe. (**Pro Tip! Don't ever build your business off other people's blocks.**)

Their vision impinged on your vision, and now you're both seeing things through tinted lenses.

However, this can be used for good!

When you see things through a more empowering lens, it will become contagious. Your consciousness will elevate the consciousness of those around you. Your changed perception will help people around you, which will help people you've never met.

No need to be the master today, babe! You have only to be willing to see.

Journal:

What beliefs did I inherit about relationships I learned from watching my parents?

_____

_____

_____

_____

_____

What beliefs did I inherit about money I learned from watching my parents?

_____

_____

_____

_____

_____

Are these helpful or hurtful?

_____

_____

_____

_____

_____

What would be the opposite of this belief?

_____

_____

_____

_____

_____

List three instances where this new, opposite belief has been true. Cite personal experiences or people you've seen on the internet/at work, etc.

_____

_____

_____

_____

_____

Lesson 19:

How I think impacts how others think.

When you squeeze an orange, orange juice comes out. The thoughts you carry on the inside will eventually manifest on the outside.

Today's lesson references the "one mind" that they talk about so much in Buddhist philosophy. Thoughts have a vibration that can attract others to them. A judgment passed on Person A in the silence of your mind, like "He talks too much" will attract another thought to it in your own mind or someone else's. This is what we call a "vibrational match" in metaphysics.

Are you then surprised when "coincidentally" Person A's name comes up in conversation with a third party, and they say, "He really talks too much?"

Sure, he may be talkative - but there are no neutral thoughts. So, is this shared judgment helping or hurting all three of you involved?

Lesson 20:

I came here to see.

I'm not gonna lie to you; changing how you see the world takes practice, persistence, and patience. But if we're not seeing the real story, what's the point? With every thought, we either support a friendly universe or a hostile universe and whichever universe we create is the one we all have to live in.

For decades I woke up in the morning feeling that my only option was to repeat the same things I did yesterday. My life was never horrible, but it was never great; it was simply mediocre all the time.

Even though it was comfortable, repeating the same actions day in and day out (plus convenient - I could drink whatever I wanted, snort whatever I wanted, and sleep with whomever I wanted), these repetitions never made me happy because I didn't come here to be mediocre and neither did you.

When someone who has never heard before receives a cochlear implant, they can hear Mozart for the first time. You can also hear a car alarm for the first time. When you choose to see, you see everything, and the world will never look the way that it used to. It can seem overwhelming, and at some point, we might wish we could go back to the comfort of what life used to be like when we were less aware, but we didn't come here to be blind. We didn't come here to be mediocre. We came here to be great, and we came here to see.

Lesson 21:

I'm determined to see what's real.

If the entire world is neutral and all we're ever seeing is the stories we project upon these neutral objects, people, and circumstances, it's hard to imagine what the real world even looks like. We are so used to seeing the story. Our entire identity, who we think we are, is all contingent on the stories we've been keeping alive for so long. And the interesting thing is that we don't even know which of these stories are true or not. We usually assume that we're seeing everything correctly and that everything our mind tells us is true.

We blame others for our experiences here, and we constantly look to the past for advice for the future. This is like making tonight's dinner out of yesterday's garbage every night.

Today, when a situation presents itself that brings you anything less than joy, ask yourself: "How much of what I'm seeing is real here? How much of my reaction to this is based on a story I have? And is this a story that I made up? Or is it a story that someone else gave to me? Regardless, can I be certain any of these stories are true?" This inquiry alone can challenge everything you know to be true.

Lesson 22:

I'm either seeing clearly or I'm attacking myself.

When we see something for what it is, without trying to change it or expecting something from it, we are completely in the present moment. When we see something and want to change it or expect it to change, we see either the past or the future. Because the past is gone and the future is uncertain, we can't be sure that either of these are real. When we're not seeing something in the present moment, we're creating an expectation about it. Either an expectation to repeat a sordid past or an expectation to be the future we think it needs to be. We're only ever underwhelmed by the present moment when we've overwhelmed it with expectations. Manifesting anything requires us to be present in this moment.

The present moment is also the only thing we can do anything about, seeing as we're not able to get the past back or able to time travel into the future.

When we see situations or people through the lens of the story we have about them, we live in fear that others aren't seeing us fully either. We think that other people are holding our past failures or potential against us as much as we are holding theirs against them.

So, if we're seeing any situation under any lens besides the present moment, we are blocking our ability to manifest our birthright. We are attacking ourselves.

Lesson 23:

If I stop attacking others, the world stops attacking me.

When you hear people say the world is a mirror, it's not a metaphor; it's literal. A mirror doesn't have mood swings (although some mirrors make us look better than others, but that's not relevant to this discussion). A mirror simply reflects whatever is projected onto it. You don't have to get with this concept right away because it's our life's work. But entertain the idea that everything you see in the world has started with and will end with your life here. When you die, can you be sure that any of this will go on existing? Does it just cut to black? What if there was no external reality and everything you see is a show put on for you? When you're done watching, the curtains close, and that's it.

A kundalini yoga mantra I love (SA TA NA MA) says, "Peace Begins with Me." I have done my best to live by this statement for years. If the mirror of the universe is reflecting my internal state, then the expectation that the world must fix all of its conflicts before I prioritize fixing mine is no longer relevant.

If I feel like I'm under attack by the world for my choices in career, fashion, politics, parenting or anything else, it's because that mirror is reflecting the way I attack others for their choices in career, fashion, politics, parenting, or anything else.

If I want to express myself however I want to, I need to make sure that I'm giving everyone else in the world freedom to express themselves however they want to. And you already know this! It's the golden rule in different words: do unto others as you would have them do unto you.

If you feel like you're under attack by society, check your weapons. What shots have you fired? What shots are you still firing?

Lesson 24:

I don't know what I want.

If you've been manifesting and it's "not working," this will help you to understand why there might be a hitch in your giddy-up.

I feel like the easiest way to explain this lesson would be to share an incident that happened in my life.

I was once engaged to a man I loved very much. I had been in love with him for close to a decade, and it broke my heart year after year when it seemed like we would never be together. Finally, after so long, we got together. All that I had ever wanted was now real! It was now my life. It was bliss for a few months, but as our differences and difficulties arose, I wasn't happy. Intellectually I felt like I "should" be happy; after all, this was the only thing I had consistently wanted in my life. But emotionally, the feelings I was feeling weren't happy ones. I was anxious, stressed, uncomfortable, and tired. I had made his heroin addiction about me, and I was trying desperately to help someone who didn't want my help, just my love. I was also a full-blown housewife. I made meals, did dishes, and planned for our one-day family.

I berated myself for my discontent. "How could I be so selfish? Of COURSE, I wanted this; I had to still want this. I would be crazy not to because this was all I wanted for the last eight years."

I wouldn't allow myself to experience my own unhappiness because I was so convinced this man would be the one that made me happy.

His untimely death from a heroin overdose was the end of our relationship. I was heartbroken. At times it still hurts. But that great sadness awakened a side nobody, least of all myself, saw coming. I learned how to trust myself. How to love myself. How to sit with the pain in myself. I learned how to run a business. I learned how to dance. I learned how I like to spend my time. I learned how to be alone and to find unshakable self-respect in the moments I felt most insignificant to the world. My healing journey has helped others heal. I became the person I loved. I became a teacher.

I have experienced the greatest joys of my life on this journey, and they're all mine. It comes from within me, not because someone has completed me. It's infinite.

Your temporal self (this body, and its limitations, this part of you doesn't know what you want.) But beyond this physicality is an aspect of you that knows all, sees all and is bringing you what will make you the happiest, however that needs to happen.

Trust the process. Trust this practice. It's bringing you closer to your Eternal Self, and you are most certainly never alone.

Lesson 25:

I see whatever storyline I value most.

We see the world and everyone in it as props for whatever storyline we've decided is most valuable. With the adage: would you rather be happy or right? We see that our mind doesn't care about us being happy if it can prove that our most valued storyline is right.

For example, a storyline I felt was valuable was that you can't trust men. In my life, I sought men who could fill this narrative for me. Men who stood me up on the first date, yet I agreed to the second. Men who I caught lying before we ever went out. Men flirting with me while I knew that they had a girlfriend. Because I had the storyline you couldn't trust men, I constantly overrode my intuition and happiness to enter relationships with men I knew would let me down. But it doesn't stop there. I used to get irritated when I saw a man walking down the street with flowers because I assumed that they had cheated on their girlfriends and we're covering their tracks with a nice bouquet. When somebody gave me a glowing review of the deeds of their trustworthy partner, I would have to poison the story in my head. I would feel bad for the storyteller because I assumed that they were blissfully unaware that their partners were cheating on them. I would ignore evidence of a good love story, yet a story of another relationship gone down the shitter would be the first thing I thought of when I woke up in the morning. I had placed the value on a toxic storyline and was forcing the rest of the world to play along.

This might seem dramatic to you, but what is your world showing you right now? What is the pattern you see with money? What is the pattern you see in relationships? What is the pattern you see with food? And what would you have to believe to be seeing a world like this?

Storylines originate in our minds way before we ever see any evidence on-screen. Would you like to try this out?

I'd like you to select something that has no emotional resonance for you. Something random. Something like chickpeas, pan flutes, or Panama City. For the next three days, I'd like you to spend just one minute focusing on something that has no emotional resonance for you. It can be anything you want, but it must be the same thing each day for one minute. You will start seeing this object everywhere because you place a value on it. Don't believe me? Talk to me in three days. I'll see you there.

Lesson 26:

All judgment is a two-way street.

Back in 2012, when I was a new and insecure yoga teacher in New York, my teacher Elena Brower told me that the only time I was insecure about being judged by others was when I was judging other people.

If I'm judging your outfit, whether I think it's ugly or because I'm jealous of it, I assume that you're judging my outfit too. When I get ready to go out, I subconsciously get ready for my standoff with you, and if I believe in this competition and judgment, I will most certainly see it. Plus, it will take me three times as long to get ready.

Any judgment we make about someone else creates equal insecurity inside of us about the exact same thing. For example:

If I'm judging how another working mom juggles success and parenting, I will assume that others are judging me as a bad mom if I have a career that lights me up, as well as children that light me up.

This also creates resistance to what it is we're trying to become. If my judgments about other successful moms have hardened into a belief I can't be a good mom and successful then I'm resisting the success that I'm manifesting.

Why?

Because if I believe I have to neglect my children to have a thriving career, I will not take the steps I need to for that success I've been manifesting because I'm scared it will hurt my children. And NONE of this is real. It all started because I thought it was my place to judge how someone is momming, based on an assumption I made on a social media post.

What are you most insecure about? Who are you afraid of becoming? And how is this directly related to a judgment you're making about someone else?

Don't forget to spend a minute focusing on that random thing you selected yesterday. You're going to see this everywhere! Tag me @everestasher on social media, or message me on The Bruja Report!

Lesson 27:

Seeing without judgments must become a priority.

We know we're not judging something when we accept it exactly how it is. We know we've accepted something when we **approve** of it being exactly the way it is.

Today you'll have lots of opportunities to judge something as being right, wrong, good, bad, flattering or unflattering, etc.

The headlines will invite a judgment, family drama too, outfit choices on the subway, a co-worker's reaction as well as the event that they're reacting to.

Instead of getting sucked into the judgment trap because it's only making you insecure, ask yourself this powerful question. Are you ready?

"How is this absolutely perfect, just the way it is?"

If you can't conclude on your own, excuse yourself however you need to and get quiet behind the eyes for a little bit. Gaze at your inner sky. When you're feeling quiet upstairs, ask again, "How can I see perfection in this, just the way it is?" The answer will always be there if we remember to ask.

When you've got your answer, observe the situation again with fresh, judgment-free eyes.

Once you do, hit it with the ultimate seal of approval!

Say "I approve of this."

Spend a minute today focusing on your totally random object and tag me @mami.onami #ltbiyb on social media when you start seeing it in real life!

Lesson 28:

I am determined to see without judgments.

Okay, so we've talked about how detrimental judging is to our growth, but over the last couple of days we've also seen how we're chronically judging things all the time. So, let's incentivize this judgment-free living a little bit more.

When we're wrapped up in judging a situation, we're basically trying to be God's (the Universe, Fate, Dark Matter, whatever you call it) boss. We're assessing what's going on and trying to determine if it's doing a good enough job, or should we swoop in and try to control it?

I will get real with you early on here. There's only ever the *illusion* of control. You cannot ever, ever control what's going on.

For example, you could jump into a river that's flowing downwards and vigorously push in all directions. You could also wear special little shoes from Rite-Aid and maybe board a steampunky little submarine thing with a propeller that creates all kinds of racket in the water. Once you've exhausted yourself, the flow continues as it was, carrying you along with it, and your *illusion* of control jumps in and is like, "Yes! Good thing you're wearing this crazy outfit and pushed the river for so long. Now we're going downwards, and it's all thanks to you!"

But the river was already going downwards... and now you're exhausted with more exhaustion on the horizon because you think you've always got to work this hard to keep things flowing, and you don't.

Judgment exists because of a desire to control, well, everything. You want others to dress a certain way, parent a certain way, and behave a certain way because somewhere in your noggin, you believe that if you're not keeping everything and everyone in line, things will slip into chaos. But people will always be people, shit will happen, and the river will always flow.

So, a question to sit with for today is: "Why do I think that if I'm not controlling everything, that everything will slip into chaos?"

Sit with it but answer it. It'll surprise you.

Lesson 29:

Perfection exists in everything I see.

When you see a couple breaking up loudly in the street, judgment loves to rear its angry little head and be like: "What an asshole! He's just dumping her like that."

But what if this man has gotten bulldozed by every girlfriend he's ever had, and after some deep internal work, he has decided that just because someone wants to date him, he need not date them. This voluminous public argument is actually a crucial first step in him asserting his boundaries as a man. And as angry as the female seems here, she's learning that when someone says initially, "I don't want a relationship right now," that she should actually listen to them! Not agree to casual sex when she actually wants a relationship, and not internally eye roll when someone says they don't want a girlfriend because she believes she just needs to be given the chance to change them, and then they'll see the light. She's learning that you can't love someone if you want to change them and that you should listen when someone says, "I'm not available," and take it as a cue to raise your standards!

They're both learning a valuable lesson, as are we.

In my travels, I've why-God-whyed about everything from SIDS to toothaches to terrorism. I won't go over each, but I'll hit these three.

SIDS teaches me to have gratitude for every moment of motherhood, especially when a manic teether is yanking out my neck hairs while screaming bloody murder. It helps me be a better mom.

Toothaches give me major gratitude that health is usually the norm, and this pain is the exception rather than the rule.

Acts of terrorism create massive waves of peace, with total strangers hugging and crying together, united by grief and determined to change.

A President that wasn't your choice being elected teaches you, "HELLO! Live by your own laws." Grab a copy of Thoreau's Civil Disobedience and live your life.

You'll probably be able to pull up several "Yeah-but-what-about-_____" for yourself right now, so ask yourself: How is this perfect?

It might take a few days or another fifty lessons in here to get the answer, but it'll come. It always does.

Lesson 30:

Everyone is doing the best they can.

Now, who did your mind just pull in as a reference of someone who is not doing their best? A lazy coworker? Your mother? An ex-boyfriend who just refuses to take responsibility for his life?

Who has the authority to decide what someone else's best is? How do you know that the worlds-worst-waitress didn't just leave a doctor's office with a grim diagnosis and cannot think of anything but? How do you know that your mom did such a bad job? Have you asked her about her childhood? Maybe she's repeating what she was taught was normal? How do you know that your ex should have done better? Maybe his heroin use was his way of coping with massive amounts of emotional pain from childhood abandonment issues, and the issue wasn't about him being less of a shithead, it's about you believing you can't have relationships built on trust and mutual honesty.

Stop forcing the world to live up to agreements it never made with you. It's not up to you to decide someone isn't living their best life. Leave them alone! Each one of us has enough shit to keep us busy for the rest of our lives, so stop obsessing over others and focus on yourself. It's not selfish, it's necessary.

Lesson 31:

I am not a victim of a hostile Universe.

Albert Einstein said: The only question that matters is do you believe in a friendly Universe or a hostile Universe?

Our culture has been steeped in the Judeo-Christian "God-the-Punisher" for centuries. Even if we didn't grow up religious, it's in the culture. Ideas like "suffer now, enjoy later" keep us at jobs we hate, with the carrot of retirement dangling out of reach in front of our faces. At our rear, the whip of societal and familial judgment threatens us should we jump ship in the pursuit of happiness.

The rules laid out in the King James Version of the Bible were necessary to establish the social hierarchies that have kept law and order all this time. For real, if it wasn't for the Ten Commandments, we wouldn't be able to walk down the street. However, we can keep the baby while ditching the bathwater. Just because society has to punish to keep us all from slipping into a free-for-all criminal chaos doesn't mean we have to convince ourselves that it's GOD punishing us. There's a big difference.

Accept that you've fucked things up in the past and that you'll fuck things up. You're human, and erring is human. You literally came here to make mistakes, and The Universe (He/She/It/You) knows who you are, flaws and all, and likes you anyway.

Things will inevitably be tough and tragic sometimes, but it's not because you're being punished. I repeat: when things are tough, it does not mean you're being punished. Want proof? Here's your homework for the day:

Today when something goes "wrong," ask: "How is this wonderful?" See what happens.

Lesson 32:

I created a hostile Universe.

You may want to sit down for this one.

You subconsciously believe that the Universe is out to get you because God created you bad, and bad people get punished.

But God (He/She/It/You) didn't create you bad; you created God bad.

You created God, and you made this creation hostile. To get what you want, you need to forgive "God" instead of waiting for the God of your understanding to forgive you.

I realize you may clutch your pearls at this, so allow me to explain:

When you were born, you had no idea what God was because you saw everything as One. There wasn't good or bad, right or wrong. Everything was neutral, and everything was new. As you grew you heard stories of a higher power, greater force, etc. You may have heard these stories from near and distant relatives, neighbors, in school or elsewhere. Even if you didn't grow up in a religious home, the concept of crime and punishment exists everywhere because our culture is steeped in Judeo-Christian archetypes. So, as a child, pre-God, when something happened and someone "got away with it," you likely heard some kind of story of someone's impending bad luck, karma, juju, etc. The idea that no one gets away with anything because Nature has a way of self-correcting and no one gets away with anything. If society cannot punish, "Something Else" will. Because we're waiting for the other shoe of Divine Punishment to drop, we'll see evidence of that person's life taking "bad" turns, and we'll say things like: "Karma's a bitch."

The problem is that God is Love, and love is not a bitch, nor does it have a bad side. Love just loves. Infinitely and unconditionally. (a great resource for this is the "Where's God When I Fuck Up?" video in the lecture archives on The Bruja Report.

So, based on what you heard and impressions that you got as a child, you started writing a story about the God of your understanding. You created it. You created a God that punishes, holds grudges, gets off on desperation and is hostile. Now you live in fear of something you created and then gave power to. You feel like your life won't improve until this Creation forgives you when actually you need to forgive It. Why?

Because you've been blaming "God" for every bad thing ever happened to you. Life sucks sometimes, and these sucky experiences always bring us where we most need to go. It's not you being punished; it's you being guided. Yes, it hurt sometimes, and because of that pain, you need to forgive "God."

What's the worst thing that ever happened to you?

For me, it was resuscitating my dead fiancé and best friend of nine years for 22 minutes while the ambulance struggled to find my apartment.

How was it wonderful?

In an instant, I learned death is not the end, I don't know what I want, I am never alone, and that there is far more to this Universe than meets the eye. I was abruptly put on the fast track to my destiny, and on this path found true love, joy, and purpose beyond my wildest dreams.

Your turn:

What was the worst thing that ever happened to you?

_____

_____

_____

_____

_____

_____

How did it positively shape your life?

_____

_____

_____

_____

_____

_____

Can you say it shouldn't have happened?

_____

_____

_____

_____

_____

_____

Lesson 33:

If I created a hostile universe, I can also create a friendly one.

If we value the storyline of a hostile Universe filled with judgment, competition, and punishment, we will always see evidence to support that.

But if we've created this hostile universe, we can as easily see evidence to support a concept of a universe that is cooperative, peaceful, and loving. It might involve taking a break from your favorite headline dispenser or asking for help in seeing the perfection in perplexing situations, but it's always possible.

Journal:

What would your life look like if you knew beyond a doubt that the universe was on your side? That it had your back completely and everyone else's as well?

_____

_____

_____

_____

_____

How would your days look if you were certain you were divinely supported?

_____

_____

_____

_____

_____

What's something cringe-worthy that went down in your life but ultimately taught you great lessons and brought you exactly where you needed to be?

_____

_____

_____

_____

_____

List three instances where you've seen evidence of a friendly Universe.

_____

_____

_____

_____

_____

Lesson 34:

I believe in a friendly Universe.

Everything is a sign.

A sign of either a friendly universe or a hostile one. As long as we're convinced that the universe is out to get us, we will have a bad time.

We won't be able to relax, expect good things to happen, or release control. Ever. If we believe that the universe is mad at us, we'll never be able to get ahead.

But if we believe in a friendly universe, everything changes. We no longer get all emotional about obstacles, racking our brains trying to find what we "did" to "deserve this." We simply see obstacles as things that need to be and will be overcome.

When we believe in a friendly universe, we don't spend our days drowning in anxiety about horrible potential outcomes because we don't see the past as a horrible history of crimes and punishment. We see difficult past moments of our lives as divinely and artfully placed and crucial detours in the right direction. With this perspective, we feel safe in enjoying the present moment.

When we believe the universe is working on our behalf, we can surrender the illusion of control (and there is only ever the *illusion* of control) and trust we can let the chips fall where they may, and it will be perfect.

Now, you don't have to be convinced that this is true now, but by repeating this statement as a mantra today, you can see evidence to support it until you've collected so many references for a friendly universe, you no longer question it.

Repeat after me: **I believe in a friendly universe.**

Lesson 35:

This friendly Universe is home to everyone and everything I see.

If there's a loophole in your friendly Universe, the only person going to fall into it is you.

The universe is 100% friendly or 100% hostile, and love doesn't have a bad side. If you see what seems to be the universe punishing someone, you will start coming up with reasons they're getting punished. What's more, you'll have proportionate insecurity to this judgment you passed. You'll live in fear that if you color outside of what you think the universal lines are, you'll be punished like Exhibit X was. It might seem like you're creating a loophole in the friendliness of the universe for this one special case, but I assure you, the only person going to fall into it is you.

Everyone and everything you see is connected, and we are all residents of a friendly universe. Would you like to make an exception to this? I didn't think so. :)

Lesson 36:

I am willing to accept the best-case scenario.

Unless you've done work to reset it, your imagination will usually default to the worst-case scenario.

When we make assumptions about what's going on in other people's noggins, we're usually assuming the worst-case scenario. All fun and games until you're paralyzed by the fear of what other people will think if you live for yourself.

When we're judging someone, it's usually because we assume they are living the worst-case scenario or trying to hide it.

When we pity someone, it's usually because we assume that just because they're in our worst-case scenario, that it's also their worst-case scenario. That they are as miserable starring in their life as we would be. Not a good assumption to be made mechanically. Some people like being homeless or working at the DMV.

We're so willing to blindly accept the worst-case scenario. The scenario encourages us to quit before we even try. We don't stop to inquire if this scenario is true or not, it comes up, and we're like, "Oh shit, that'll happen. Forget it."

Sometimes we'll even think others (inevitably people close to us) are cold and irresponsible when they're not willing to fantasize about worst-case scenarios with us. I've felt abandoned and subsequently hostile when Patrick refuses to accept that my son's runny nose is the first stage of double pneumonia.

Whatever we're focusing on, we get more of, especially when we're feeling the worst-case scenario. Pit in your stomach? Check! It's also easy for us to make a full meal out of a fleeting worry. We had one little thought go by, and the next thing we know we're deeply analyzing her posts...from five years ago.

Here's some good news. With all this worrying, you've proven that you have a real knack for visualizing outcomes that haven't happened yet, and really FEELING as if it's already happened. All you need is a bit of practice indulging the **best-case scenario**, and you'll have this whole manifesting business on lock in no time.

What's something that's been keeping you up at night?

What is the absolute best-case scenario? Spare no detail! Bring in the ripple effect and any other extras.

Do you realize that you can choose from an assortment of potential outcomes based on what you're focusing on?

Are you willing to accept the best-case scenario?

Say it loud, say it proud! **I AM WILLING TO ACCEPT THE BEST-CASE SCENARIO!**

Or tag me on the Bruja Report Slack or on social! I'll know exaaaaactly what you're talking about.

Lesson 37:

I'm willing to see a pattern of perfection.

This won't work unless you answer out loud. But if you answer out loud and don't skip a single question, it will really really really really really really really work.

What's an incident where you feel like you've been done wrong? This could be someone doing you wrong or the universe doing you wrong.

What actually happened here?

What's the story you gleaned from it?

Have you seen other incidents of this story being true?

What positive thing happened because of this wrongdoing?

How was it great?

How was it one of the best things that ever happened to you?

If it was something that positively shaped you, is the story still true?

Can you know that it's true?

What would be possible for you in a world where this story was never true and will never be true for you? What could you achieve without the weight of this story?

Write a new story:

_____

_____

_____

_____

_____

Lesson 38:

Why do I think this shouldn't be happening?

No matter how deep into discomfort I am, this question always brings me into a higher state, where I can clearly see a solution that wasn't there before.

I will introduce you to a concept that we'll revisit repeatedly, it's the concept of the triangle.

Any time we're feeling uncomfortable or like we're up to our eyes in stress, family drama, or financial woes, it's because we're playing one of three roles in the triangle. The three roles are:

The Victim, The Rescuer, and the Judge.

When we're in the role of the victim, we cry, "Why is this happening to me?" When we're in the role of the rescuer, we cry, "Why is this happening to you?," and when we're in the role of the judge, we try to find "Why is this happening?"

We don't stand a chance at achieving enlightenment if we have no energy to focus on our soul. One of the main ways we leak vital energy is by freaking out in the triangle, as opposed to stepping out of it altogether and seeing it from a Divine perspective.

If you're in a state of discomfort, you're in the triangle. If you ask yourself, "Why do I think this shouldn't be happening?" you are viewing life through the eyes of the Divine. From that perspective, anything is possible.

So, where in your life are you feeling like things are not as they should be? Family, business, or financial drama? Your weight? Your mediocre relationship? Recognize the role you're playing in each one.

Now, visualize yourself from the top of the room, looking down at yourself. See the top of your head. See yourself in relation to the problem. "I'm here, and the drama is there." Ask yourself, "Why do I think this shouldn't be happening?" Feel in your body how the tension simmers down.

Take it even deeper. Ask yourself: "How is this great, just the way that it is?" Take it even deeper. Ask, "What can I do to enjoy this, just the way that it is?"

Collect your answer and with this new, heightened state, let your day return to you.

We always have the opportunity to see things as God sees them if we can just remember to ask the right questions. If we're seeing outside of the triangle, there's no problem. Today's question is your visa for getting out of the triangle

Lesson 39:

The Universe supports what I want.

I could write an entire book on why the Universe likes you, but what would be way faster is if we just get to the bottom of why you think the Universe doesn't like you.

I used to feel like the Universe wanted me to be in trying relationships to "grow." My BFF trashed my house, made fun of me for being a teacher and teased me endlessly about getting sober. I also was dating someone who wouldn't call me back, never followed through on his promises to visit, and had a list of reasons why he wanted to fuck me but couldn't. To clarify, he absolutely wasn't my friend because he made it very clear that he wanted to talk about fucking me, but he wouldn't fuck me because he wanted to "be my friend" and didn't want me to get the wrong idea. I played this game with him for a YEAR because I thought this "BFF" and this "boyfriend" was the best it would get.

So, I started asking myself difficult questions and forcing myself to answer them. I'll give you my answers, but I encourage you to ask yourself the same when you're done with today's lessons. Where in life are you tolerating sub-par experiences because you think the Universe doesn't want what you want?

Q: Why do I think this is the best the Universe has for me?

A: Because I'm not supposed to have better than this.

Q: Why are other people supposed to have the best, but not me?

A: Because there's something wrong with just me.

Q: What is so wrong with me?

A: I'm dirty.

Q: Why am I dirty?

This was the hardest question I've ever had to answer. Turns out all that sexual abuse I experienced as a child was a big deal and wasn't just going to go away no matter how much I ignored it.

Experiences out of my control created a deep sense of shame inside of me, and I was convinced that the Universe didn't like me. I spent my life trying to hide the disgusting person I was sure lived inside of me. I tolerated disrespect from everyone because I didn't think dirty, disgusting me deserved anything from anyone. I felt like the Universe was toying with me, plaguing me with huge dreams and desires that I could never achieve. Once I asked the right questions, I saw that I believed a lie. But I took twenty-nine years to ask the right question: Why do I think the Universe doesn't like me? What bullshit reason is cutting me off from Universal support?

It'll be the hardest line of questioning you've ever put yourself through, but if you can be brave enough to find the lie of why you think the Universe doesn't like you, I won't have to write a whole self-help book trying to convince you why it does, we can just keep waking up here.

I know you can do this. So, ask. You'll say, "I don't know," at first, and your job is to force your ego to spit out its little piece of bullshit so you can see it for what it is. A lie, keeping you from everything.

Lesson 40:

I am not alone.

I was in a lecture with one of my professors in Nutrition School, Deepak Chopra, and he said this: "There is only one source of pain and illness in this world, and that is the sense of separation."

The sense of being alone.

Your spiritual path brings you closer and closer to your Source. I889So close that you realize it is inside of you and can never, will never abandon you. It IS you. You ARE it. As you realize how not alone you are and the mighty force that goes with you absolutely anywhere and everywhere you go in your life, all depression, anxiety, and pain ends.

Today, try one meditation. As long as you can early in the morning. Allow yourself to reflect on memories of your life when you felt alone. Watch yourself from above, like a movie, as you see all the times when you felt like there was no one there. As you lovingly reflect on these instances, notice your own presence in these memories. Notice how, from your perspective now, you can see that even though you felt like everything was falling apart, it all worked out eventually. Notice in these memories how when you finally stopped crying or first got out of bed, there was a little voice inside of you, so small that hinted at "It's all going to be okay.." And even if it had to tell you repeatedly, eventually, you listened, and it was okay. Notice in your life now where you feel like you are very alone and see yourself from above, just like we did in your memories. See if you can hear this little voice talking to you now. What's it saying? How does it feel to hear it?

The soul speaks softest, but she speaks just as much. Under the catastrophizing loudspeaker of the ego yelling about what a failure you are, it sure seems like the weaker voice - but it's not.

This little voice has always been with you and always will be with you. No matter how alone you've felt, you've never been alone. Not for one second.

Lesson 41:

When I see as God sees, anything is possible.

There are three forces required to create something new, and this is what the expressions of holy trinities symbolize. The first force is active, the second force is passive, and the third force is neutralizing. The first two forces are like a game of ping pong; one says YES, and the other says NO.

So, for example, you decide you want to have a business that you love, that never feels like work. You serve the ball into the Universe, and that's the active, desiring force. Without fail, the ball gets smacked back to you as all your doubts. "You'll never be able to make a living off of this." "You're not qualified enough." This passive, denying force can also show up as unexpected bills, your family being "concerned." It feels like a no everywhere you turn.

Now, this doesn't mean it's a sign that you're not supposed to have a delightful and fulfilling career, it just means that every time you want to reach a new level in your life, you will have to blast through all your doubts about doing it. As long as you're alive and desiring, you will interact with this denying force. It's a sign that what you want is on its way.

Anytime you feel like you don't have an option, you are stuck at the ping pong table. This back-and-forth also looks like being a slave to your likes and dislikes. For example, feeling like Rocky Balboa when you have money and feeling like absolute bottom-of-the-barrel scum when you don't have money. Or loving it when someone calls you smart and hating it when someone calls you crazy. If we get inflated when things are going our way, we'll get equally deflated when things aren't. These are always proportionate, which is why you can go from believing you can soar in business one day, and then one little thing goes wrong, and you never try again.

Most people aren't aware of the third force that is a requirement for anything to manifest, ever. The force that is neutral. The force that doesn't freak out when that first payment clears and doesn't freak out when you have a shitload of unexpected expenses. The force that says "Sat Nam, thanks" when someone calls you their mentor and says "Sat Nam, thanks" when someone calls you an egotistical weirdo. This force is impervious to the ebbs and flows of the ping pong table because this force sees this battle of the yes and no as exactly what it is. A ping pong game that you're choosing not to play. It's the preliminary back and forth leading to the manifestation of something new. Instead of becoming so identified with every passing incident, taking things personally and behaving as if your entire life is now ruined forever because someone on the internet said something mean to you, or feeling like you're beyond human form because someone on the internet said something glorious about you - this neutralizing aspect is permanently chill, in on the big picture, and always available.

When we're tapped into the neutralizing aspect, we think as God does. We're able to see the "good" and "bad" as part of a beautiful story unfolding. We relax our obsessive grip on the desire, like squeezing your date's hand until it's sweaty and awkward, and instead gently keep the contact, knowing it's gonna be here because it wants us to. Like resting your hand on your partner's leg while they're driving. Because nothing can flow through an obsessive grip, and it feels stressful to hold onto anything that tightly, what we want can finally flow to us easily in this state.

So, how do we get to this state? It's simple! You need to practice it. Here's the meditation I use all the time to get myself in this state. Read the description, then do it when you have time.

Notice the area in your life that feels like it's starting and stopping, not making any progress. It could be a business, a relationship to a person or thing, your broken-down car, money, whatever.

Sit in a way that feels relaxing to you. Breathe easily and imagine yourself at the top of the room. See the top of your head, the part in your hair, your open palms, etc. Rise higher. See the whole room, like from a drone perspective. Take a few breaths with this, watching yourself meditate from above. Now, from this aerial view, notice where the problem is. If it's your partner in the next room or 3 miles uptown, take in that distance. See like on Google maps, you're here, and they're there. If it's a negative balance in your bank account, take that in. Some set of numbers somewhere on the internet is stacked against me. Okay. Take a few breaths seeing your desiring force (you) and your denying force (the problem) in relation to one another. Now, see you and the problem, aerial view, in relation to time. See this day of your life in relation to how long you've been here and how long you vaguely assume you'll be here for. For example, if I was born in 1987 and plan on living till I'm 120, this problem on this day is like a small blip on that timeline. Give yourself the gift of observing from an aerial view other instances where you were certain your life was over. Notice, in the great scheme of things, how short those moments actually were. Yeah, things might be a little more exciting than you would care for them to be, but it always passes, right? And when they pass, something better usually comes of it, right? And you're usually grateful that it went down the way it did, right? So, if you're going to be grateful down the road, could you just skip to that right now? Maybe? How would that change your experience here, now?

Come back to Earth when you're ready and notice how you feel.

Lesson 42:

If the Universe doesn't punish people, I won't either.

Nobody ever behaves with the intention of being evil or doing badly.

Think about some horrible choices you've made in the past. At the time, you felt like it was the right thing to do, the most joyful, the most fun. Even if you knew that it wasn't "right" per se, you decided that it would make you happy to do so, and so you did.

Right and wrong are subjective concepts; they're not a fixed set of rules. What supports your aim, you consider to be "right," and what hinders your aim, you consider to be "wrong." Everyone has their own set of rules based on their aim.

When I was a child, I remember watching 101 Dalmatians in the theater. There is a scene where the puppies are watching TV, a show about cops and robbers, or maybe cowboys and natives. From a young age, I questioned everything. Blind trust has never been my forte. I realized, at three years old, that if the cop is the person telling the story, he's the good guy. If the robber is the one telling the story, like Robin Hood, he's the good guy. This bothered me because the Bible at the time determined my whole life in the cult I grew up in. I knew that all the stories were being told from "God's side.." I figured that if I read a Bible written from Satan's side, I could also side with it. (I have since browsed the Satanic bible, and it is fascinating.). I understood that right and wrong were subjective arrangements.

Here's a concept about Satan, the origin of all evil that may interest you:

Free will is God's gift to man. If the right choice were appetizing, and the wrong choice was labeled as a highway to hell - we wouldn't have free will. It would be like me offering you a plate of pasta and a plate of rat shit and clearly explaining to you that one was delicious and one came out of a rodent's ass and asking you to choose which one you would prefer for dinner. If the choice is obvious, did you get to choose?

Satan was God's right-hand dude, appointed with the difficult task of making the "wrong" choice extremely, appetizing. An apple, so to speak. If we always made "right" turns, consciousness could not expand because it would never face new obstacles and have a chance to expand. God loves us so much and wants us to be free so much he sent his right-hand dude to Earth to bless us with free will.

Deeper still, you can't make a "wrong" turn. Think about a time when you were sure you made a wrong decision. I berated myself for accruing debt while starting my business for a long time, especially a 7k investment in a business coach promising 10k months, when I was emotionally frazzled, and I didn't have a business to apply this methodology to. I felt like I had wasted money, and I would be punished for my "wrong" choice by never being granted cash money again. I felt horribly guilty about my debt, was certain I was being punished with poverty, and damn near gave up on my dreams.

But that 7k mistake became my biggest blessing. I realized that I didn't want to be a "life coach" the way I had seen other people doing it. I didn't want to rely on Facebook ads, have thirty clients a month, or 180k in debt doing so. I dusted myself off and began my career as a spiritual teacher.

I was determined that my new career would be everything hers wasn't. I stalked her frequently-ish on social media, determined to see her get punished for what I thought were inflated sales stats, money hungriness, and heckling. I felt like now that I knew I was "right," that she had to fail for me to succeed. My constant surveillance of her and her business led me to make some highly sabotaging judgments about how business should and shouldn't run. I judged her for "selling" all the time, assumed she was embellishing how much money she made, assumed that all life coaches did so, got annoyed at her ads, and strove to see every new sales post as proof she wasn't meeting her goals and was being punished.

I wanted to believe that she was being punished, but I was only punishing myself.

Because of this I never advertised, wouldn't sell, didn't read business books or hire a coach (not that I could afford it, with no sales from my business.) I meditated and did nothing else, feeling righteous, and watched her "fake it" on social media. Plus, I was also convinced that life coaching wasn't a profitable industry because all life coaches "lied" about their income.

The Universe doesn't punish anyone because a: right and wrong are subjective concepts, and

the Universe doesn't have a bad side. Ever. But if we're looking to see proof of punishment for someone's "evil" deeds, we'll punish ourselves and live in fear of doing what we actually need to do or want to do because we think we'll get punished too.

So, what's your aim? What do you want to accomplish here? Anything that supports that is good for you; anything that hinders it is bad for you. Your job is to fulfill your aim and not bother with trying to change anyone else's aim to suit your preferences. If you're trying to manipulate someone else's aim, you will be "bad" for them and will be treated accordingly. Mind your own business.

See you tomorrow :) and do my mini-workshop Jelly if you want to move those jealousy blocks that are seriously obstructing your money flow!

Lesson 43:

Acceptance is 20/20.

I try not to use the terms love, unconditional love, or forgiveness too much because I feel like we overcomplicate them. We have too many ideas of what we think these things look like. The biggest block to consciousness is the assumption we're already there. You're not going to go looking for a new rubber spatula if you already have the same one at home, right? I have heard many people speak about how they've forgiven their ex-husband, mother, or business partner *despite* all the horrendous things they've done. Let's remember that these wrongdoings were always violations of the victim's aim but were actually quite aligned with the perpetrator's aim (so the right move for them at that time). Saying you've forgiven someone when you haven't is like lying about what color shirt you're wearing. Everyone is onto it but you. Saying you can't stand the way your boyfriend drinks his face off and starts fights with homeless people, *but you love him,* is not love.

Love, unconditional love, and forgiveness are all ways of saying "acceptance."

Think about it like this: a friend is Miss Inspirational. She juice fasts four days a week, works on her website every night from seven-sharp to nine-sharp, does yoga every single morning, and always has a piece of advice for you in regard to reaching your potential.

You have to be in the mood to hang out with her because every time you leave, you're like, "Okay! I'm going to dump him, stop eating sugar, do yoga every single morning, and work on my website from seven-sharp to nine-sharp.." While it's nice to get 40ccs of go-get-emtiger straight into your arm and strategize your next plan for action, it wears off. You never do everything on your to-do list, that's the nature of to-do lists, and every time you hang out with Miss Inspo, there are five new things on your list.

Then you have a friend that's your bestie. When you go to your house and sigh yourself down onto her couch, you feel like you're totally at home. You can have a big bitch, and instead of her problem-solving with you, she is just there with you. Feeling the feels. You can order $70 worth of Thai food and cry watching Lemonade together. You accomplish nothing on your to-do list. You may finally send a squad-endorsed text that ends a relationship that had it coming for some time. You can fart openly, watch another episode, and pass out on the couch without worrying about being rude. You text her the next day, "I love us." and you really do. Why? Because she accepts you as you are. She doesn't motivate you to be more like her; she motivates you to be more like you! She gives you permission to show up just the way we are. Tag your bestie with the passage from this book! (and FYI, Bruja Report is all women you could fart around)

Often we have so many expectations of others that we never even see them for who they are at this moment. Similarly, our vision is clouded by how we think that they've failed us in the past and punish them because we feel like they haven't held up their end of an invisible bargain they never made with us. When we don't see people in this exact moment, exclusively, we're not seeing them clearly. We're forcing them to live in their failures (the past), or their unfulfilled expectations (the future), and we're missing out on the real them, which is beautiful and real - right now.

The most loving or forgiving thing we can do for anyone is to accept them exactly where they are right now. Accepting that they may have done you dirty in the past, but that was then, and this is now. Imagine if you cheated on one boyfriend that you didn't even like that much when you were nineteen, and at your wedding day, ten years later, about to marry the love of your life, someone says, "I OBJECT! She's a cheater! Once a cheater, always a cheater!" How horrible would that feel? We're doing this same thing to people all when we refuse to accept them for who they are today.

We constantly punish people for not living up to our expectations. We keep asking them to show up for things to prove to us that they've changed, and then feel hurt anew when they do the same thing they've always done. Like a family member that you've never gotten along with because they always shoot down your dreams, and every time you go home, you try to arrange a meeting because you think this time will be different. So, you go, and they have too much to drink, and they shoot you down again, and you're devastated. We say, "How could you! I gave you another chance *because I love you*, and you ruined it again!" In a situation like this, it's more loving to NOT go out of your way to see this person because you accept that they will not change. Y'all might be oil and water forever, and that's okay! Just because they have a hard time with you doesn't mean it must hurt you.

If your boyfriend can't stop getting drunk and fighting with homeless people, it's more loving to say, "I can't be with you without trying to change this. As long as I'm trying to change you, I'm not accepting you, which means I'm not loving you. I'm instead going to wait for someone I wouldn't change anything about because I'll know that it's really love."

All it takes is one person, you, operating differently to change the outcome.

When we accept someone as they are, asshole or not, it gives them permission to show up differently. It's unconditional love because we're saying I accept you exactly as you are, you can fart around me. If you're seeing someone repeat the same painful things to you repeatedly, it's because you haven't accepted them. If you've been trying to talk less or lose weight for ten years and it's still not happening, it's because you haven't accepted that you might be a talker with an abundant ass - and that is fine!

A Universal truth is that whatever we resist will persist.

We're always afraid that if we accept someone or something, we will be stuck there forever, and that is not true. When we accept something, we finally stop resisting it, and it is no longer obligated to persist. It is only when we stop trying to change something through acceptance that it can finally change.

Lesson 44:

I'd prefer to think like God thinks.

When you're faced with a problem, and you can see no possible solution, you're seeing as your ego sees.

Let me give you an example:

A few years ago, I was getting mediocre attention from two different guys, but what I really wanted was to be in a spiritual partnership, move to the woods, and have some kids.

The one guy was successful, worked for a liquor company that flew him all around the world, well dressed, good taste in music, good relationship with his mom, long hair and lots of tattoos. He also didn't keep his word around visiting or calling me back, sent me mixed messages, and we actually didn't get along that well. I believe in a cooperative universe, and he believes in a chaotic universe.

The other guy was a talented and famous artist from Los Angeles who I had met in Austin. He was sober, interested in my work, an avid sexter and paid me a lot of attention. After a fair bit of X-rated attention, I found out that he had a nineteen-year-old girlfriend.. and according to him, "it was complicated." I find that cheating usually complicates things, right? He also called me fat, multiple times.

I was trying to decide which one of these guys was going to get the boot. I had committed to not fucking with anyone who was unavailable, and both these guys were unavailable. I had been gnawing on this decision for some time. I was disillusioned with both of my options. I thought as my ego thinks.

I went to a crappy Chinese massage parlor in Austin I used to love going to because I had learned at that point that when I put myself in a situation where I'm receiving, the answers I need always come.

I was face down on the massage table, thinking about how I wasn't even really attracted to either of them and that the best-case scenario with either one of them would be me in another long-distance relationship, which I didn't want. My primary love language is you actually being here. AKA quality time. If I don't get that quality time, I need A-L-L the other languages at a ten. I need the gifts, the words of affirmation, fulfilling my morbidly large sexpectations if we ever see each other after talking about it for so long, and you should probably do me a huge favor too. I only have unreasonable expectations when the person I love is not actually here in my life.

I was frustrated or ping ponging between Guy 1 vs Guy 2, I suddenly said out loud: "Is this seriously the best it's going to get?"

This question brought me to the mind of God, as a good question will do.

I felt the Universe winking at me. I heard in my heart: "That's a very good question. Do you think that this is the best it's going to get?"

I realized that I was the one keeping my options limited. That I was the one settling for less. That I was convinced it would have to be a compromise, or that I was too weird to be loved.

I went home, dumped both, and wrote out what it was that I wanted. I wrote out what would become some of the most powerful signature processes I teach today. I got real about why I thought I had to settle for less (having thick thighs and being a spiritual scholar? Please. These are assets!)

I wrote in my journal I wanted somebody who was here and here to stay. I wanted them sober. I wanted them hot from every single angle. I wanted them to understand me and understand how important my work was to me. I wanted them to be spiritual. I wanted someone who would beam, waiting in the wings for me as I walked offstage from a mic-dropping lecture. I wanted someone who wasn't intimidated by me, all of me.

I also decided that I would not be waiting for a man any longer to fulfill my dream of moving to the woods near water. Because the only thing I could do to prepare was to practice swimming, I did that every day. Juice cleanses and exercises did nothing for the persistent 20lbs of travel weight I put on. I would leave at 7 am to go swimming before anyone else got there, get home at 10 am, and not leave the house for the rest of the day. I told God, "Whoever's going to be with me is just going to have to like my ass like this, and they're going to have to come to find me where I am because I am not going looking anymore."

Not even two weeks after I made that decision, I met my husband, swimming early in the morning. He saw me from behind before I saw him and was like, "Yup.." He walked straight up to me out of the water, and we've been together ever since. One of the first things I said to him was, "I want to buy land on the water, so I'm here practicing swimming." and he was shocked. He said, "I just wrote that down in my journal."

So, where in your life do you feel like you're stuck between two mediocre decisions? It's a sign you're stuck in the ego brain. The yes/no, desiring/denying.

Why do you think this is the best it will get for you?

Use that question and think in the mind of God.

Lesson 45:

Love is Freedom.

I used to have a lot of ideas about what I thought love was. I thought it was helping someone reach what I had determined was their full potential. I thought it was taking care of someone. I thought it was being the perfect housewife, there all the time, obsessed with my partner's happiness. I thought love was marriage, committing to stay and not leave no matter what. All my versions of love were some leash. I didn't think that what I loved would stay if I wasn't holding onto it.

A leash of any length is not love.

Love is freedom.

Freedom to be who you are today and who you are tomorrow. Freedom to fuck up, learn, and fuck up again. Freedom to go explore. Freedom to wake up ten years from today, say, "Who am I?", and start over. Freedom to change your mind. Freedom to express yourself fully, at that moment, every moment for the rest of your life. Freedom to be as many versions of yourself as you want and know that they're all loved by me. Freedom to be vulnerable. Freedom to need help sometimes. Freedom to not have it all figured out. Freedom to be in a bad fucking mood. Freedom to get fat, shave your head, and move to Thailand. Freedom to want more. Freedom from your endless expectations. Freedom from your concept of what their potential is. Freedom from your help. It's giving you the freedom to be yourself unconditionally and giving others the same freedom.

We are made of the Universe, and the Universe is infinitely expanding, growing, and changing. It is our inherent nature to expand, grow, and change. There is no shortage of people you can love "but you wish they would just..."

There is no shortage of people in the world who will love us as long as we can keep singing their favorite song, wearing their favorite dress, and being there next to them at their favorite bar, but what happens when you outgrow this?

Rumi says: A mask worn when the face has grown becomes a wall that rubs and cuts.

At some point, we realize that we can't keep being that same old person, doing that same old song and dance for people. When we live for ourselves and shed the old masks that others "loved" and came to rely on so much, we can see the true colors of the ones who claim to love us the most. I lost nearly all of my friends when I made a commitment to hang out with my soul and try to emulate her more. They couldn't handle it. They didn't want the new me, and they made it clear how much they wished I could go back to being the old me.

But we cannot live our lives for other people. We cannot permit ourselves to be rubbed and cut every minute of every day just so the friends we've well outgrown can be more comfortable with their construct of us. We must give ourselves permission to grow.

While I was devastated to lose so many friends, I found that the person I had finally allowed myself to become could get closer to a cashier in five authentic minutes than I ever got in fifteen years of some friendships. It's been said, "That is real what never changes." Who I was at my goal weight, on tequila, at 17, 22, and 27, when I was insecure, when I felt safe - these were all different people! They did only change! But when life shook me to where I didn't have the energy to fake one more smile, all of those identities fell away, and all the people who "loved" those versions of me fell away too. When I got real about what had always been true for me and started letting her shine (as we'll do in the upcoming Identity Game), I never had to decide who I was going to be anymore. I just am.

What do you feel will slip away if you're not holding tightly to it? Working for it? Your dress size? Your salary? Your partner? Your schedule?

Answer this question in your journal, filling in the blanks as many times as you want.

What would my life look like if I loved my _____ and my _____ loved me?

Lesson 46:
The Universe is friendly.

Repetition is the mother of skill, and I'll hammer this home many times during this year.

The Universe is friendly and conspiring on your behalf.

We have the best deal ever as humans here on earth; we're basically guaranteed to win. It's like bowling with bumpers. Every great thing we focus on will eventually grow into reality. And you're protected from all the horrible, paranoid outcomes you focus on by ego default. Getting in a head-on collision with a semi-truck, your house burning down, or a winter chill turning into frostbite, gangrene, and amputation - those things don't happen! A few shit things happen here and there to wake you up, but overall - the good things always manifest, and the bad things rarely do. In addition to this, we're protected by time. Time allows things to arrive in a way that feels natural and stable. When a million-dollar paycheck arrives gradually, as opposed to you winning the lottery, you don't worry that it will all disappear as quickly as it appeared. Three out of five lottery winners file for bankruptcy within five years, did you know that? That's because if we're not equipped with the wattage to handle a big change, it fries the system. When things show up gradually, through the Divine operating system that is time, we feel as if we've done it all ourselves with a great assist from something beyond us. That's because the Universe is SO friendly it doesn't want you to feel indebted to it. Like it says in the Tao Te Ching, "the great teacher works without self-interest and leaves no trace. When the work is done, the people say: "We did it ourselves. ""

We're also protected from what we think we want, too, by our soul. If we did something like settle for the wrong life partner, thinking they were the one for us, the universe will make sure we don't do that. Something will dissolve the relationship, so you can be available for The One. It is always this or something more.

The sun stays the perfect distance from us to keep us warm but not cooked. Circadian rhythms keep us at our peak by not setting us up to rage for 72 hours and sleep for two.

Oceans stay beautifully contained, rarely overflowing and wiping us out. Rain comes when it needs to and not before. Entire ecosystems, no matter how unkind the food chain can seem to be, run in perfect harmony. And inside your body, with no direction from you, your heart beats, and your lungs respire. Whether you're in a good mood, bad mood, on a juice cleanse, or furtively stashing your bag of VHS tapes because you've been on meth for four days - your body has your back.

It's easy to want to wail, "Why is this happening to me?" when things don't go according to plan - but it's not because the Universe is hostile. It's because to get from where you are to where you want life to be, things need to change. Because it would be way too much work for you to manage all the moving parts that create change, the Universe does it for you in its own perfect way. All you have to do is stay happy because you know that you're always grateful in the end that things went down the way they did, and the Universe takes care of the rest.

So, why is it so hard to just feel good? We'll get into that later. For now, be willing to see evidence of a friendly universe. It will show its true colors left and right when you're willing to see it.

Lesson 47:

I am safe in a friendly Universe.

When we feel inside like we're not safe, no matter what the outside looks like, we'll always feel this way.

For example, I felt unsafe without money for a long time. I felt like I would literally die without it, alone on the side of the road. The fear of being evicted would haunt me on the second of every month. Sure, I paid this month's rent, but what about next month? Flash forward a few years, and I'm making tons of money, but because I still wasn't feeling safe, I worried about being robbed, or my kid held for ransom or going to tax prison for an error on my accountant's part.

If you don't feel safe inside, no matter what happens on the outside, you will not feel safe.

Some of us got the impression as children we weren't supposed to be here. Maybe you were an unexpected pregnancy? Maybe you got brought into the world 3-4 weeks before you were ready through Caesarean section? Maybe your mom gave you the impression that her life was over once you came along? Maybe as a child, you felt like it was your fault that your parents fought or split up? There're myriad ways we can get this impression as children, and if no one is around to give us an explanation, we'll often blame ourselves for something that had nothing to do with us. If we blame ourselves for something we think we did, that's guilt. If we blame ourselves for something we think we are, that's a shame.

When we suffer from guilt and shame, we become convinced that the world is out to get us. We become chronic survivors, barely eking through, unable to rest. When things are bad, we're afraid it'll never end. When things are good, we're suspicious and afraid to enjoy it because we're terrified we only get good things because it hurts us more when we lose them, and the Universe wants to hurt us because we've either done bad or we are bad.

When we suffer from guilt and shame, we interpret obstacles as signs that we'll never get what we want, when obstacles are a part of life. We'll see everything as a sign that the Universe is out to get us. If whatever we focus on grows, with each passing day, we see more evidence to convince us we are in danger in a dog-eat-dog world.

Regardless of how valid your qualifier for guilt and shame seems to be, know that your original state is not this, and there's nothing you can do to damage your original state. All you can do is believe false stories about your original state, but your original state abides. Your original state is blissed out and filled with joy. Your original state is bright-eyed and bushy tailed. Pure, carbonated, unfiltered Source consciousness. You can always return to this, and this is how the Universe has always seen you. This is your natural state; fear is the stranger.

No matter what impression you were given by yourself or others about the quality of who you are or how you are, those are just impressions. They aren't real.

As we work through this book together, we'll keep returning to this concept, so if you don't get it today - don't blame yourself! Repetition is the mother of skill.

For today, I'd like you to entertain the idea that safety is an inside job. Let's answer some questions!

1.) What does "safe" look like?

2.) What does "safe" feel like?

3.) I feel safe every time I _____

Lesson 48:

I am always bigger than my fear.

In life, there's one battle. It's the battle of you vs. your fear. Today we will break down what fear is, so we can recognize it when it comes up.

No matter how elaborate of a disguise it's wearing, it's only ever fear. No matter how big the fear is, you always have the tools to make it your bitch. Fear never gets smaller as we learn and grow - but our ability to make it our bitch gets bigger. We can expect to always interact with fear every time we're about to do something great or every time things are great (google: Upper Limit Problem). We're never going to run fear out of town permanently, and that's okay! Every time we send it packing temporarily, we get SO strong.

I love the acronym F-E-A-R. False Evidence Appearing Real. It's never real, and it's also never validated. What I mean by this is there's never a good reason to feel fear. As a mom to a two-year-old in 2020, I'll google health stuff occasionally. The predictive text on whatever I'm googling often comes up "teething fever, when to worry?" - as if there's a time when it's responsible to put yourself into a frantic state and expect it to help someone else. Sure, we can investigate something but there's absolutely never a good time to worry.

And what is fear, actually? Let's start with what it's not:

1.) Fear is not a "sign" from the Universe warning you of impending doom.

2.) Fear is not true. No matter how scary it is, it's not true. That's why it feels so bad when you're afraid. When you eat rotten food, your body feels bad because it's rejecting what doesn't belong. When you're feeding yourself rotten thoughts, it feels bad in your body. You may even feel like you've eaten rotten food! It feels bad because it doesn't belong

3.) Being afraid doesn't make you responsible. Someone (you) need not be worrying all the time to keep things from falling apart. Worrying is one of the main killjoys we have. When things are going well, and we don't believe things go well for us, we'll gravity bong some worst-case-scenario fantasies to cut our soul down to ego size. How much joy can you take? You'd be surprised.

4.) Fear is never, ever stronger than you - but that doesn't mean you won't let it win.

And what is fear, ultimately?

It's a mood you're in. A sneaky mood you get yourself into that can keep you from doing anything meaningful unless you exert some power over it. That's it. It's not real, it's not a responsible thing to do, and it's not a fixed state. You can change it anytime you want to. Yes. You choose your mood, and if being afraid and never moving forward in your life isn't working out for you, you can change it anytime.

For feeling shit, it's also ALWAYS fear. There is no neutral. If you examine any feeling, you'll see it's either rooted in 100% faith (which feels good) or 100% fear (which feels horrible).

So, how do we make fear our bitch? There are infinite methods because, as I said, this is always the battle, but my favorite one to do is this:

List ten things you can appreciate right now. A full ten. The reason we go appreciation and not gratitude is that sometimes we'll do gratitude like: "Well, I'm grateful for my health because I could have some kind of galloping face rot, and I guess that would actually be something to complain about."

Does that sound like 100% faith to you?

Appreciation doesn't contrast or compare to anything yucky to try to titbully you into feeling grateful. When we're in a state of appreciation, it's impossible to feel afraid or angry. I guarantee that by appreciation #4, you'll feel better, and by #10, you'll be in a different state, where new options will be visible to you. Also, it's a law: Whatever you appreciate, you get more of. I'll show you my current ten, so you can see how uncomplicated it is.

1.) the smell of my tomato plants omg

2.) the little flowers on my tomato plants

3.) my son's chubby cheeks

4.) biscuits

5.) this beautiful windy afternoon

6.) good strong coffee

7.) my husband's ridiculous jokes

8.) naptime

9.) the fact that I can learn anything, anytime with the internet and books now

10.) my teeth! Spiritual dentistry, baby!

Resist the temptation to wimp out at #3 because you can't think of any right now. You must use the power of your mind to consciously focus on these things instead of fear, and fear is easy because, in life, it's easy to be a little bitch instead of acting! SO HUP-TO! You got this!

Lesson 49:

I am never too busy to ask for directions.

What would your life look like if you were divinely guided? If you had a guide who knew the way, never got annoyed by you, and was waiting for you to ask.

One of the main reasons I get when I'm encouraging someone to meditate is: "I don't have the time."

Let's put this on a storyboard for you.

Let's imagine that you're trying to get somewhere very important to you as soon as possible. Maybe it's meeting the love of your life, or reaching your next financial epoch, or building the career of your dreams. For this storyboard, we'll make the goal "getting to your job interview," but please adapt to whatever is hot on your vision board right now.

So, you have a job interview that you're very excited about and you very much want. You decided your outfit yesterday. You're appropriately caffeinated and ready to go five minutes early. You've never been to this address, but you're sure you saw it across from this other place. You consider googling it, but you're now only two minutes early, and you don't have the time. Off you go.

You encounter some traffic because there is always a denying force. You don't want to be late, but you're sure you can take side streets, so you zip off at the nearest exit. You have fifteen minutes to get there.

Problem is, it's one of those weird exits that get you all turned around and has you driving for like ten minutes before you can turn around. You're also noticing that you're low on gas, and you're supposed to be there in five minutes. You tap the steering wheel nervously, cursing as you catch yet another red light.

You're now officially late. Whatever, what's five minutes. Traffic, right? That weird feeling in your gut is making it worse, however. That weird little voice saying, "Are you sure you're going the right way?"

You're about to turn around and ask for directions, but you see a setting that looks mildly familiar. "A-HA! It's a left here! I knew I was going the right way. And I'm only ten minutes late, and my hair has collapsed a bit, and I feel like I need a third cup of coffee, but I'm almost there!"

You take your series of turns, and sure enough, you end up right across where you thought this interview would take place, only to discover - it's not there. You're also about to run out of gas, and there doesn't seem to be one anywhere soon.

You are PISSED. You shake your fist at the sky. "WHY CAN'T I EVER GET WHAT I WANT?!" You decide the Universe hates you, that no matter what you do, it'll never be enough, and are now crying with frustration that everyone else gets everything and you get nothing.

And none of that is true.

What actually happened?

You were "too busy" to ask for directions.

Your guide, your soul, can never intervene on your behalf unless you ask. Once you ask, you have to listen. If you have little time, that's okay. The answers will reveal themselves as the day goes on if you remember to ask. But you can take ten deep breaths, about one minute, to listen.

Once you get the directions, you would be wise to follow them! If your guide says, "Turn right," and you say, "Well, I don't really think you know wtf you're talking about, so I'm going to turn left." then there's really no point in asking. You can laugh, but you do this all the time!

In addition to guidance, there are also signs indicating that you're headed in the right direction. If you're too busy running your own show, you won't see them. You need to ask to see signs (you can specify how you would like to get them. Some of mine are grizzly bears, the smell of laundry, repeating numbers, Prince songs), and also that you recognize them for what they are.

Another note is that the voice of your soul will always give you an option that feels very doable for you today. Something that gives you a sense of "Oh yeah! I could totally do that." It will never tell you something like, "it's time to work past the point of feeling good, you lazy asshole." While you're getting accustomed to the sound of your guide's voice, please use joy as a GPS. Your guidance and joy will always direct you to the same place, so if you don't have a clear message, go with what feels the most joyful for you.

Here's a prayer I use every single day, which will radically improve the quality of your life every time you remember to use it. I recommend tattooing this on your hand, but if you don't have a hand, you can use a post-it.

My soul, I trust you to guide my life. I trust you more than anyone or anything to guide my life because what's good for me is good for you. I don't want to figure this out on my own, and I don't want to waste our time. I want to be on the express lane to my greatest joy. Please tell me today what I can do to align with our highest purpose. Please show me the steps I can take today and give me lots of signs indicating that I'm on the right path. Please help me to trust implicitly in what you tell me and to see and follow all the signs you put in my path. I don't want to do this without you for even one day. Please show me the way.

Lesson 50:

I trust my guide. I will follow directions.

Trust isn't something we wake up and decide we have one day. It's something we build, brick by brick. How do we build trust? We educate ourselves on what it is we're trusting in.

Think about it this way. If a random guy comes up to you on the street and says: "Hi, I'm Lefty Carmichael, and I think you should trust me to handle all your money, income and expenses from here on out."

You're going to be like: "No ways! Who the hell are you? You could be an ax-murdering con artist; there's absolutely no way I'm going to trust you with my money. Get away from me, weirdo."

You don't know them, so how can you trust them?

Whereas if it's someone you recognize as a world-famous financial advisor, who handles trillions of dollars in assets and has doubled and tripled the income of everyone they've worked with, it's a different story when they suggest you trust them to handle your money.

You say something like, "Hey, I recognize you from TV! And I've seen the results of your work in so many different publications! I took just a little bit of your advice one time and had a total breakthrough. Would you please manage my money?"

For you to trust your inner guide, we've got to get y'all very comfortable with each other. You also have to get very comfortable with letting your inner guide handle the little stuff, so that when it comes time to ask for guidance with bigger stuff - you'll know she can handle it.

The voice of our inner guide is very quiet. She doesn't argue (that's your brain), she'll just repeat what she said. She works like a muscle. The more you work it, the bigger it gets, and the easier it is to hear. Because this can be difficult, I'd like to give you a practice you can use for the next ten days to get you comfortable with how your inner guide communicates. Every day of our review period, you'll be using this feeling like an internal GPS. Commit to this 100% because if you do, you'll be able to go to yourself for guidance on the spot, always. You won't have to consult your oracle cards or wait until Mercury stations direct first. It's just ten days, and you won't end up in Central Booking if you listen to your inner guide for ten days.

The main way your soul communicates that you're on the right path is through the feeling of joy. Yes, joy.

Contrary to the impressions you may have picked up in church as a child; suffering does not indicate you getting closer to reward. Like my favorite massage therapist says: "No pain, no pain."

Whatever we focus on grows. It's a Universal law that applies to all things in this Universe. If we shift our priorities to feeling more joy - that grows. You get more joy!

Now when it comes to big decisions like leaving your fiancé or job, you might be a bit trepidatious about letting joy make these decisions for you, which is why for these next ten days, we're going to ask joy to guide us with every single decision.

Get out of bed and go to the gym or sleep in? What would bring you more joy?

Sugar in your coffee, or no? What would bring you more joy?

Black turtleneck or yellow dress? What would bring you more joy?

Go on a date or Netflix at home? What would bring you more joy?

Joy is guiding you all the time, but you must be able to take directions.

Now sometimes you're in the worst mood ever, and maybe you have been for the last thirty years. That's okay. Here's how you proceed...

If your brain is saying: "I'm miserable, and nothing sounds good, everything sounds horrible, and I hate all of my options."

You need to treat yourself like a baby you're soothing. Like this: "Oh honey that sounds horrible, I'm so sorry. Is there anything, anything I can do to make it better?" Baby will likely say, "No! There's nothing."

You'll stay super soft here: "Oh baby, I know. I wish there was something I could do. Is there anything at all I can do to make it better?"

And baby will probably say, "No. All I want to do is stay right here in bed."

And that's your ticket! If the only thing that sounds good is wanting to stay in bed - that's your ticket. Of the things you COULD do, that's your top pick. So, instead of berating your baby by calling yourself a lazy asshole for being in bed, acknowledge that right now, you're choosing the bed, and when something better comes along - you'll do that.

What if you have to do something like go to work, and you hate your job?

When it's something we need to do, ask, "Is there any way I can bring joy into this?" Would leaving early, wearing an outfit you love or waking up early to have a long coffee before going in bring a sense of joy into it?

What if you quit your job today, and even if today wasn't your last day or even the day you put your notice in, you knew that your exit strategy was being developed and your days there were numbered (if you need help with this, you can do my workshop How To Start A Business From Scratch). If you knew you wouldn't be stuck at this job forever, would that bring joy into it?

Maybe you need to call out of work today? But what would you do with your day if there wasn't work to go to? Plan out a free day for you, and if that's radiating with pure, fizzy, joy - then that's your ticket!

Ten days letting joy guide you and following where she leads. I know these ten days will change the course of your whole life. Just watch. :)

All right, let's review. If something is calling out to you, make a post it! We'll review five lessons a day.

Lesson 51:

Review 1-5

1.) **Everything I see is neutral.**

The world is a blank canvas I project my thoughts onto.

Where is joy leading me today?

2.) **Everything I see is neutral until I give it meaning.**

I write a story about everything I see.

3.) **I don't understand what I'm seeing.**

I only see this story.

4.) **None of these thoughts mean anything.**

This story only exists inside my head.

5.) **I'm never angry about what I think I'm angry about.**

It's always the same story with me.

Lesson 52:

Review 5-10

Where is joy leading me today?

6.) I'm upset because I'm believing something that isn't true.

I've never questioned this story until now.

7.) All I see is what's behind me.

This story clouds my vision and mind.

8.) I'm always thinking about the past.

I live in a world that doesn't exist.

9.) I'm not seeing the real story.

I'm just seeing MY story.

10.) I am not my thoughts.

If I'm not the body or the mind, what am I?

Lesson 53:

Review 11-15

Where is joy leading me today?

11.) Each thought I believe creates a world I see.

My thoughts are doing something in my life.

12.) I'm upset because I believe a thought that isn't true.

My thoughts are not bad, they're just not accurate.

13.) My unchecked thoughts empower fear.

If I'm not in charge of them, they're in charge of me.

14.) Fear is not the natural state of things.

God has not given us the spirit of fear but of power, and of love, and of a sound mind.

15.) The thoughts I choose determine the experiences I have.

I can choose my thoughts.

Lesson 54:

Review 16-20

Where is joy leading me today?

16.) The world is neutral; my thoughts are not.

I have to be vigilant over my unchecked thoughts.

17.) I see nothing as neutral.

I make a story about everything I see.

18.) How I see impacts what others will see.

When I heal, I am not healed alone. - A Course in Miracles

19.) How I think impacts how others think.

When I heal, I am not healed alone. - A Course in Miracles

20.) I came here to see.

I am no longer willing to live a false existence.

Lesson 55:

Review 21-25

Where is joy leading me today?

21.) I'm determined to see what's real.

Resist psychic death!

22.) I'm either seeing clearly or attacking myself.

It's one or the other.

23.) If I stop attacking others, the world stops attacking me.

Repeat after me: If I stop attacking others, the world stops attacking me.

24.) I don't know what I want.

I will accept that I don't know what I want, but God does.

25.) I see whatever storyline I value most.

I need to place my value wisely.

Lesson 56:

Review 26-30

Where is joy leading me today?

26.) All judgment is a two-way street.

I am never "getting away" with judgment.

27.) Seeing without judgment must become a priority.

I am willing to take responsibility for my judgments.

28.) I am absolutely determined to see without judgment.

I will work on this until everything improves and then continue to work on it.

29.) Perfection exists in everything I see.

Let it be beautiful.

30.) Everyone is doing the best they can.

Love is freedom.

Lesson 57:

Review 31-35

Where is joy leading me today?

31.) I am not a victim of a hostile Universe.

I'm always grateful down the road.

32.) I created a hostile Universe.

I give everything all the meaning it has.

33.) If I created a hostile Universe, I can also create a friendly one.

I have the power to change how I feel.

34.) I believe in a friendly Universe.

Cosmic forces are working on my behalf, at all times.

35.) This friendly universe is home to everyone and everything I see.

We are all safe, and where we're meant to be.

Lesson 58:

Review 36-40

Where is joy leading me today?

36.) I will accept the best-case scenario.

If I can accept the worst case, I can also accept the best case.

37.) I will see a pattern of perfection.

Let it be beautiful.

38.) Why do this shouldn't be happening?

I'll sit down and give it a think.

39.) The Universe supports what I want.

It's safe to want what I want.

40.) I am not alone.

I've never been alone.

Lesson 59:

Review 41-45

Where is joy leading me today?

41.) When I think as God thinks, anything is possible.

I'm open to infinite possibilities.

42.) If the universe doesn't punish people, I won't either.

I am freed from the fear of punishment.

43.) Acceptance is 20/20.

I can see only through acceptance.

44.) I'd prefer to think like God thinks.

This is an option I can always choose.

45.) Love is freedom.

I am free to be me. You are free to be you

Lesson 60:

Review 46-50

Can I trust my joy based on the last ten days? Stop and consider.

46.) The Universe is friendly.

This is the bottom line.

47.) I am safe in a friendly universe.

It has always been this way.

48.) I am always bigger than my fear.

I win every time I step into the ring.

49.) I am never too busy to ask for directions.

I can't afford to go at it alone anymore.

50.) I trust my guide. I will follow directions.

I will ask, I will listen, I will apply.

Lesson 61:

I am good.

The ego will tell you that this is the most egotistical thing you can say about yourself and that you have no right to claim this about yourself. While there might be a voluminous internal argument about if this statement is okay or not with you, it doesn't matter. It's just the truth. The truth will always be the truth.

I will give you a spoiler alert, so this can sink in for you right now. To harness your I Am power right now and accept that you ARE inherently good and have no barriers to manifesting anything you want into reality - you need to know why you're so special. Why do you get to be good?

You are special. And good. So am I. And so is every other person in the entire world. You'll get bonus points and be able to apply this to your life now by deciding that everyone, everywhere, like you, is good. Even if it's hidden.

Lesson 62:

Forgiveness is what I'm here to do.

Forgiveness is the first and most powerful miracle you will work in this lifetime, and it will change the way you see your past, present, and future instantaneously.

The Course teaches that for every discomfort we ever experience in our lives, all we have to do is ask, "What needs to be forgiven for this to go away?" Forgiveness is powerful, and it is your function. To be free in this life, forgiveness will need to become your lifestyle.

Forgiveness, initially, teaches you how to reframe an upset. Forgiveness as a lifestyle means you forgive someone BEFORE they upset you so they aren't able to hurt you. Reflexive forgiveness changes the way the world looks to you, and it shows you a world of miracles.

Forgiveness takes practice, but you're practicing so you're well on your way. It's your function. If you forgave as a sole function, you would have a rich and meaningful life as a fully enlightened being of Supreme Consciousness. While full-blown enlightenment at the top of the Himalayas may not be this life's particular story for you, you can allow forgiveness to release the pain of unfulfilled expectations and resentments.

Lesson 63:

The best way to teach is to be.

In grief recovery, I learned that you should never ever tell someone that you've forgiven them, it's condescending and a major trigger.

Have you ever met someone with such a good vibe? Just being around them made you feel peaceful, and calm, and that everything was going to work out. This is what good energy looks like. Good energy comes from being free from fear (aka not stressing out), from being free from judgments (aka not throwing shade or being two-faced) and seeing everyone as a reflection of yourself and treating them accordingly.

Close your eyes and visualize the most loving version of yourself in all your affairs today. I mean it. Really do it. When you see that being loving is a simple choice you can make that requires no cooperation from anyone or anything, and you visualize what that would look like for you today - you can achieve it easily!

Lesson 64:

If I am angry, it's my responsibility.

Responsibility: respond + ability. The ability to respond to a situation.

We "know" that we're in charge of our feelings, but we don't use it. We say, "well actually, it's not my responsibility I'm mad because of society/the President/God/ my family/the economy/ he's a dick and they need to change before I can be happy." No.

That's not how this life works. If you poison yourself with anger, Donald Trump won't die. If you poison yourself with anger, you will die.

It feels like falling to your knees to actually accept this statement as true, but if you do you will grow, oh my God, you will grow.

If I am angry, it is always 100% my responsibility.

Lesson 65:

Please remind me I came here to learn.

You need not attend every argument you're invited to, and you will be invited to many. The world you are seeing has a goal, and that goal is to make you forget that you have a choice to create it. When you're forgiving as a function, you are constantly questioning the reality of what you see by reframing it. It's easy to forget, and the more you start to live with forgiveness as your function, the bigger the obstacles will get. Don't let this discourage you; you'll be getting stronger every day.

Today's mantra is just like the "lead us not into temptation" clause of the Lord's Prayer in the Bible. You're just sending a memo to your subconscious to please let you not forget the choice you have to react differently. When you can remember this, joy is inevitable.

Can you set aside ten minutes today to meditate on this with your eyes closed? Get comfortable. Breathe deeply. Like how I taught you.

Breathing in 2-3-4, Hold 2-3-4, Breathing out, 2-3-4, Hold 2-3-4

May we always remember the great choice we have.

Lesson 66:

Forgiving makes me happy.

INCENTIVE!!

Forgiving the world will make you HAPPY. It's not going to feel like work.

The ego is constantly fighting, but Spirit is permanently chilling. Ego chases its own tail looking for anything to keep the fight going.

Ego has given you so many functions in your life. The judge, the disciplinarian, the voice for the underdog, the overachiever, the failure, the survivor, the caretaker, the rescuer, the "good" girl or boy, and the "bad" girl or boy. None of these roles represent your true function. Your true function is just BEING as perfect as you naturally are and letting other people BE as perfect as they naturally are.

Lesson 67:

Love created me loving.

It's so easy to forget who you are, where you come from, and what you're capable of. As you progress on a spiritual path, there are going to be a lot of people who aren't such big fans of The New You. If you change positively, it means they can too, and that's threatening for people who don't like change. There have been situations in the distant and recent past where people have said horrible things about me, and it's hard not to take some to heart.

But then I remember who I am and where I come from. I remember why I'm here and that when I heal, I am not healed alone.

The beat of your heart, the magic of your vascular system, the rhythm of your breath - you were designed perfectly by something perfect.

Let every breath today be a reminder:

Love created me loving.

Holiness created me holy. Kindness created me kind.

Helpfulness created me helpful.

Perfection created me perfect.

Lesson 68:

There are no justified resentments.

I repeat: there are no justified resentments.

I'm not denying that people have done horrible things to you in the past, I'm not denying that life can be profoundly shitty at times and that the world can be cruel.

But every resentment you carry, you carry alone. You are the only one who designed it, and you are the only one who can destroy it. Every resentment (or grievance) is an incompletion in you, a place where YOU can do something to heal it. An incompletion that will take up way more space and energy than you give it credit for and will continue to hurt you until you can let it go.

I will guide you clearly into your meditation here:

Scan your mind for the major incidents you recall being hurt; they should pop into your mind immediately. Now you will look for some of the smaller ones, a side-eye from someone, a rude lady at a grocery store, etc. There is no one whom you hold no grievance against in some form. Who you feel owe you nothing. These resentments make you feel alone in this world.

Now, I know this is hard. But love created you loving. You were not created by resentment; therefore, you cannot naturally be resentful. Gaze at the people who have hurt you in your mind's eye and say:

"From now on, I send you love."

That's it. Yes, you may have felt some crazy things in the past, and yes, maybe they owe you an apology, and yes, they fucked up, and if we were in the judge's seat, we were right, and they were wrong BUT - from now on, you send them love.

Lesson 69:

My resentments block me.

Underneath the sadness and confusion we face daily lies a force so pure and so infinite it can solve any problem, heal any illness, and answer any question we might ever have.

It's always there, no matter what. But it can seem hidden, and what it's hidden behind is our judgments, fears, and lack mentality.

The Course has such a beautiful way of guiding this particular meditation, I will include it here as it is originally written in the first edition of *A Course in Miracles*.

Quietly now, with your eyes closed, try to let go of all the content that generally occupies your consciousness. Think of your mind as a vast circle, surrounded by a layer of heavy, dark clouds. You can see only the clouds because you seem to be standing outside the circle and apart from it.

From where you stand, you can see no reason to believe there is a brilliant light hidden by the clouds. The clouds seem to be the only reality. They seem to be all there is to see. Therefore, you do not attempt to go through them and past them, which is the only way you would be convinced of their lack of substance. We will make this attempt today.

After you have thought about the importance of what you are trying to do for yourself and the world, try to settle down in perfect stillness, remembering only how much you want to reach the light in you today, now! Determine to go past the clouds. Touch them in your mind. Brush them aside with your hand; feel them resting on your cheeks and forehead and eyelids as you go through them. Go on; clouds cannot stop you.

If you are doing the exercises properly, you will feel a sense of being lifted up and carried ahead. Your little effort and small determination call on the power of the universe to help you, and God Himself will raise you from darkness into light. You are in accord with His Will. You cannot fail because your will is His.

Pretty cool, right?

Lesson 70:

Only I can rescue me.

You are the only one who can bring peace to your mind because you are the only one who created what you see.

The Course has hinted at the notion you and the Universe are one and the same, and even though it's the nature (or Tao) of the Course to keep referencing God and Christ, in this lesson, it does emphasize that you and God are the same.

The Universe wants what you want. The Universe is neutral and reflects to you whatever it is you choose to see with no bias or judgment. It simply is. By cleaning up your view of a lack-filled world, an abundant one can be shown to you because YOU created it.

If you practice removing the clouds in front of your own vision by a commitment to seeing differently, you WILL see a different world. It WILL be shown to you because that is how you designed it. Everything starts with a thought.

Lesson 71:

Only God's plan for me will work.

The default setting of the Universe is love. It's always going to come back to this. It is its natural state, and yours as well. As much as the ego loves to create a story in opposition to this and tell us we must interfere with the Tao (or natural way) of things, that's a choice we make.

Here is where you are introduced to the prayer practice I have been keeping for some time now. How do we align ourselves with our highest self and ask to be guided by our own internal guidance system?

Every morning, first thing in the morning (before you even open your eyes), ask yourself these four questions from *A Course in Miracles.*

Where would you have me go?

What would you have me do?

What would you have me say?

And to whom?

The answers will arrive as the day unfolds if we open ourselves to the idea that every person we meet is bearing a message for us, and it's to us to find out that message.

Lesson 72:

Resentments block me.

When we're upset with people, ourselves, or the world, it's based on a judgment we've made about how we feel they might have let us or others down. Our ego makes this determination based on the ego side we have seen in someone else.

Salvation is when a mind is freed from fear. If I'm judging you, it's my ego running the show and trapping you in an ego state you don't deserve to be in either. If I see myself as I truly am, an expression of Source consciousness, and you as the same - I cannot be upset.

Feelings happen, of course, people hurt us, and it's important to honor our feelings but there are no neutral thoughts. Every upset is promoting more fear or promoting more love - which is the road to salvation.

There are no justified resentments, and each blocks you from experiencing the joy of salvation, which is the default setting of the Universe.

I like today's lesson because it's a simple equation. Hanging onto resentments, no matter how validated they seem, is an attack on yourself and blocks you from miracles. The end.

Lesson 73:

All change begins with me.

Today, you decide what you see.

Have you ever shone a flashlight on a mirror? Try it.

This is how the Universe works. The Universe doesn't judge you; it simply reflects you. If today you make your commitment to being the love you feel is missing in the world and shine it out as clearly as possible by really letting the judgments go - it is the Law that it must be reflected back to you.

On the day, this lesson came to me, there was a regular at the bar who I couldn't stand. During our tenure together, I had kicked him out multiple times, had overheard him saying all kinds of awful things, and I was carrying what felt like highly validated resentments towards the guy.

On the day of this lesson, I was determined to project something different out onto the world, and he was the perfect challenge. I did my best to treat him with warmth and patience, and he completely opened up to me about the difficulties he had been experiencing in the last few years and became an exemplary customer from then on out.

These shifts are miracles, and miracles can become a lifestyle.

You have the power to create a world brighter than anything you have ever seen that you and everyone you know can live in.

Let me pass along this sweet practice from a teacher I love, Sadhguru. It's written above my bed. He asks only that when you wake up in the morning, think one thought: "Today I will create a loving world."

And so, it will be.

Lesson 74:

There can only be one plan.

Your eternal aspect knows what will make you happy in the long run, even if sometimes it feels like you're not getting what you want. Your will and God's will are the same; they are both aimed at bringing you to your highest level of happiness.

If I feel like my will is separate from God's when things aren't as I want them to be, I'll see a lot of conflict in my life, and I'll feel like I'm in it alone. If I can remember, there is only one way things will go down, and that's the way the Universe will have it - I can breathe and relax into the idea that I'm exactly where I'm supposed to be. That I'm not being punished, and that everything is going exactly as it should, then the suffering in my life is immediately lifted.

If you're having a difficult time seeing The Plan, ask those same questions from the other day.

I pray this every morning:

Where would you have me go?

What would you have me do?

What would you have me say?

And to whom?

The answers will appear as the day unfolds, as long as you remember to ask.

Xoxo

Lesson 75:

This is what peace looks like.

Congratulations!

The wait is over, the time is now, and you are ready - right now.

This is good to write on your hand so you can reference it many times a day.

This is a day of total and complete gratitude for the present moment. The pain of the past is gone, the anxiety of the future is gone, and we are simply here in the light of the present moment, giving thanks. Any situation that we're present in becomes pleasant in its own way. It's a choice we can always make if we can remember.

The text of *A Course in Miracles* mentions the *holy instant* a lot. We can spend a long time learning something, or we can have a quantum shift in one holy moment. Let today be a day filled with holy instants for you. Imagine that all the pain and suffering of your life has ended abruptly. Sure, terrible things may have happened - but that was then, and this is now.

Take a deep breath into your surroundings. Sigh it out through your mouth.

Enlightenment is the ability to see peace in any situation - Nisargadatta Maharaj

Lesson 76:

I can choose to see what I want.

You're the boss, applesauce. You decide the rules you live by. You design the quality of your life by what you allow, stop, and reinforce. As much as ego or external forces might want to make you think that you are living by someone else's rules - you create the standards you want to live by.

At some point, if you want to be happy, you must stop negatively fantasizing about what other people might think of you. Try to stop needing the approval of others so much. If you do that, you'll be able to move from a place of honesty without always needing verification from others that it's okay to be you. Ask for the answers and trust in the guidance you're given.

How often are you asking for divine help in your life? Spirit cannot intervene on your behalf unless you specifically ask it to. You can ask for help all day long. It's never a bother.

You are the prayer, you are the one who prays, and you are the one who answers. But also, there's God. God speaks in silence, and I really can't explain it - you have to experience it. The course says something like, "I will sit and listen for the wisdom that is beyond my own."

You can rely on that wisdom to guide your life, but you have to make a lifestyle out of deep listening. Start today. Listen.

Lesson 77:

You don't need to do anything to be worthy of miracles.

Honestly, I didn't really understand this until I had a kid. Seeing how perfect and spirit-filled my kid is, just naturally, was the first time I realized that I wasn't born bad. That actually I was born perfect. Then I had to do all kinds of work around remembering I was never a "bad girl," those were messed up situations I was left to explain to myself.

I was worried about Rainer because of a minor health issue, and I tried everything in my power to control it. After three decades of deep self-work, I had managed to convince myself somewhat of the Universe's love for me, but I was doing "good things" and being a "good person." I was earning it.

I had never seen Rainer do Sobagh Kriya or write a translation of *A Course in Miracles*, so I wasn't sure I could trust God with his healing. How could I be sure God loved my son, too? How could I know miracles were his birthright too?

He taught me that none of us have to do anything to deserve miracles. They are our right; all we have to do is claim it.

Miracles are your right because that's who you are. You are the source of all miracles because your inherent nature is miraculous.

You create miracles as you would paint a picture or write a song. You are indisputably entitled to your creation because it is yours. You don't ask if you've earned or deserved what it is you have created - it's yours.

Your inherent nature creates miracles naturally, and every miracle belongs to you.

Today you will practice claiming your miracles. Come into the space of listening and allow yourself to envision the situation you would most like to see unfold for you. This is you designing the miracle, much like painting a painting. It is your creation. From here, ask that your miracle be granted this or something more, and it will unfold in the way that serves you best.

Remind yourself all day today you are entitled to miracles, that they are your right, and allow yourself to claim them.

Lesson 78:

I'm willing to swap resentments for miracles.

The miracles you've been praying for are underneath all your judgments of how you think they need to look. (Read that again.)

It doesn't matter what you choose to see, the miracle exists regardless because it is the true state of the Universe, but we can certainly focus on lack instead and see more of it as a result.

The Course helps us to practice seeing things differently, trusting in the perfection of the unfolding situation, just as it is. We could easily look at our lives through the lens of lack and have a terrible time, or we could pray.

Prayer is a memo to the part of your mind you think you can't control. You are the prayer; you are the one who prays, you are the one who answers.

Today's prayer is simple.

Universe, I ask to see miracles wherever I used to see pain. Heal my mind. Where there is chaos, let me see calm. Where there is lack, let me see love. Blow my mind. Thank you. Amen.

Lesson 79:

Let me recognize the problem so it can be solved - ACIM

I was explaining this concept to a new client the other day.

When we know what to fix, we can fix it. It's like a breaker box.

A trauma happens, maybe during the night while we're sleeping, and one of the breakers gets switched off of its natural setting - love. 99% of the time, we don't know what flipped this switch.

Anyway, we walk into our kitchen, and the light doesn't work. It's not our priority right now, so we ignore it. Later on, we'll go to plug our phone in, and it won't work. Is it the charger? OMG, is it our phone? We start to panic. Everything is going wrong. Next thing we know, the hallway light is out, we can't find our tweezers, and we're in what Rumi calls the "furnace" of anxiety, which sucks.

When we know the breaker is flipped, all we have to do is go back and fix it. It's as simple as that. The problem is that we're living in pain until we realize what is actually wrong. (I do this).

Today the Course asks us to make a new practice of asking to re-cognize the problem for what it really is. There is truly only ever one problem, and that is the sense of separation from love.

Sent on an infinite wave of peace

Lesson 80:

Let me re-cognize my true self.

Let's focus here on the word "recognize" because it's one of my favorites. Re-cognize. We have to cognize, to process something over again because we had it a little wonky the first time.

We ask our highest Source today to help us cultivate a new mindset, to create a new belief by thinking it over and over into recognition.

If there is only one problem, and it is an illusion of separation, we are realizing today that there is no problem because we can never be separate from something that we are. It is as logical to assume your head can be separated from your neck while you're still alive as it is to assume that you are divisible from God.

So, breathe a HUGE sigh of relief. This is not spiritual bypassing. We're not Namaste-ing off into a pink cloud of denial. You're still going to have tough days in life, there are still going to be situations that frustrate and perplex you - but if you can just remember that there really is only one problem ever and that it's technically not a problem at all - you can really change the day for yourself.

It's going to take time to re-cognize this, but practice makes progress, and I know you know how different you are 80 days in, so stick with it. I love you.

Lesson 81:

Review 61, 62.

61.) I am good.

I can illuminate everything and everyone around me by being the change I want to see.

62.) Forgiveness is what I'm here to do.

You have one job. Forgiveness. That's it.

Now look, it's okay you don't understand forgiveness yet! You're still learning it, but at the core of every discomfort, we can ask the question, "What needs to be forgiven for all of this to go away?" Forgiveness will free us - so let's accept our roles even if we're not sure how we will do it.

Lesson 82:
Review 63, 64.

63.) The best way to teach is to be.

We can solve not just our problems but the world's problems with our forgiveness. Who can you extend this to? Who can you send a silent loving thought to? Here's a little tip I learned in grief recovery. Unless someone asks you to, never tell someone you forgive them. There's no need.

64.) If I am angry, it's my responsibility.

Let me not forget there is an option to see this differently. Forgiveness is real vision, and if I'm feeling less than fabulous, I can forgive and see this differently. Today I pray that I don't forget this option.

Lesson 83:

Review 65, 66.

65.) Please remind me I came here to learn.

I might usually try to self-appoint as either the victim, the rescuer, or the judge - but these are not my true functions. My only function is to be the love.

66.) Forgiving makes me happy.

I do this because it will make me happy. Even if I thought stirring up some drama would be more fun, that was then, and this is now. I am determined to see.

Lesson 84:

Review 67, 68.

67.) Love created me loving.

I'm a slice of a bigger pie. It's where I came from. My conscious and my subconscious are two aspects of one Source. It's not up to me to decide if this is true or not. I am that I am.

68.) There are no justified resentments.

I choose to stop attacking myself. I'm over it. My judgments and grudges are an attack on myself, and I choose to have a different experience. I am determined to see this differently.

Lesson 85:

Review 69, 70.

69.) My resentments block me.

Inside me, there is a light that heals the world. My judgments and upsets hide it. These judgments and upsets are a choice, and I can opt them out.

70.) Only I can rescue me.

This light is with me everywhere I go, at all times. It comes from inside me, not outside of me. I can't escape it, can't leave it at home, and can't ask someone else for it. It is mine, and it is me.

Lesson 86:

Review 71, 72

71.) Only God's plan for me will work.

Fear is a sign I am relying on my own strength, on my own plan. I don't have full faith in my plans, and I feel fear, I choose to rely on God's plan for me. I will stick to my determination to see this differently and allow the best option to be shown.

72.) Resentments block me.

Hanging onto these grievances doesn't help me out, it actually makes my life difficult because it's an attack on my goal for legitimate happiness.

Lesson 87:

Review 73, 74.

73.) All change begins with me.

Today I turn the light on and experience vision for what it truly is. As simply as I turn the light switch on in my house, when I will there to be light, I will there be light in my mind. And so, it is.

74.) There can only be one plan.

I will step back and ask myself why I think this shouldn't be happening. What will happen, will happen. I can keep the mentality of "I must use all of my effort to keep my head above water," or I can let go, float, and allow myself to be carried.

Lesson 88:

Review 75,76.

75.) This is what peace looks like.

The light has always existed, it has always been on, but we have obstructed it. Wasn't our fault, doesn't make us bad people, but now we are clearing the way for the light which has always been and will always be. This world cannot show you darkness because the light has come.

76.) I can choose to see what I want.

I suffer because I believe laws that are not divine. I can always see peace instead. I am entitled to miracles, and they flow to me freely.

Lesson 89:

Review 77, 78

77.) You don't need to do anything to be worthy of miracles.

My vision designs miracles in place of suffering. I create miracles, and they are mine. I don't "deserve" them, I haven't "earned" them - they are mine, I created them, and they are supported by the cosmos.

78.) I'm willing to swap resentments for miracles.

I will have all the pain in my life replaced with miracles. Spirit cannot intervene on my behalf unless I ask it to, so I'm asking. Heal my mind, help me to see the perfection in this situation exactly as it is. Where there is sorrow, bring me joy. Where there is lack, let me see abundance. And so, it is.

Lesson 90:

Review 79, 80

79.) Let me recognize the problem so it can be solved.

There is only ever one problem - the sense of separation (which creates the illusion of lack).

There is only ever one solution - returning to your natural state.

It is SO hard to remember sometimes that we can choose again, that we can see this minus the struggle. But we can always, always return to love.

80.) Let me re-cognize my true self.

And here's the icing on the cake - there's no problem.

The illusion of lack causes pain, but it's an illusion. It's not that the struggle is bad, it's just that the struggle isn't real.

Lesson 91:

This is not vision.

We've established that judgments obscure miracles and that, most of all, we want to see clearly what truly is. Miracles are not a psychedelic experience where you see something totally new and unrecognizable. It's a shift in perception and change in energy, which allows you to recognize all that has been there all along. The miracle exists regardless, it's there no matter what. Like anything else, it's easier to see when the light is on.

I'm not a real stickler about meditation. Should you meditate every day? Ideally - but I would rather get you comfortable with being in a meditative state all the time. How is the best way for you to keep each day's lesson at the forefront of your mind? Write it on your hand? Have a reminder that goes off on your phone every hour? Every time you check the clock, check-in? Do your best, it's enough.

Today when you sense discomfort of any kind, remind yourself: "This is not vision. I choose again. I choose to see."

You can do it; you're three months in already.

Lesson 92:

I can ask to see.

Cognition is software, not hardware. We usually have this confused. Eyes are hardware but seeing is software. Ears are hardware, but listening is software. So, what is it that creates the software?

What is it that looks out from our eyes, translates sounds into meaning? That's consciousness.

There is nothing stronger than consciousness. The brain is so strong it named itself.

This enhanced vision, this determination to see is the greatest asset you have. It is what makes you strong. This vision sees only miracles because what sees from behind our eyes IS miraculous. Miracles are a lifestyle for our soul. We're exercising your consciousness a little more every day, and you and I both know it's getting stronger.

Lesson 93:

I'm naturally good.

You think you are the home of evil, darkness, and sin. You think if anyone could see the truth about you they would be repelled, recoiling from you as if from a poisonous snake. You think if what is true about you were revealed to you, you would be struck with horror so intense that you would rush to death by your own hand, living on after seeing this being impossible.

This one really hit home for me. Intellectually I knew that yeah yeah, I wasn't a total failure, waste-of-space of a person - but I didn't emotionally understand it.

Today I remind you that your natural state is perfect. That you were never bad.

This is guaranteed. Your opinion on it doesn't matter.

I was ugly, crying on the train in Toronto, tears literally streaming down my face. I had just left a powerful past life reading, where I had learned that my soul was wild and trying to be "good" would never work for me because God made me wild. The car was filled with men who were terrified by this blubbering, bawling mess. A woman got on a few stops in, took one look at me, and immediately asked if I was okay.

"Yes," I said. "If you can believe it, these tears are a good thing."

"What happened?" she asked.

And I said, from the bottom of my heart:

"My whole life, I thought that I was sick and couldn't be healed. I just found out today that there's nothing wrong with me at all, that I'm totally and completely whole."

One stop later, we were both crying on the train.

Lesson 94:

You do not have to be good.

In loving memory of the wild and precious Mary Oliver.

You do not have to be good.

You don't need to be different, better, or more than you are.

You do not have to walk on your knees

for a hundred miles through the desert, repenting.

You were never in trouble. You never made a wrong turn. God loves you. Now.

You only have to let the soft animal of your body

You're a lot more primal than you give yourself credit for

love what it loves.

Let. Desire. Lead.

Tell me about despair, yours, and I will tell you mine.

We could go back and forth about our problems, traumas, and regrets all day.

Meanwhile, the world goes on.

Meanwhile, the world goes on.

Meanwhile, the sun and the clear pebbles of the rain are moving across the landscapes, over the prairies and the deep trees,

the mountains and the rivers.

When you know your direction, everything can flow to you.

Meanwhile, the wild geese, high in the clean blue air, are heading home again.

Whoever you are, no matter how lonely, the world offers itself to your imagination,

You can choose to stop seeing that.

calls to you like wild geese, harsh and exciting - over and over announcing your place in the family of things.

All is well in my world.

Lesson 95:

There are no "other" people.

Only one quote today, only one thing to keep in mind.

If you can't see God in all, you can't see God at all.

Where can you write this so that you'll be reminded of it in every interaction today? Who do you have the hardest time seeing God in?

Lesson 96:

I can be free.

You've already won the fight that you think you're in. Your success has already been established. We feel at times like we're embroiled in a conflict between our ego-mind and our Source mind, that there are these two opposing sides inside of us, and we're not sure who's going to come out on top. **That's all just the mind talking.** You don't have to attend every argument the mind invites you to.

Enlightenment isn't a flash of light and new experiences suddenly appearing. It's a re-cognition of what has always been and always will be. Enlightenment is the journey of experiencing a vision free from separation and lack. It's the ability to see peace in any situation.

Your capital-S self is not asleep waiting to be woken up, your body is. All that confusion, that's just your body, your mind talking. This energy, this life force inside of you is fully charged, ready to work miracles for you, as you. It is ready to go all the time. You can ask for answers at any time and receive them if you are willing to a: ask, b: listen, and c: trust in what you hear.

Lesson 97:

I can ask for help, and it will arrive.

All the mesoteric or second-level spiritual teachings (what all religions agree on) are paradoxical, meaning they seem to contradict each other. One of the hardest lessons I've ever had to learn is the paradox of affirming and behaving as if something is already here and asking for help (acknowledging that it's not here).

One of the great reliefs of life is realizing that you can ask for help, at any time, no matter what your spiritual practices look like. But there are two ways of asking for help, and I call this praying to Divine Masculine and Divine Feminine. As a personal practice, I talk to Divine Feminine most of the time.

When we ask Divine Masculine for help, it's telling God what to do. Like men, who need a clear problem so they can develop a clear solution, Divine Masculine does well when you tell him exactly how he can help you and with what. This is how most of us were taught to pray. If I was struggling to reach a new financial goal, this is how a prayer to Divine Masculine would look:

"Please show me how I can make 1k every day. Help me to make wise business choices and to put my own oxygen mask on first before helping others."

Divine Feminine despises being told what to do and loves a vent (the opposite of a clear problem). The reason she hates being told what to do is because she's probably already doing it, and better than you're suggesting. She also knows what you want better than you do, and everyone owes her a favor, so anything is possible. When you pray to

Divine Feminine you just tell her all your problems and let her sort it out. I can't tell you how important this is. Here's an example:

"I feel like I'm never going to make 1k a day and that I'm not making decisions like an executive. I feel tired and overwhelmed, and I'm sick of listening to other people's shit."

Trust the Gods understand both and notice how you feel after each one. If you're a woman and you've never prayed to Divine Feminine, try it for 40 days. You will be floored.

Lesson 98:

I'm a teacher. I am here to heal.

The great teacher speaks little. He works without self-interest and leaves no trace. When the work is done, the people say, "we did it ourselves" - Tao Te Ching

ACIM says that the call to teach is heard universally, but very few respond. There is no greater calling, no higher honor than healing others through your own healing. And you, yes, YOU are a teacher. Now.

An idea, when shared, gets stronger. Your healing will heal the world. When you teach something, you master it. ACIM says "when I heal, I am not healed alone."

The best way to teach is to BE different. To bring a conscious response where an automatic reaction used to be. By doing the work on you, you're becoming a teacher. Your healing inspires others to peel away their own layers. When you're authentic, people are authentic with you. When you are vulnerable, people present their vulnerability to you.

Today's lesson asks you to accept that you are now playing a role in the healing of the world. Your story contributes massively to the healing of our collective consciousness. It has the power to heal the world as it heals you.

How have you overcome fear to become the person you are today? Who can this story serve?

Be who you needed when you were younger.

Lesson 99:

I have one job. See the miracle.

The Sistine Chapel, right?

God is reaching for Adam with everything he has, every muscle and a legion of angels. Adam is reclined, soft, and looks bored, like "Huh? God?"

If you zoom in to the fingers, almost touching, you see that all Adam has to do is fully extend his finger, and he would touch God, he would access all God's power. He's just too lazy.

This is us. Laying around complaining about what is, focusing on what we don't have, and refusing to consciously engage with our lives. It doesn't matter how far God reaches, how many miracles surround us, if we're refusing to see, we're refusing to see Extending our finger means asking to see the miracle in any moment. When we see the miracle, we touch God.

Our number one purpose in life is to see the miracle.

Lesson 100:

My voice as a teacher matters.

You resonate with me because I'm someone who speaks the same language as you. There are certain concepts you wouldn't be able to learn from anyone but me, and your healing is expedited when working with someone you understand.

For a long time, I felt as if I had failed in my life. My life had been painful, I had made a lot of mistakes, and felt as if I had been let down by the world and, worse, that I had let myself down.

All of these difficulties taught me how to be a good teacher for you, and your difficulties will make you a good teacher for others. As you grow and heal and change, you will reach people no one else could reach. You will bring peace and clarity to people who thought they would be stuck in this alone. Your healing is so important, and your role here is crucial.

While yes, we're all reading the same text here and learning that forgiveness is ideally all of our function - nobody does it quite like you. Your people need you. They've signed contracts to suffer until you get over your insecurities and teach them.

Lesson 101:

Delight is in the heart of the Almighty.

What would your life look like if you knew you were divinely guided?

You can't make a wrong turn with the Universe. God's plan is the only plan you want sis, trust me.

I was sitting on the floor smoking a blunt in Austin, feeling some weed guilt, when I heard a thunderous voice say, "Delight is in the heart of the Almighty.." I nearly fell over. I asked, "Who said that?" and before I even finished the question, the answer came, silently. Archangel Michael.

I'm not really an angel person. Hot gods? Sounds like something made up to keep moms busy. This was my first interaction with an angel I was aware of, and the message confused me. For months I thought about this, and finally, it was revealed. God's favorite thing is me, delighted.

The desired outcome for both God and you is your joy. Even when it seems like things are going "wrong" it's happening in your best interest. Trust is relying that something or someone will capitalize on your best interests.

From the small temporal self, it seems as if the things we want aren't unfolding and that our will is being blocked. Well, sometimes it is blocked by your capital S Self, who knows that instant gratification would hinder the universal entelechies working on your behalf to bring you the greatest amount of joy.

To align yourself with God is to align with your joy, trusting that your deepest desires are the signal that what you want is already approaching. So, how can you lean into that knowledge today, trusting that the Universe has your back and that Spirit capitalizes on your best interests?

The same way we do it every day, we remind ourselves over and over again. A belief is just a thought you keep thinking.

Lesson 102:

I'm good with God's plan.

This exercise helps you to see "to me" vs. "for me." If you're trying to live God's will, you need to understand that it's also your will and in your best interest. When something we want seems to have escaped us, the mantra is: "This or something more.." If the "this" seems blocked, it just means that would prevent us from the "more."

Your dream role for right now could have you tied up on location for the next twelve months, missing out on the bigger role you were truly born to play. This lover that has you frustrated and perplexed is teaching you the lessons you need to learn so that you can truly be available for your soul mate.

The entire Universe is rooting for you and wants you to be as joyful as possible. This is a promise. This or something more.

Lesson 103:

I always know how to find my path.

Joy leads to love leads to God. The plan is you being happy. To return to love or get to God or however you want to express it, you can follow your joy to get there. The trick is honoring what makes you happy and trusting that it's okay to be happy.

God is the energetic presence of pure love. Joy is a symptom of being free from fear and in the presence of pure love. You have three forms of GPS for returning to your natural state:

1.) Where would God have me go? What would God have me do? What would God have me say, and to whom?

2.) Where would my joy have me go? What would my joy have me do? What would my joy have me say, and to whom?

3.) Where would inspiration have me go? What would inspiration have me do? What would inspiration have me say, and to whom?

All roads lead to Roma, and Roma is where you want to be.

Lesson 104:

I don't have to earn it.

Miracles are your right, and on the spiritual path, they are a lifestyle. They are available for you any time, any place, and infinitely. You don't have to worry about asking for too much. You can have as many as you like.

This is like the Amazon Prime analogy those of you who have worked with me are familiar with. You can order as many packages as you want on an unlimited gift card; they can be delivered right to your door in two days or less. But unless you're trusting that you can open the door and truly receive all these miracles and bring them into your here and now, you're just going to have a stack of packages outside your door, which is as good as a million miles away if you're not open to receiving.

Here's some examples of beliefs that block miracles:

"Hard work = Money"

"Closing on a house is hard."

"Relationships are work."

"That which gives light must endure burning."

"Nothing is free."

Don't worry, miracles that are deflected by us are held in time until we're ready to receive them. Today the lesson is to simply remind ourselves as frequently as possible that what we want also wants us, is looking for and attracting us, and that it is our right. It is your inheritance.

Lesson 105:

Peace and joy are my gifts to give.

The gifts of peace and joy are ours and can be accessed at any time. They come from infinite resources as well, so we need never worry they will tap out on us. When we share our peace and joy with someone else, OUR peace and joy get stronger. To give to others is truly to give to ourselves.

Because we were raised and conditioned on the terms of a finite Universe, we cannot imagine ourselves not being depleted as we give of our time, energy, and resources. It's hard for us to practice authentic generosity because it feels to us that if we give it, we will not have it. We will feel the lack of it in our lives and will live at a deficit.

It takes practice to cultivate a new mindset based on an infinite Universe, but this is why we're here. This is what your soul has been craving, been nudging you about. This is what makes you feel alive. When you can truly share the resources inherently yours, that never run out, and will get stronger every time you share them, your life will have a purpose you could have never imagined.

Lesson 106:

I will listen instead of think.

Half the time you think you're listening, you're thinking. The answers are always available, right under the surface, if you can be still long enough to listen. Even if you don't have time to sit for 20 minutes, asking the question alone is enough.

"What is the most elegant way to do this?"

"How can I handle this with grace?"

"What is the option I'm not seeing here?"

Learning to listen to a new narrator in your life takes practice, but as the Course says, for every five minutes you listen, a thousand minds are saved. There will always, and I mean always be an answer, but it can be so hard to take the time to ask. This is our work.

Remember this line from the Tao Te Ching - "Even the muddiest water clears when still.."

Today we take a breather from the brainstorm and invite the brainstill.

Lesson 107:

Truth ends worry.

According to Swami Nithyananda, the best way to stop worrying is to share your truth with someone.

An idea, when shared, gets stronger. When you're feeling doubtful, overwhelmed, and destitute tell someone what you believe in. Write a post on Instagram, call your mama, or tell the person next to you on the train. The opportunities will be everywhere.

When we vocalize our truth, doubt disappears. It's the winning thought. Remembering the truth of who you are has the potential to eradicate all doubt and discomfort from your mind.

Do you believe in what you say you believe in?

Say aloud what you believe in. Affirm it to yourself until it becomes a truth and you're not afraid anymore.

"I believe in a friendly Universe."

"God is good.."

These self-evident truths will correct all errors in your mind, and you'll be granted true vision.

Lesson 108:

To give is to get.

In various sacred texts, we're encouraged to treat all people as we would like to be treated. Zooming out a little, we would practice seeing others as an extension of our own self and committing to treating anyone around with as much grace, gentleness, and integrity as we would want to be treated with. We would recognize that being excellent with others is being excellent to ourselves.

Tipping generously opens the floodgates of abundance in your life. Forgiving others for the way they've hurt us allows us to trust that all the heinous things we've done are forgiven as well. The teacher learns from the student as much as the student learns from the teacher.

What helped this particular lesson gel with me was the mantra, "Everything I give is given to me." I would remind myself of the sacred selfishness of generosity and excellence to all. Giving taught me how to receive, and once I learned how to receive - I felt the support I always thought was lacking.

Try.

Lesson 109:

I rest in God.

This is truly my favorite lesson in the entire Course.

Rest was not a big part of my life, neither was God. Everything that I had in my life, I worked for, and hard. Every project, relationship, and home I had was evidence of the blood, sweat, and tears I poured into everything. I was a chronic survivor, and survivors have no chill. I slept with one eye open, I worried about the future, I made plans, to-do lists, and scheduled my life out to the minute. I was always working, striving. Surviving, and not thriving.

Once you know what holds you, you have permission to move freely. Once you know what the beat is, you can play jazz. Once you know what you are orbiting, you can explore who YOU are. You can relax. You can rest, finally.

Every time you say this, your peace is instantaneously granted. It doesn't matter what is going on at home, at work, or in the bank. You can now rest in God.

Not work in God. Not plan in God. Not 90 minutes of Ashtanga Primary Series in God. You rest. You find your home, even if you've never had a home in the world before. You are quiet, you are still, you are safe. It is your refuge and your strength. This intelligence within you that never leaves you and is never pissed off at you is where you can hang your hat, put your dogs up, and trust you are being protected.

Even if the whole world has hurt you, abandoned you, let you down, and laughed in your face - you can now rest in God.

Even if everyone you've ever loved has left you, you've been stranded at the grocery store with no money for food and watched your home burn down around you - you can now rest in God.

Even if you have no reason to trust that anything or anyone could have your back ever - you can now rest in God. Close your eyes and breathe in deeply, paying attention to the rims of the nostrils. Place your hand on your sternum and feel the expansion of presence in your heart. Feel peace washing over you like a glossy wave, soothing your mind and grounding your bones. Feel the silence between each breath. Feel the intelligence of your cells. This is what God is, and this is where you will find your rest.

On an infinite wave of peace,

I rest in God.)

Lesson 110:

I am a part of the whole.

You were created in absolute perfection. Your natural state is absolute perfection.

If we observed the Dalai Lama with all spirituality aside, what we have is a child raised without any trauma. This child is specifically chosen before birth and raised in an environment fully supportive. No shame, no fear of money, no opportunity for inadequacy. When there is no room for fear to grow and love abounds, you have an enlightened person on your hands. The original state of perfection is amplified and maintained throughout life. He is AWARE he is still as God created him.

You can have this too, although your childhood might require clearing some trauma to relax into this knowing fully. At your core, you are God. You are as God created you. You are perfect, enlightened, joyful, and peaceful. Your wealth is constantly increasing. Your vitality is constantly increasing. You are a beacon of love and light. You are not any story that the world has given you about yourself; you are not any story you have given you about yourself. The truth of who you are is perfection. Source created you like itself. Kindness created me kind. Love created me loving.

You don't have to become anyone new, all you have to do is remember who you are. Use forgiveness to create a world that reminds you of who you are. Adjust your social circle to one that supports the truth of who you are.

Wherever you are right now, I'd like you to commit to ten breaths with me. Place your left hand on your heart chakra (the sternum) and place your right hand on top of that. As you breathe in feel the start of your inhale at the rim of your nostrils. Feel your heart expanding under your hands. Watch where the breath goes into the body. Does it end in the belly? The sacrum? The bumbum? No judgment, just observe where it goes. When you exhale, ask yourself where the breath departs from and where does it return to. Feel the beat of your heart, the spaciousness of your breath. Ten breaths are all you need. Feel the intelligence that supports you, that made you, that maintains you. Remember this intelligence and say thank you.

Lesson 111:
Review 91, 92

Ideally, over the next ten days, you'll be able to keep two ideas at the front of your mind through reminders, notes on your hand, or any other method you like that keeps you from losing the plot.

During this review period, the first lesson we'll hit up hourly (bonus points if you add a glass of water to this routine), and the second is every thirty minutes (or every time you check the clock).

91.) This is not vision.

Today we ask that we see all the choices we have at any given moment. Allow this inner intelligence to illuminate our surroundings and show us clearly the infinite support that has always existed for us.

92.) I can ask to see.

This wisdom is your greatest strength. It is stronger and more important than anything.

Cultivating this light, this intelligence will give you superpowers. Literally.

Lesson 112:

Review 93, 94

93.) I'm naturally good.

You already have the gifts you are seeking and they go with you wherever you go.

94.) You do not have to be good.

Your natural state is absolute perfection. You were created as the embodiment of Source energy.

Lesson 113:

Review 95, 96

95.) There are no "other" people.

If you can't see God in all, you can't see God at all.

96.) I can be free.

This awareness has the power to improve everything that you see.

Lesson 114:

Review 97, 98

97.) I can ask for help, and it will arrive.

You are God. You are Spirit. You are the Big Bang. You are the Creator.

98.) I'm a teacher. I am here to heal.

Forgiveness is your portal into a saved world. A saved world is the experience of "heaven" right here right now. Your healing heals others. By working on yourself first, you create a ripple effect that heals the world.

Lesson 115:

Review 99, 100

99.) I have one job. See the miracle.

Even if you think it's your calling to be the rescuer, victim, or judge - Salvation is your only function. It's why you came here.

100.) My voice as a teacher matters.

There are people in the world who will not ever be healed unless you show them how you have healed. You are needed.

Lesson 116:

Review 101, 102

101.)   Delight is in the heart of the Almighty.

God wants you to be happy.

102.)   I'm good with God's plan.

This friendly Universe wants what you want. It is in the best interest of the cosmos to make you happy. Happy wife, happy life.

Lesson 117:

Review 103, 104

103.)   I always know how to find my path.

Joy is a clear sign of an aligned life. God is the absolute presence of love and its primary expression is happiness. When you're happy, you're God. Again, happy wife, happy life.

104.)   I don't have to earn it.

You're not looking for anything you don't already have. All you're doing is remembering you have had it all along.

Lesson 118:

Review 105, 106

105.) Peace and joy are my gifts to give.

You are entitled to peace. You are entitled to joy.

106.) I will listen instead of think.

Half the time you think you're thinking, you're listening. Be still and know that you and God are the same.

Lesson 119:

Review 107, 108.

107.) **Truth ends worry.**

The best way to end worry is to tell the truth.

108.) **To give is to get.**

All that I give is given to me.

Lesson 120:

Review 109, 110

109.) I rest in God.

I rest in God. I rest in God. I rest in God. I rest in God.

110.) I am a part of the whole.

Let me remember who I truly am, and not the stories that I have about myself, and others have about me. My inherent nature is as God created me, and it is perfect.

Lesson 121:

I can receive only as much as I forgive.

Of all the awe-inspiring things I've seen in my life, nothing moves me more than the human capacity to forgive.

Your capacity for receiving miracles is in direct proportion to your ability to forgive. In layman's terms, when you forgive someone for the heinous things they've done to you and see how it transforms the "reality" of the situation, you'll be able to ask for the moon and trust you can receive it freely because all your heinous sins have been forgiven.

Like it says in the Lord's Prayer of the Bible, "Forgive us our debts as we forgive our debtors.."

We're constantly running a list of people who owe us an apology, or better behavior. Maybe it's a family member one day, a rowdy driver the next day. At some point, if you want to ever achieve peace, you have to clear the balances. When we forgive others, forgiveness is granted us. A guiltless life where no one owes you anything is a paradise, and there, miracles are natural.

Lesson 122:

Acceptance is the shortcut.

I lost everything I loved in tragic and dramatic ways, and when I learned to say thank you for it - everything changed for the better. In saying thank you, I forgave God for all the painful and terrible things that had happened to me. When I forgave God, she showed up differently. I could trust her with my life because I didn't see my past as a track record for God failing me anymore.

They say in the Course that we can seek and destroy the core of every discomfort by asking the question, "what needs to be forgiven for this to go away?" It's always true.

Forgiveness allowed me to fully accept my life with gratitude, graciously receiving and playing the hand I've been dealt as opposed to begrudgingly "accepting" that the terms of my life were painful and traumatic (and thus always will be).

Forgiveness changes the relationship to the past. The picture may look the same, but the frame is different. When you forgive the past, you stop being concerned with a negative history repeating itself because you genuinely feel nothing bad happened. Yes, I accept that it was sad and difficult to get through at times, but I see the ways these events have positively shaped my life, and I wouldn't change them.

When you forgive the past, you release anxiety about the future, and you create a space now in which you and the world can present their best selves.

But you can ONLY forgive the past if you've accepted how much it hurt and how long it's taken you to "get over it." It's impossible to forgive unless you're very honest about what it is that you're forgiving. The incident, and the impact of it.

Lesson 123:

Gratitude keeps it coming.

Gratitude is essential for manifesting. Without getting too deep into this (I could go for chapters), the ultimate way to be in the space of receiving is to live from a place of authentic gratitude.

When you say, "Thank you," you are signaling to the Universe (aka your subconscious) that you realize you can manifest everything you desire. The words "Thank you" translate as "Keep it coming."

Have you ever been to a churrascaria? A Brasilian steakhouse? Go. I hail from Brasil, and churrascarias are a family tradition, even when I was vegan.

When you go to a churrascaria there's a little thing you put on the table that looks like a wooden sand timer. Green on one side, red on the other. As long as you have the green side up, hot waiters will cruise around with SWORDS loaded with all kinds of barbecued meat on it, carving it right onto your plate. (I'm fanning myself).

The second you flip it to red, the service stops.

Green is gratitude. "I'm loving this, keep it coming!"

Red is waking up in the morning thinking about all the shit you DON'T have. It signals: "No, thank you."

As long as you have said "No, thank you.," you'll sit in the restaurant all day long wondering why everyone else is getting all the food they want except for you. You'll use it as proof of your fears and sink deeper into The Hole. You'll watch others in the restaurant get EXACTLY WHAT YOU ORDERED and feel left out. Forgotten. Hungry. Hangry. PISSED. Sad.

To receive an endless supply of all that you want, you need only to flip your signal to green. That's it. "Yo, I'm loving this, keep it coming.," and the miracles flow. Any time you're feeling a lack in your life, imagine that you can change your signal to green. Grab a pen, or the notes on your iPhone and write down five things you're grateful for. Acknowledge that you have wonderful things in your life because you designed it that way, and from this green light, allow yourself to desire more and trust it is on the way.

Five things. Gratitude. As much as possible. It's a cliche for a reason.

Lesson 124:

God likes me.

As we've talked about before, there's only ever one problem, and that's the idea that God doesn't like you. That you have to call on God and hope that she likes you enough to want to back your plans, but she probably doesn't. This is a huge issue.

What you want, God wants, and God goes with you anywhere you go, and she has your back no matter what. You both want the same things. You both want you to be as happy as possible. You cannot be apart from God because you are in God, and God is in you. You are a part of the whole, just like everyone else, with no exceptions.

You will never be left alone. You will never be in danger. You cannot fail. You are safe.

Lesson 125:

Even the muddiest waters clear when still.

Half the time you think you're thinking, you're listening to the mind talking incessantly to you. You can listen to your true Self, outside of the mind, best when you're still and quiet. Even the muddiest waters clear when still (Tao Te Ching).

You receive an answer every time you ask for it, the work is learning how to trust what you hear implicitly and follow through. If you don't know what to ask, ask to see what you most need to see at this time - and it will be granted.

What would your life look like if you knew you were divinely guided? Would you ask for directions? Would you trust each step? Would you relax? You are divinely guided in every moment, and if you need a word, simply be still and know that you are God.

Lesson 126:

All I give is given to me.

When living in the illusion of lack (learn more about this in my YouTube video on Scarcity Mindset) we cannot imagine the idea of receiving what we give. We feel that if we share what we have, we will feel its absence in our lives, that we will no longer have it and our life will feel the deficit.

From a very zoomed-out perspective, there is no world outside of you. Generosity to all beings with all things is treating others as an extension of your own self because we are all one. Generosity is the key to unlocking the flow of abundance into your life.

Giving is kicking scarcity in the ass while singing.

Now look, I definitely err on the side of being too generous, and it backfired nearly every time (honestly). Turns out that when you're giving to someone because you want to change their situation, it can easily be motivated by sneaky codependency and attachment to results instead of "give it and forget it." Here's some of the rules for conscious generosity I've learned the hard way.

Give as much as feels GOOD when it feels GOOD to do it. Never give out of guilt or shame because you feel like you "should" or because other people do. Don't give 10% because TR does, or 5% because DDT does. Give what feels good when it feels good.

Avoid giving because you're trying to "help someone." Look I know it seems like, "wait, why else would I ever give anyone money besides wanting to help them?" but here's how you can spot the difference:

If you give money to a homeless person, you're not expecting to come back the next day and see them employed and clean-shaven. You accept that that's where they've lived their life and assume the thought of "get a job" has crossed their mind, and they're obviously not interested. If you live in New York, you don't give to homeless people every day (you'd be broke in a week), it's really just when someone catches your eye or tugs a heartstring, and it's just like bam, bam, here's everything in my pocket, bye. It feels good, seems like the right time, and you have the money and are happy to give it whether it's going to beer, food, or continuing education. You have no attachment to the outcome. This "give it and forget it" is the ONLY way to give, the ONLY way that sends that clear signal that more is always right behind it. You never wake up at night feeling broke and wishing you could go take that $3 back from the homeless man, you feel me?

It's way better to have an awkward conversation about how you won't be giving more money than giving when it feels shitty.

Lastly, don't give when you know it would sabotage you. If you don't know how you're paying your rent, figure that out first. I know so many people who finally get that paycheck and then insist their sibling/parent take the whole thing because "plenty more where that came from."

Pray for the person to see all their options, and you can respond, "I'll pray for you" if you need to. If you feel like everyone would prefer money to prayer, that's cause you obviously don't think prayer is that valuable, and you would probably prefer money because YOU NEED IT! Not a good time to give. But prayer is very valuable, just make sure you actually stop and pray for them.

"May they see all their options" is a great prayer when you don't know what's right for someone (all the time)

Lesson 127:
Today, I will create a loving world.

There is one source of all things, and this is what people call a Higher Power. You decide on what it is for you. It can be spacetime, dark matter, Buddha, Source, or love. It's all going to lead you to the same spot. If you contemplate anything in nature (God-made) for long enough, you'll awaken. Whether it's contemplating the innate GPS of the monarch butterflies, fungal networks and microbiomes, the origins of any stone anywhere, or the way the oak leaves arrive year after year no matter how worried you are that the New Mexico frost has taken them out - if you look at anything God has created long enough, you will see her unfathomable wisdom and presence in all things.

If we zoom out and look at the universal conditions that allow us to thrive on Earth without getting sizzled by the sun, flooded by the oceans, or floating off into space, it's easier to assume that maybe the entire universe is conspiring on our behalf.

Whatever/Whoever God is to you - it loves you. You're here. You're well. You have access to teachings that will forever change your life in a positive way. You are good. You are loved.

Sadhguru, who gave me today's lesson title says:

"Every day, 150,000 people die. When you woke up this morning, were you alive? Was everyone you know still alive? Why don't we rejoice every day we remember that we and all we love are still alive, and well."

What does love mean to you? Is there potential for it in all experiences? Do we possess it? Is it inside of us? Is it inside of everyone else? Does everyone want it? Does it run out? Can fear exist in it? Can it be shared?

At the end of the day, we all want the same things, to love and be loved unconditionally - as we are. Because we all share one common desire, it can all be satiated with one common energy - love.

In ACIM, it says that all communication is a cry for help or a loving response. If it's not a loving response, it's a cry for help. Everyone in every situation is only ever asking for one thing, and that's love. Love is accepting someone as they are today, not who you think they could be with a little work. You cannot love potential. Potential is your expectations of someone else that they never agreed to. It is absolutely not love.

When I read this, I visualize the most loving version of myself handling all my affairs, and when I see an image of it, I realize I could feasibly do it. Now listen, I forget almost all the time. I'm usually 100% convinced that I'm right, and I boss my husband around even when I'm sleeping. Yes. In my sleep, I've even got demands. But I'm trying every day to be softer, slower to react, and more patient. So, even after all this time, I've still got this mantra written above my bed.

Where will you take yours?

Lesson 128:

I don't want what I think I want.

This can be a really hard concept to integrate because we have the order of manifestation confused in our heads.

We believe that obtaining objects (e.g., Ferrari) will generate feelings of success, and it is not so. It's actually completely the opposite. You have to first feel successful to be able to buy a Ferrari and not feel like you'll be a poor impostor in a rich woman's car.

Here's another example: I want to feel loved and desired. I think that if I can select what I want from the world, a.k.a. Mr. Right, then he will make me feel lovable, which will then create the belief that I am lovable, and I can take this shortcut to build self-worth. This is not true and is also going to waste my time until I set it right. If I tried to get a Mr. Right before believing I deserve someone who treats me like a queen, I will sabotage the relationship because I think someone like that has to be crazy to love someone like me.

The first confusion is I think I want "Mr. Right" when actually I want to be loved, and that work must begin with me.

That work looks like this:

I must first come to believe that I am inherently lovable (a belief is just a thought you keep thinking). I have to locate and diffuse all the reasons why I think I'm not lovable so that it doesn't feel like I'm lying to myself when I say, "I'm lovable." If I can do this, I will naturally generate feelings of worthiness and desirability with no one else being there, and only then can I attract someone who will reflect the truth of this new belief. I am happy in the meantime, and even if

Mr. Right is only Mr. Right Now - my belief won't be shaken if this person leaves.

In a few days, we'll get to the one true wish for life, but for now, let's remember what the first week of this work taught us. We give everything we see all the meaning it holds for us. We assign so much value to our external circumstances because we think it holds the key to our happiness and enlightenment, and this is not how it is. Everything we could want is inside of us and not outside. Until our vision is cleared and we see the oneness of all that is, we will continue to be eluded by lack and desire more outside solutions for an inside issue.

This will be hard to understand right now, but we're practicing. For now, affirm to yourself frequently, even if it seems strange - "I don't want what I think I want."

Lesson 129:

There is more to life than just this.

What this lesson aims to teach you is that when you adjust your perception to show you a world where lack does not exist, you tap into the natural infinite and abundant nature of the cosmos. In this world where we feel like everything (time, money, love) is always running out on us and we are racing against the clock trying to hold on to what we love the most - we are constantly craving things, wishing we had them, and sad that they aren't here. Say you want a Fendi sweatshirt, and you're convinced you'll never be able to have it. Every time you see someone with a Fendi sweatshirt, it will support this idea of lack you have, making it feel further and further away from you. This is the world we are certain we have to live in. Some serial pessimists will even look at these illusions and tell you matter-of-factly, "That's life.."

Acceptance is a portal that allows us to see the perfection of the world exactly as it is right now. When we honor the way life's profound suffering has positively shaped us, we stop thinking we've made some mistake or that our terrible history will repeat itself and we'll never be happy or safe again.

When we accept and forgive that story, we can enjoy the present moment without constantly replaying our and other people's failures. It aligns us with the concept of infinity. It shows us a world where nothing runs out, where losing is impossible, where pain dissolves. Grey looks silver, and yellow is gold.

When the great Eastern sages refer to the maya or illusory nature of life, they're not saying that your home, family, possessions, and environment are all a dream. They're saying that you're never in your home, with your family and things in a safe environment. Where are you? You're in your head, living in the past. You're replaying everyone's faults and failures, judging situations, and being hard on yourself. That's the maya. That's the illusory world you're living in.

May you see all your options ;)

Lesson 130:

It is impossible to see two worlds at once.

It's impossible to see two worlds. The concepts of a fear-based and hostile universe are diametrically opposed to the concepts of a love-based and friendly universe. Every thought supports one or the other, and you cannot see two at the same time.

We get so used to looking at a world filled with lack and pain we convince ourselves that the series of coping mechanisms we call life is filled with compromises and that we must just accept all kinds of "facts" about our lives, such as "Men will lie to you.," "Hard work equals money," etc. You cannot look at an abundant world and a lack of world at the same time because where light is darkness cannot exist.

Be open to it being black and white today. Does this thought help me or hurt me? Does this thought reinforce duality or oneness? Who would I be without the thought?

Lesson 131:

You'll win every time you step into the ring.

For a long time, I avoided long, hard looks within because I was afraid that if I dug deep enough, I would come across something broken. If I acknowledged there was something broken inside of me, I worried that I wouldn't ever be able to fix it. I also figured I was damaged enough as is and didn't need to add one more issue to my batch of neuroses. This is what shame looks like.

Additionally, I worried that if I trusted too much or let too much go, that I would lose touch with reality. That my faith and love wouldn't be enough to protect or support me and would find out once I was in over my head I had been too trusting, God had forgotten me, and I was out on my ass instead of loved and protected.

What would you do if you were certain you couldn't fail? What would you attempt, and when would you start? What would your life look like without the voice telling you it can't be done?

Today I encourage you to go beyond fear. Fear passes through you; it doesn't have to stop you. Go beyond doubt. If you knew what walked with you, you could not fear. Your will has been honored by the cosmos. You have already won. Failing is not a possibility on the road to enlightenment because no one can fail who seeks to reach the truth. You're exactly where you're supposed to be. Always trust more. Always say thank you more.

Lesson 132:

I'm willing to let the world show up differently.

Forgiveness allows the world to show up differently.

At the beginning of these lessons, we reviewed that we have assigned the meaning to everything we see. We determine if it is lack or abundance, fear, or love. Is the glass half empty or half full?

For the new story to emerge, we must first release the old. Cultural conditioning, social stigma, and childhood traumas create deep neural pathways constantly projecting onto the mirror of the world our beliefs about it and who we seem to think we are in said world.

The quickest shortcut to living this is through aspiring to be present in every moment, which is possible when you work hard at it. It's very fucking hard work, I'm telling you. The past isn't here, the future isn't here, and technically none of it exists or serves us at all in this present moment. If you treat yourself as if this is the only moment you've ever been here and treat others the same (holding no grudges, judgments, or typecasting others as the next cameos in today's episode of History Repeats Itself) then you'll be living in reality for the first time. "Be here now" is a cliche for a reason - it works.

Remember that when you change the way you look at things, the things you look at change. If you can let the guilt from the past stop holding your idea of the future hostage - you will arrive into the present moment freed from fear and in the hot seat for miracles.

Lesson 133:

I'm willing to redefine my value systems.

It's easy to decide what's valuable and what isn't because we give everything all the meaning it has for us. Because we assign value, we decide what is valuable and what isn't. We're usually chasing something we unconsciously value, so we just want to check in and make sure that what we're valuing is current and still desirable.

My teacher asked his teacher, "What is real?" He said, "That is real, which never changes.." This is a key step in establishing value. According to Darwinism, whatever has been around the longest is the strongest and most valuable. They're saying the same thing. What is constant is valuable.

The first step of understanding if something is valuable or not is to ask yourself. "Will it last? How long will this satisfy me?" If it has a temporary value, a high that will eventually wear off, then it's not valuable. There's no neutral here, either. We've seen this happen many times in our own lives. We finally get something so important to us, that we wanted so badly, and then it's not enough. It needs to be added to, adjusted, maybe even replaced altogether.

The second part is that if you want something someone else has, then that's not really valuable. There's enough for everyone, and if we're jealous of someone else's something - we're tapping into finite resources.

"There is only one, and they have it, therefore, I never will. I want to be a yoga teacher, but she's already doing it. There can only be one success, and she has it.." The idea that if someone else has something you want, it becomes less attainable for you (because if they have it, you can't also have it) - this is a problem. This supports the idea of a world that isn't all that friendly to you. I recommend my workshop Jelly for this!

As we go on, I will introduce you to something that is more valuable than anything else you could imagine, and when you realize this is all you want, you will value nothing else as much. Don't get me wrong, you'll always want nice things, and you will always have nice things - but you'll know how to satisfy that soul craving. Everything else is icing on the cake.

We only want REAL things. So, what is real? What never changes? That's for you to chew on today! Enjoy it.

Lesson 134:

Let me remember forgiving is for me.

We think that forgiveness means we'll have to turn a blind eye to the truth of things, roll over, and let people walk all over us. That we'll have to just accept that people were crappy to us, turn the other cheek, and deal with it. We'll have to call someone, do some ninth-step kind of stuff, and it will be humiliating and one more nice thing we did for someone who has never been that nice to us.

The forgiveness we do for US. Not for other people, but for us. Anyone who's done forgiveness work with someone that isn't alive anymore can tell you this. It's not about changing the relationship to the person; it's about changing the relationship to the pain you have connecting you to this person.

Imagine that everyone in your life is holding a cord that you have designed and are using it to connect the pair of you. If you have decided this cord is resentment, competition, lack of trust, etc. - that will be what connects you. With family members or people we know we will be dealing with for life, forgiveness frees us from having to stay bound to people in a negative way. Forgiveness allows us to hand them a different cord and lets them show up differently.

Forgiveness is a blessing for US. Not them. It benefits them too, but your life is really only about you. It doesn't matter what they did or how validated you feel in the resentment. Until YOU let this cord go and replace it with something that serves you, this person (living or dead) will hurt you, and you decide when it ends.

So, you're not doing anyone any favors. You're doing YOU a favor. Today is about remembering that.

Lesson 135:

If I defend myself, I'm attacking myself.

The great playwright Anton Chekhov said that if in the first act you have hung a pistol on the wall, then in the following one, it should be fired.

This is how our defense mechanism works. When we walk into situations armed and ready, we're asking for a fight. We have it in our heads that the Universe is hostile, and we must be prepared for an attack. We prepare ourselves for arguments that haven't happened yet, create long and detailed explanations for our choices (just in case), and arm yourself with as much information about our opponent (meeting an ex?) as possible to be extra prepared for what we're certain will be a standoff.

When we show up defensive, we force it to be an attack. If we show up with a gun, we're liable to shoot it.

Vulnerability is the seed of strength. This softness is your greatest strength. This openness is your protection. I don't just mean spiritually, either. I won't recommend you drink snake hooch with a biker gang in Vietnam to prove this, but if you were to - see what happens when you're not choked up with fear and trying to defend yourself by being closed, tough, and judgmental.

Become very, very conscious of your defense mechanisms. Just ask yourself: Why do I feel like I need to defend myself right now? Who do I think is judging me?

Consider defensiveness your new red flag and see if you can't swap it out for a white one. It's only weird if it doesn't work.

Lesson 136:

What's the value of being sick?

I will hook you up right now. I will give you the meaning of this lesson, but at a higher level, you can handle this. Today's lesson is really closely linked to teachings from the Teacher's Manual of ACIM. Are you ready? This is big.

Anything, anything can be healed the second the victim stops seeing the value in being sick.

Everything we hold onto because it has value to us. While we might say, "being broke has no value to me, having a broken body has no value to me," but it does. It's frustrating to hear, but it does. We design what we see, assign it meaning, and ask it to be here.

Can you dig deep? Think about what you don't want to dig into. Grab your addictions, your sorrow, your longest-standing-discomforts, and ask yourself what story they allow you to keep.

An unavailable partner might be valuable because if someone who doesn't love you is who you've decided you must have (in a world with billions of people) - then you can keep an old story alive. The story of "I'm not worthy of love." Is it true? No. Did you know that was what was going on behind the scenes? Of course not. That's why questions are so important. You know the answer, but you HAVE to ask.

Those last ten pounds are so valuable because they're that last little thing keeping you from being lovable as is. Even if you punish those ten pounds away, you'll find something new to keep you juuuuuuust far away enough to think someone could love you exactly as you are.

Being broke is amazing because you don't have to try. You don't have to push yourself. If you "know" you can't get paid for what you uniquely bring - then you can atrophy away in your comfort zone and never change.

I believe anything can be cured if you're willing to look at why it's valuable to you. I have seen it in my life and the lives of others. I have seen miracles, and they all occurred in this lesson right here. Anything is possible if you're willing to examine it. The Biblical miracles of Christ looked like him saying to a cripple: RISE UP AND WALK. The authority of this statement overrode the person's "I can't" belief system. To a blind man who he laid hands on and healed, he said, "It is YOUR faith that has made you whole.." Jesus never took credit - he showed people what they could do all along. Like they say in Verse 17 of the Tao Te Ching

"The great teacher speaks little, He never speaks carelessly. He works without self-interest and leaves no trace. When all is finished, the people say, "we did it ourselves.."

This is high-level healing, folks. As a warning, I will tell you to keep this information to yourself until you have practiced it so completely in your own life you believe it enough to heal others. It's a slap in the face to someone struggling to tell them that they're doing it to themselves, even if it's true.

Magic is spending more time on something than anyone else would reasonably expect. Anyone can heal anything. What good healers do is lead by example and live a life that exhibits this miraculous radiant power so fully that when you tell someone who has never walked to rise up and walk - they do. Psychics will tell you the same thing as a drunk man on the bus might: "Do what makes you happy.," yet you'll believe it more from someone you BELIEVE has special powers, powers enough to invest in. What makes them special? Practice. Study. Devotion.

Here's your homework: Identify your biggest discomfort. The biggest pain in your life at the moment and ask yourself why you are hanging onto this. You may contemplate this for many months, many years - but to ask is enough. If you want to expedite it, call a teacher.

Lesson 137:

When I heal, the world heals with me.

There is no better way to teach than to be different. The best way to lead is by example. I will ask you to read that again, especially if you've been trying to help your family.

By living defenselessly, especially around people accustomed to the old you - you are the greatest possible advertisement for the Universal entelechies. Your healing is the spark that lights the fire, reminding others of the choices they forgot existed in their life, and questioning all you know to be true.

Once you see there's an option to do things differently, it's hard to accept that this is "just the way it is." You're wordlessly inciting a spiritual riot in others through your own healing, and it is magnificent.

Go out and BE it.

Lesson 138:

I have to CHOOSE to see Heaven.

There are many ideas of Heaven being a problem-less world surrounded by pearly gates (?!) where we get to see everyone we've loved and lost. Another example, if you practice Islam (as a man) you get 72 virgins, and if you're a woman, you get to pick one husband (but it can be anyone you want).

There are so many descriptions of "heaven" and to save time and segue helpful teachings from outside the Course into it, I'll explain it like this:

We came to Earth to add to the expansion of an infinite Universe by learning through contrast. When you're all conscious, all-seeing, all-knowing it is all "good!" But when you have nothing "bad" to contrast it against, it is a neutral state, which gets old. So, So, we came to Earth, choosing to forget all we know and interact with people, places, and things that will press us to REMEMBER the choices we have as co-creators in a universe of infinite expansion. Heaven is less a place we're trying to get to and more the reality of the present moment if we choose to believe in a friendly Universe where all resources are infinite. Heaven. Is. Now.

So, when I tell you, "you have to CHOOSE to see Heaven," it's true. There isn't a decision to be made because it has been scientifically proven that we live in a Universe that is, by nature, infinitely expanding. Infinite expansion creates infinite expansion. All things on this Earth have an infinite nature if you CHOOSE to see it as such and act accordingly. That means you have to work hard to drop all the thoughts that keep you enslaved in a walking hell. We must choose to see abundance over lack, peace over chaos, and love over fear.

When you choose to see it differently, right here, right now - that everything you want really is here, you have just walked in the Pearly Gates. This life, just as you know it, but with infinite possibilities; infinite power - that is Heaven.

Lesson 139:

I forgive myself.

Atonement is the decision to accept the gift of forgiveness for yourself. You've done so well thus far with the Course, learning how to forgive others, see differently, and work miracles. When you forgive others for the hideous things they've done to you, you can fully release your past stories of the hideous things you've done in your life, knowing they will all be forgiven. You don't have to call anyone and apologize; you don't have to even journal it out (but I recommend it.). Today you accept the gift of forgiveness for yourself.

Think of all the things that you feel the worst about and let them go. The same way that you've let others off the hook, you now release yourself. You are free to arrive in this world differently. From now on, you send yourself love. Yes, there might have been hideous crimes you've committed in the past, but that was then, and this is now. You are free.

So, celebrate today.

Lesson 140:

If I remember myself truly, I can heal anything.

Your brain is so powerful it named itself, and it can do anything it is commanded to. We forget this all the time. Millennia of social conditioning have trained us to forget this. Sickness is a convincing illusion, and if you "cure" an illness without curing the illusion, you haven't cured anything.

In 1952 Dr. Albert Mason cured a fifteen-year-old boy of an "incurable" case of warts through hypnosis. He was hailed as a hero, and he went on a tour to teach others how to do the same. On one of these panels, a doctor challenged his method, claiming this was impossible and that if it worked, why wouldn't he do it again.

Look, there's never going to be proof of miracles outside of your own mind. You'll always be able to explain it as getting lucky or a strange coincidence. Sometimes, you'll even just call it inexplicable and leave it there. It's easier to fear than it is to love because the confusion of life has made it this way. Whatever you plant in your subconscious grows, and the deeper defaulted neural pathway (fear, in most cases) will be where this seed of an idea ends up. Dr. Mason was not only unable to heal any further patients, but the fear-based belief that this truly was incurable was so strong that the patient's warts returned.

In some Sufi traditions, meditation is called "remembrance," simply remembering you are whole. This is what salvation looks and feels like. The only way to truly cure anything is to believe once and for all that you are whole and complete, and you have everything you could want or need. This is the only way and the only cure.

Lesson 141:

Review: 121, 122

The theme for these review periods is the lesson "I want to see as God sees." The clear presence of your mind in its natural state is God. Free from the fluctuations of the mind, fears, and worries.

Give yourself permission after you read each lesson to focus all of your attention purely on the breath. Allow yourself to go beneath just the awareness of the present moment and into the deepest silence in yourself. This is God.

121.) **I can receive only as much as I forgive.**

122.) **Acceptance is the shortcut.**

Lesson 142:

Review: 123, 124

123.)   Gratitude keeps it coming.

Gratitude is the way.

124.)   God likes me.

You. Are. God.

Lesson 143:

Review: 125, 126

125.)   **Even the muddiest waters clear when still.**

Be still and know that I am God.

126.)   **All that I give is given to me.**

We are all one.

Lesson 144:

Review: 127, 128

127.)   Today, I will create a loving world.

Love comes from one infinite Source.

128.)   I don't want what I think I want.

I choose a different world.

Lesson 145:

Review: 129, 130

129.)   There is more to life than just this.

Beyond this fear is something I want.

130.)   It is impossible to see two worlds at once. (no neutral thoughts, remember?)

I can't live in two worlds at once.

Lesson 146:

Review: 131, 132

131.) **You'll win every time you step into the ring.**

It's law.

132.) **I'm willing to let the world show up differently.**

I want to see the truth of my life.

Lesson 147:

Review: 133, 134

133.) I'm willing to redefine my value systems.

Getting it backwards happens, I can always correct my thinking.

134.) Let me remember forgiving is for me.

I'm doing this for me.

Lesson 148:

Review: 135, 136

135.)   If I defend myself I'm attacking myself.

If I arm myself, I'll shoot myself.

136.)   What's the value of being sick?

There's always something keeping it around.

Lesson 149:

Review: 137, 138

137.)   When I heal, the world heals with me.

138.)   I have to CHOOSE to see Heaven.

I could always stop seeing miracles.

Lesson 150:

Review: 139, 140

139.)   **I forgive myself.**

I've made mistakes, it's cool.

140.)   **If I remember myself truly, I can heal anything.**

My true identity is God.

Lesson 151:

Anything anyone says is God talking.

This is a fairly complex lesson, but I feel it can be wrapped up succinctly if you're willing to contemplate these two notions and allow them to grow. Read each one several times so it can sink its hooks into your mind.

All people come to you bearing a message, and it's up to you to figure out this message.

The miracles you've been waiting for are hidden under all your judgments about how you think they need to look.

If you can't see God in all, you can't see God at all.

Lesson 152:

I can't make a wrong turn.

I will explain to you the Universal concept of free will.

If the "wrong" choice looked horrible and the "right"

choice looked great; you wouldn't have free will. This is the significance of Eve's Apple.

However, you cannot make a wrong turn with the Universe. The choice is eternally yours, and the GPS of the Universe recalibrates. You can choose longer routes that teach you different lessons in harder ways, but honestly, you'll learn 10x faster from one dumb mistake than ten right choices. This is because we will always do more to get away from pain than to go towards pleasure.

What would your life look like if you knew you were divinely guided? Would you ask for directions?

I ask every single day.

To receive Divine assistance in your life, you have to ask for it. Spirit cannot intervene on your behalf unless you allow it to. When you recognize that you can trust Spirit to capitalize on your best interests, you can trust it to lead you towards the decisions for the highest good. However, the choice is always yours.

Many times, we are waiting for the Universe to make a move when in fact, it is our turn. Any prayer we say, such as "Universe, when are we going to get started with this?" can be turned 180 degrees. "When am I ready to get started with this?"

If you feel like you are at a standstill in your life, just make the call. Make the decision based on what will make you happier. If it's the "wrong" decision, you'll know right away. If it's the "right" decision, you'll know right away. If you do all things with integrity, gentleness, and excellence - if it's the "wrong" decision, you can go back and adjust. The Universe will honor your decision. This is the beauty of co-creating.

If you do not want to make the decision and you want to be sure that you are moving toward your highest good, the only way you can be sure that you are in total alignment is to be in an active state of non-resistance, aka surrender.

Lesson 153:

ACIM - In my defenselessness my safety lies.

This is one of the quotes in the Course I use the most frequently.

Like I wrote about in previous posts, like Anton Chekhov said: "If there is a gun on the wall in act one, scene one - it must be fired by act two, scene one.." By having defenses ready, you force the world to spar with you.

Our overt explanations for our choices, our apprehension about going to the high school reunion, our need to "mentally prepare" for the task at hand - these are all defense mechanisms. Defense mechanisms are diametrically opposed to a benevolent Universe. Einstein says the most important decision we must make is whether we think we believe in a friendly universe or a hostile universe. While your mouth may say, "friendly universe," your defensive actions say, "hostile universe."

The amount of ease I've been able to find in my life, in addition to the eradication of fear (I have been in some scary places in this world and have walked fearlessly and defenselessly) is because of my defenselessness. Defenselessness has led me to a space of radical vulnerability, of total honesty. This vulnerability, this openness - is the highest form of bravery. This is the *je ne sais quoi* that people can't figure out about me. People I have never met before open up to me within moments. They think it's magic, but it's not. It's a conscious choice to be defenseless. When I'm not on the lookout for misogyny, competition, judgment, and affirmations that I'm alone in this world - I am open to everything. I can treat people equally.

I cannot stress the importance of this lesson enough. It is the ultimate mantra for vulnerability, and vulnerability is the seed of strength.

Acceptance and honesty allow the world to present its best self through all the many selves that make up our fellow humans.

Today, walk defenselessly. Do everything you can to let today's mantra motivate your words and actions and see what happens.

Lesson 154:

I am a Teacher.

In the teacher's manual of the Course, it says that the call to be a teacher is Universal, but only a few respond to it.

Now, spiritual dexterity is essential for survival. The world cannot have enough teachers, look at the news. We need all the help we can get.

Whether you like it or not, you are a teacher.

Remember, the greatest way to teach is to BE different. Words are unnecessary, your energy alone will transmit the tools for change. So, don't worry! You don't have to fling your laptop out the window and eat, pray, love your way through a third-world country. You don't have to record hours of video on radical vulnerability - all you have to do is learn yourself.

What breaks your heart?

Answer, and you'll see your mission clearly.

So, what have you learned? And who can you share it with? Who can you allow to arrive, as is, into a presence free of judgment, guilt, and control.

Who will your next student be?

"I help people as a way to work on myself, and I work on myself to help people... To me, that's what the emerging game is all about."

Ram Dass

Lesson 155:

I will ask.

Have you ever spent a day asking your inner guide where you should go and what you should do?

Have you ever attempted this on an event-by-event basis?

"How should I take my coffee? Where should I go? What should I do? What should I say? And to whom?"

LET THIS BE THE DAY YOU REALIZE WHAT POWER YOU HOLD!

A quicker way?

What would bring you the most joy?

Joy is a sure sign of the presence of God, and if it makes you happy, it's the right thing to be doing.

If you cannot comprehend what joy feels like, you have work in the heart to do.

If you're convinced that what makes you happy is bad (and you hypothesize on this externally like: "kids make pedophiles happy, right?"), you have work in the sex center to do. (I teach teachers all strategies for all centers in my teacher training Wheels: Reinvented),

But if you CAN learn to listen to joy implicitly, you can move so much faster, and the journey will be fun. Spend some weeks using joy for small decisions, and you'll soon find you can trust it with the big ones. Check-in all the time to see how you're feeling. If you're feeling bad, you're out of line. Feeling good? Carry on!

Even if joy feels a long way away (been there), the right answers will appear if you can remember to ask. With time, you will be in the space of listening all the time without the spiritual foreplay of asking first. However, no matter how far you get, there is magnificent potency in asking for guidance as much as you possibly can.

When you are in this state of surrender, asking what to do instead of just charging forward, stepping BACK from your precious plans and your desire to control, the road can rise to meet you - but first, you must step back and ASK.

Another great resource for this is Video Two in my workshop Spirituality 101, titled The Emotional Guidance System.

Lesson 156:

Where I am, God is.

Everywhere you go, no matter what you do, no matter how undeserving you feel - God goes with you.

Ask yourself: "What would my life look like if I knew I was Divinely guided?"

You have been guided safely and precisely to this moment here, and you are exactly where you are supposed to be. You cannot make a wrong turn.

When you forget who stands with you, problems seem real. When you forget who stands with you, worry prevails. When you forget who stands with you, you're insecure and doubtful. When you forget who stands with you, you're lost and uncertain. When you forget who stands with you, you take shit and get overwhelmed.

When you remember who stands with you, anything is possible.

As it says in the Bible, "If God be for us, who can be against us?"

Lesson 157:

The sooner I remember I'm not alone, the better.

This is where you choose to join forces with your own infinite capacity.

I will share with you how I integrate this lesson into my life.

By aligning myself with Spirit first thing in the morning, before anything else takes priority, I can walk through my day assured that I have connected with my Higher Self. If the classic questions of the Course (where would you have me go? what would you have me do? what would you have me say? And to whom?) feel a little external to you, try this.

I wrote this initially in 2017, and now in early 2020, much has changed and will change again. I'm always looking for shorter and more effective ways to guarantee the success of my day.

My morning routine is like a mala that falls off when it's served its purpose, whereas it used to be a very perfectionistic, Capricornian regime. Now that I wake up with my bairn and scheduled activities, I've altered a bit. I'll include both, so you can see how the contact remains, but the grip is gone.

Every morning, before I open my eyes or leave my bed, I ask myself these questions:

"What is the most important thing to me today?"

This question allows me to set my intention for the day easily. When I have a theme, I can keep it. From a Course perspective, I am asking my Highest Self how I can be of the most service.

2020: I usually wake up 45-90 minutes ahead of the rest of the bed, so I'll jump right into whatever I'm inspired about and can get done while keeping a boob in my kid's mouth. I can usually handle all my daily internet duties from here and then, while the house is waking up, ask, "What would I LIKE to do today?" with an open schedule. Letting pleasure lead is a priority for me now.

"What are five things I'm grateful for today?"

This daily practice allows me to feel supported before I have a chance not to. Gratitude reinforces surrender and is the Universal signal to keep miracles coming.

I haven't done this in ages because I wake up with the most gorgeous husband ever and the cutest babies (I already know the one in the belly is cute) ever in the most comfortable bed ever in the most beautiful room ever, and I manifested the whole thing. This is appreciation, which I prefer to gratitude because gratitude can get comparative. For example: "I'm happy I have money cause I'm not broke anymore" doesn't have the same texture as "I LOVE MY LIFE!!" for 15 minutes straight. Can you feel that? Whatever you appreciate, you get more of.

What's ONE question, request, or thought prompt that could set your day on the right path right from the beginning? Feel free to switch it up all the time.

Some other ones I've loved have been:

What do I WANT to do today? (pleasure-oriented, and very different from "What do I **have** to do today?")

Bring me who you would have me serve.

Today I will create a loving world.

What does the most loving version of myself look like?

How do I want this day to go?

If I could accomplish only one thing today, what would that be?

What feels good?

What am I inspired about?

Lesson 158:

I receive freely, I give freely.

The Universe is constantly expanding, infinitely. To live the fullest expression of this life, we have to tap into our own infinitely expanding nature.

This is difficult if you grew up broke, ignored, abandoned, forgotten, or had hard-ass parents you had to prove yourself to over and over again. This gets us very familiar with the idea of finite resources, and we start to become wary of giving because we feel like if we give it, we will not have it.

The legs of finite resources will then grow up and make an ass out of themselves in the form of full-blown lack mentality. For example, you really want to be a yoga teacher - but you live in New York, where there are countless yoga teachers. If you have a finite belief system, you will assure yourself that the roles of yoga teachers have been filled, that as many people that can get paid and succeed at it have already been paid and are successful at it. The well is tapped out, and you have been robbed of your niche in the world.

To access our own infinite nature, we must cultivate this idea of "there's plenty more where that came from.." To give freely of our time, love, and resources because we are certain that there is more on the way.

I could explain this deeper, but you can give yourself a massive shortcut if you use the secret mantra "there's plenty more where that came from" any time you have an opportunity to share what you have. Imagine the looping icon on your iTunes or Spotify. When it gets low, more will arrive. Always, always, always.

You don't have to believe it today, but you can start practicing.

Lesson 159:

My healing heals others.

Instead of explaining all of the ways you have received miracles in your life, I'm going to incentivize sharing your truth for you so you can experience the true gift of giving for yourself.

The biggest thing we must overcome in our life is fear. A classic by-product of fear is worrying. Worrying is the furthest thing from trust. This is an incompletion with your third chakra, the Manipura chakra. Worry is praying for the worst-case scenario. Whatever you focus on grows. The more you get into the power of choosing useful thoughts, the less tolerance you have for a negativity machine-like worry.

The #1 way to END worry is to share the truth with someone.

Some truths like:

The Universe has my back.

I am fully deserving of love exactly as I am.

When I stop trying to control things, what I want flows to me.

There's plenty more where that came from.

It's so powerful! It's the greatest gift to reaffirm your strength to yourself, to reinforce supporting belief systems instead of damaging ones. The best part is, the better you get at speaking the truth, the more of a career it can become. Imagine that. Getting paid to become the best version of yourself.

Remember, an idea, when shared gets stronger. Everyone comes to you with a message, or ideally a question. When you are generous with your time and take the time to listen to people, you are often granted an opportunity to grow by sharing your truth.

If you believe in what you say you believe in, there is nothing to fear. What better way to remember what you believe in than to say it out loud to someone? It ENDS worry.

Everything you give is given to you, my darling, everything that you give. Your time, your love, your money. A teacher is nothing without a student, and we are all learning from each other.

And, as always, there's plenty more where that came from ;)

Lesson 160:

Fear is not my natural state.

As you adapt to a different way of thinking, it's easy to feel that this PMA is the "new" mindset and that it still needs beta testing, troubleshooting, a few kinks ironed out. What today's lesson seeks to clarify is this peace is your natural state of mind. This is the power you were born with. Fear is the stranger, the creation, the illusion.

All we are doing with this work is returning to our natural state - love. We aren't learning anything new; we are allowing ourselves to forget what no longer serves and remember what does.

Enlightenment is less a flash of light and more of a slow burn. Instead of being floored by new people, places, and circumstances - we are awakening to what has been here all along.

Lesson 161:

I don't have to fight all my own battles.

Today's lesson encourages us to start turning inwards and requesting guidance from our Innate as opposed to journaling out all our problems or trying to fix them on our own. When faced with a difficult situation or a conversation that challenges us, we can ask our inner guide to show us what it is that we should see here.

We can receive any of the direction we want, but we have to ask to see it.

How can you put this into practice today?

When a crisis arises stop, put your hand on your heart, and ask your highest Self: "how would you have me see this? How can I see this differently? What is the loving way here?"

Be open to any message that arrives. Receiving the answer is the easy part, after all, it is ever-present. Remembering to ask and trusting in what has been given - that's the work.

Lesson 162:

It ain't broke.

We spend so much time trying to fix ourselves, forgetting the adage "If it ain't broke.."

We were created perfectly. We're simply returning to this blueprint. We're remembering who we are, where we came from, what we walk with, and what we hold.

There is nothing wrong with you, my darling. There is nothing keeping you from having all that you want. You are eligible, entitled, and deserving of all that you want because all that you want also wants you. Can you remember that?

To assist in the contemplation of this idea, I will give you a piece from the great Sufi father, Rumi.

When I run after what I think I want,

My days are a furnace of distress and anxiety.

If I sit in my own place of patience,

What I need flows to me,

And without any pain.

From this, I understand that

What I want also wants me,

Is looking for me

And attracting me.

When it cannot attract me

Any more to go to it,

It has to come to me.

There is a great secret

In this for anyone

Who can grasp it.

You are good because God doesn't make shit. If you can bask in this idea, all that you want will come to you.

Lesson 163:

Death is not the end.

I thought I understood this lesson until I directly experienced the gravity that death is.

Grief comes from the French grever, which comes from the same Latin root as gravity. It means to be under the burden of a great weight.

How can I tell you death is not the end, those of you who have loved and lost? Those who have had to accept that something they treasured is no longer an option for their life.

In the Rider-Waite Tarot, ominous-looking cards like Death, the Ten of Swords, and the Tower indicate a great change. The cycle of life/death/life is accepted as truth. When we see the elements of death in the patterns of our life, we realize that while the end of something may be profoundly painful - it is the beginning of something much more.

We fear death because it symbolizes the complete loss of control. We cannot cheat it. It comes when we least expect it to those we least expected it to come to. It is the one thing we are certain of in this time-space continuum, yet we find ourselves -funeral after funeral - gobsmacked and unprepared. Evidence of the finality of life, the resource you thought would never tap. We believe in death being the end.

I can explain this more as we go on but to summarize - let me tell you what I know to be true.

Death is not the end. No, you cannot physically hug a loved one, to see with your first and second eyes the freckles on their face. You will feel them, you will hear them - but, maddeningly, you won't be able to prove that it really happened. Your entire relationship after death will rely on your faith and ability to love.

Death exists in that way, but it is not the end. Death signals the beginning of a new life. Although painful - obstacles and tragedies are detours in the right direction, and with forgiveness and patience - you will realize that. It is always this or something more. Always. Always. Always.

Lesson 164:

God doesn't make mistakes.

God isn't mad at you, and she has never been.

When God created Adam and Eve, she knew that they would do the one thing they were told not to do, and she loved them anyway. We're all here, right?

We can spend decades on the spiritual path trying to obsessively fix what was never broken. We came here to make mistakes because God doesn't. If it wasn't for us making "wrong" turns, we would never learn, and consciousness would remain at a fixed level. That means you, with all your flaws, were created on purpose, and you haven't made a wrong turn even when you're sure you did.

In the work I study (Fourth Way), the Law of the Octave states that nothing in nature follows a straight line, that it is law we will fall off course. To get back on our path, we'll need a shock. I teach these laws in my workshop, School of Unified Spiritual Laws. The lessons we learn off course are crucial for that next level of a person we're growing into. It's good to fall off course, and it will always happen.

You can't make a wrong turn in this life; you're meant to "fail" sometimes, and that's how you learn.

Lesson 165:

My love affair with brokenness is over.

We get so comfortable with our discomfort. I used to coach people all the time who would rather argue through the pricey minutes of our sessions they had already forgiven their parents or that they were already grateful, remembering to breathe, and are surrendering.

Because I know this beast well, I can tell when it's an untruth. My clients would cling to some variation of "I tried it, and it didn't work; therefore, something is broken with me, and I can't do it. Everyone else can, but I can't.."

In the Fourth Way, they say, "You only have to give up one thing, your favorite brand of suffering."

I have to ask them, "Why do you not want this to work?" even though I know the answer.

If this works, you will have to admit that there is a mental action you can take, for free, right now, that will change your life.

In the Fourth Way, they also say that the primary block to enlightenment is believing you're already there. If you think you've already forgiven, already grieved, already heard it all before then you're not able to receive new teachings cause you don't think they apply. The problem is that it's a lot quicker and less painless to solve the untruth of "I've already forgiven them." than it is to solve "Forgiveness doesn't work for me."

Clinging to the idea that all of this could be BS, that it doesn't really work, that it can't be that simple, that you've already let go enough (love this one), and above all, God has forgotten you - is your ego's favorite way to tell you to quit before you even start.

If there's something we can prove is wrong with us, we can stop trying. If we accept the power that we have, we realize there are no limits, and we are forced to persevere. It's much easier to give up, trust me. But you get to a certain stage in the game where turning back is no longer an option. At this new level, you meet your new devils. You learn as you unfold that it's always forgiveness. Always love. Always gratitude. Always breathing. You've never done "enough" surrendering, you can always breathe more, say thank you more, love more, and let go more.

Don't forget the choices you have. This is denying the God that you are. Sometimes you may miss the old you, someone that could dump all the blame on someone else, wash your hands, and deem the situation "unfixable." You have more responsibility now, but it means that every day is a new start, that you are the only change needed.

Lesson 166:

I have gifts.

You have what Beyonce has. You have what Neil deGrasse Tyson has. You have what God has. It is your gift.

Coming to Earth in human form is the greatest gift imaginable. You are at the tippy top of the energy food chain. You aren't an ant or an opossum. You have enough cognitive awareness to be at Lesson 166 of 365. You are breathing. You are here. And you affect the world around you.

You have the power to create anything that you want. You have the gifts of God. Once you realize this you manifest many things, sometimes things you thought you wanted- but when they unfold, you realize that you don't want them anymore at all.

So, this is where we turn our plan over to Spirit. My eldest sister taught me this prayer:

"You're in control, you love me, and you do all things well.."

This is a prayer of surrender, where we align our will with God's will. We stop using our power to manipulate what's going on around us and offer what we have to the highest good of all. This is surrender. This is strength.

Lesson 167:

If there's life, there's God.

In Swami Nithyananda's lecture on a vegetarian diet (which I do not currently keep, heads up) he mentions that the argument is not on the existence of life in all things, it is the degree of life in all things. Grass lives. Chickens live. We live.

Through science, we understand that everything is still vibrating with the energy of the Big Bang. That Big Bang was enough to create everything that we know. It creates a presence in all things, a commonality.

In Advaita Vedanta, we ask ourselves what separation exists outside of our perception? Are we all not breathing together? Is everything happening in a sacred sequence, all roads leading to the Roma of one common goal? Are we all on the same side here? If everything is on the same side, nothing can be against you.

Finally, through my own conscious sojourns into the higher realms, I understand that we are all connected. That everyone is here because I asked them to be here, yep, even sadistic fuckers that abused me as a child. If I am connected to greatness, we are all connected to greatness. If I stop questioning the greatness of others, I stop questioning my own. That there is one life, one goal, and we are all doing the best we can to get back home to that.

I say frequently, we are all in this together. And we are. We are all co-creating this experience together as Organic Life on Earth, and we're all part of the same grand organism.

Your highest good, your highest joy, will align with the highest good for everyone. A rising tide lifts all ships. If anyone sits still long enough, they will conclude this. All religions I have anything to do with will lead you to this concept. We are all joined in one life, one love, and one mind.

Lesson 168:

Today I will be graceful.

Grace is a calmness, a peace, a slow steadiness that allows you to pause before you make a decision and confirm that it is truly the choice you want to make.

The most important thing that I've gotten from my meditation practice is that extra bit of reaction time. That extra 1-3 seconds before I open my mouth, interfere, or make that call. In this grace - I choose my reaction. I choose my reality. I choose my experience.

We have eternal access to this grace; it is our gift. It is our calling. We have only to claim it.

Before you leap, take advantage of this gift. Stop. Breathe. Ask. Then move. Even if you ONLY do this once, in the morning, you'll see huge results.

The answers are always there if we can remember to ask.

Lesson 169:

If I can do it, I can also do it elegantly.

Grace is the texture our life softens into when we slow down, stop trying to get somewhere, stop trying to change everyone, and instead experience our current presence here, in this moment.

We can make grace, elegance, and beauty themes for our life. It's DIVINE. A great softening. Sensuality. Poise. We show up differently in the supermarket, allowing others to go ahead of us. We don't honk and scream when a car cuts us off, we choose a Mona Lisa smile of enlightenment instead, nonplussed. People in a rush are bad in bed, everyone knows that. Isn't it so funny? What a world. We can assess a ranting stranger on our social media comments with amusement before elegantly and with no loss of energy blocking them from your page. You don't let bad drunks scream at your birthday party, right? But you also don't have to fight them in front of the whole bar and mess up your hair over it.

Grace is not about being the sweetest, nicest shit-taker in the whole world and calling it enlightenment.

Grace is disarming, beauty is power, and love is the strongest force there is. Unlike anger, love charges you up. You can be elegant in all your affairs without being a doormat. It's just a different way of handling life. Nothing is worth ruining your hair over. You've spent half a year studying why to do this; now try it. Surprise yourself. If it can be done, it can also be done elegantly,

Lesson 170:

God doesn't get mad.

Many people I talk to in different stages of distress tell me they realize the Universe is testing them. This is an interesting concept for me because the story they seem to describe is the Universe purposefully placing them in a situation that is challenging and uncomfortable to coerce them into making an unusual decision or punishing them for seeing how much they can take before freaking out.

This doesn't align well with the principles of a friendly Universe.

Additionally, I have heard people describe situations where they felt Universally compelled to rise to the occasion and defend themselves (sometimes aggressively) or interfere defensively on behalf of a party they've deemed as unable to defend themselves.

One of the primary characteristics of a spiritual teacher is gentleness, which is the opposite of cruelty. I was told in early 2016 that the word to answer all of my life's problems always was and always will be gentleness. Personally, this grossed me out. Gentleness to my type-A, Pitta mind seemed flaccid, artificial, and unsustainable. Also, no matter how gentle I try to be, I'm still a bitch at heart. God said be gentle, not be perfect. I can tell you, though, the desire to learn in me is way, way larger than the desire to say mean shit to people "just because." The number of things I say that I regret goes way down just from the intention of being gentle, even if I'm very, very far from perfect. I got it tattooed on my head; you should definitely get a tattoo on your face too ;)

We come to the Course to learn about the options we forgot about. Defensiveness comes from internal hostility, not external hostility.

Your defenses are usually prepared around what you think people might say to you and not what they're actually saying. Hostility is cruelty, and it poisons you. Fortunately, if it starts with you, it can end with you. No one else has to change first.

These are the forgotten choices we have. If it is your choice to do so, may it also be your choice to do so differently.

Lesson 171:

Review 151, 152

"God is but love, and therefore so am I" is the theme of the next segment of review. Choosing love only is the primary choice we must make in our life, and it is not the easiest one. I have the symbols for "be love" tattooed on my hand as a reminder for myself; that's how intense this gets. These review periods will help the ideas from the last three weeks settle in deeper. They're dense statements, so chew on them.

God is but Love, and therefore so am I.

151.)   Anything anyone says is God talking.

Everyone comes to you with a message.

152.)   I can't make a wrong turn.

You have free will.

Lesson 172:

Review 153, 154.

God is but Love, and therefore so am I.

153.)   In my defenselessness my safety lies.

There is no need for defense, ever.

154.)   I am a Teacher.

I am a teacher.

Lesson 173:

Review 155, 156.

God is but Love, and therefore so am I.

155.)   I will ask.

Step back.

156.)   Where I am, God is.

We are one.

Lesson 174:

Review 157, 158

God is but Love, and therefore so am I.

157.)   The sooner I remember I'm not alone, the better.

How would you have me see this?

158.)   I receive freely, I give freely.

All that I give is given to me.

Lesson 175:

Review 159, 160.

God is but Love, and therefore so am I.

159.) **My healing heals others.**

By being different, I show others what is possible.

160.) **Fear is not my natural state.**

My natural state is peace.

Lesson 176:

Review 161, 162.

God is but Love, and therefore so am I.

161.)   I don't have to fight all my own battles.

I can ask for guidance, and I will receive it.

162.)   It ain't broke.

I have what Beyonce has.

Lesson 177:

Review 163, 164.

God is but Love, and therefore so am I.

163.) Death is not the end.

life/death/life

164.) God doesn't make mistakes

You are good.

Lesson 178:

Review 165, 166.

God is but Love, and therefore so am I.

165.) **My love affair with brokenness is over.**

Let me remember the choices I have.

166.) **I have gifts.**

I am a conduit for Divine energy.

Lesson 179:

Review 167, 168.

God is but Love, and therefore so am I.

167.)   If there's life, there's God.

We're all in this together.

168.)   Today, I will be graceful.

I accept a simpler way of doing this.

Lesson 180:

Review 169, 170.

God is but Love, and therefore so am I.

169.)   If I can do it, I can also do it elegantly.

Be love.

170.)   God doesn't get mad.

Love is always the appropriate reaction.

Lesson 181:

I have no enemies.

The aim of the upcoming lessons is to help tear down the defensiveness even more. Why? Because it's hard. It's also called authenticity, radical vulnerability, receiving and being judgment-free. Defenses are useless. Intellectually we get it, but we truly have to live it and understand it. It creates fearlessness.

It's also going to help you identify what is valuable to you and what isn't. We can get really stuck on material wealth over emotional wealth. Having material wealth is great because it's a natural result of emotional wealth. If you can feel rich, you'll become rich in all areas of your life. That's why all the cards that show the most abundance are in the suit of emotions (Cups) in the Tarot. Whether it's the jubilee of the Three of Cups, the riches of the Seven of Cups, the well-deserved pride of the Nine of Cups, or the overflow of wealth and health of the Ten of Cups, it reminds us that material wealth comes after emotional wealth, it always starts with the feeling.

Here we go:

We're all in this together. Everyone is here to help you on this path and is here because you asked them to be here. Additionally, everyone is doing the best that they can in their life right now, and it's a waste of your time to try to assume what someone's best is and then decide that they're not doing it. Even if they're addicted to drugs, and you feel to your heart that they're wasting their resources - they're doing the best they can, just like you.

What would the world look like if everyone loved you? How would you be if you loved everyone back? Would you test it out?

If you were to BE LOVE for today, to practice being defenseless and asking yourself, "How would I treat this person (my spouse, my barista, the car that just cut me off) if I loved them?" before you do anything, it would transform you.

Whatever you put out, you'll receive it.

Lesson 182:

I will be still for a minute.

Pick a thought. Right now. Stop what you're doing and pick one thought right now. Isolate one, and let's look at it.

Did you know you can do that?

Look at it. Is it a helpful thought or hurtful thought?

Who picked the thought?

This is deeper than "Be here now." You're not just observing the now, you're diving into the wormhole of it. Mining.

This is a small example of what is possible when you allow Spirit to direct your life. There are endless entelechies at your disposal, but you are scared of being needy or asking too much or people thinking you're "crazy." Ask Spirit EVERYTHING. Just do it. Try it. Make it the new normal. Ask for guidance every day.

Where would you have me go?

What would you have me do?

What would you have me say?

And to whom?

The answers will unfold every time as the day goes on, but you have to ask.

Lesson 183:

Ratchet Bible Stories: Moses

In the Bible, there is only one instance where God says its name. Let me create a setting for you.

Moses had a relatively difficult go of things. His mom sent him down the Nile in a basket to save his life when a psychic told the Pharaoh he would be overthrown by a Jew. Pharaoh was so pissed he had the psychic executed and ordered all the Jewish sons to be killed. This made perfect sense to him. Turns out the Pharaoh's wife would be the one to find baby Moses and raise him as the Prince of Egypt. He kills an Egyptian and has to run for his life. At this point, Moses is done living such a crazy existence, his life is extra weird, and he wants to live a quiet existence minus the nagging voice of God he's heard his whole life. He gets married, starts working for his father-in-law, herding sheep, and settles down. No news is good news for a while.

Moses is out with the sheep, and he comes across a burning bush in the desert. It's glowing.

Basically, a neon sign. Moses goes to get a closer look, and the bush says to him, "Moses."

Moses is like

"Oh shit. It's God."

Moses can't hide in the desert, so he hides his face like a toddler. God is amused, but also God is annoyed. Moses has been hitting the leavened bread and the wine bag a bit too hard to listen, so now God has to come down here and burn some bushes to get Moses to pay attention.

God says, "Yes, it's me. Your God, the God of your fathers and forefathers. Yep. Me. You know it's me. Now take your shoes off, this is my land, and I've been trying to get a hold of you."

Moses knows that when God talks, it usually means there's a big change coming, and he's rightfully nervous.

God speaks:

"Okay, Moses, you've been diddling long enough. You're now to go back to Egypt and tell the Pharaoh, a.k.a your stepbrother Ramses, that you're taking 100% of his workers and then you're going to bring them all right back here, and you can all worship me together."

Moses is gobsmacked:

"WTF? You mean I'm going back to Egypt. First of all, I'm wanted there. Second of all, free all the Jews? With what? My stick? What? No. No way. I realize Noah built an ark when you told him to, but this is definitely different."

The bush said nothing but the heat of it burned so bright that Moses's face felt like the skin was melting off. Moses knew he could not say no. He also knew orientation was about to end abruptly, and he had better get the specifics fast.

"So, IF I go to Egypt, who am I supposed to say is leading this expedition? I'm not taking the fall alone. Also, I'm not just worried about the Egyptians; I'm worried about the Jews. Yeah, Chateau Giza sucks, but I'm asking them all to leave their entire lives to come into the wilderness with me and worship something whose name I don't even know."

God says: "Tell them I am that I am sent you."

Moses is like: "What? That's all I get? That's basically me telling them that I'm God. When I say, "I am," they will think I'm talking about myself."

God says: "First of all, don't assume what others are thinking. It's a waste of time. I don't think, I know. With time you can practice this, which leads me to my next point. You are me, but I don't have a body, so I need to use yours. Which reminds me, please stop with the leavened bread and the wine bag. My name is your name. When you call my name, I answer no matter what. If you call my name and someone else is there with you, it makes the red telephone ring in my office. Seriously. Praying with someone else is a direct line to me. I have given you my name just like a father would give his name to his son. You can tell people who your dad is, and they won't fuck with you ever again."

Moses is like: "Yeah, but that still doesn't solve the issue of your name being something that I feel is going to create a lot of difficulty for me. To assume your identity is going to piss a lot of people off."

God says: "Yes, but everyone can do it because everyone has this aspect. They just forget it."

Moses sees a loophole and jumps for it.

"So, if everyone can be you, why don't you get someone else to do it."

God says: "Because last time we were watching Earth together, and you saw the psychic predict this baby, you wouldn't stop bugging me until I gave it to you."

Moses is not convinced, but God shows him the contract he signed with Jochobed and Nefertiti and Ramses, and even the Egyptian soldier he killed, and Moses understands.

Moses accepts. He has no choice, really, but he accepts. Plus, God has convinced him of his ability to perform God-powers. Even though God is demanding change, he can feel how much love this message is conveyed on, and he agrees.

As he moves towards his sandals, he asks God once more,

"Seriously, can we renegotiate the name thing in a few months? It's going to take me like forty days to get to Egypt, and I'm sure we'll have a lot of talk time. Just one word, maybe, like Madonna, or Beyonce?"

The bush glows, for a moment, Moses feels like he's gotten off the hook, but the heat gets hotter. Desperate to avoid the face-peeling sensation again, Moses steps back.

God BOOMS: "This is my name forever,

the name you shall call me, from generation to generation. I'm never not you. The scroll keepers cannot seem to get my words straight, and y'all are constantly misquoting me for your own gain. You can't fuck this up. In Hebrew, it's Ehyeh Asher Ehyeh. It can't be lost in translation. Now quit hiding your face and get the hitch out of your giddy-up."

So, that's how God's name became your name, and if you want to see how God's name became my name, you can see my video here.
https://www.youtube.com/watch?v=jC4UV9fA8kE

Lesson 184:

They're not your type, they're your pattern.

Your idea of what your type is might be clamblocking you from what you want. It's not your type, it's your pattern. For example, if you are certain you like the bad boy type yet are frustrated with being stood up, ignored or lied to- that's probably not the mate you want, you just think you do out of habit. Your ideal mate is the person you choose to be the one you BREAK the pattern with, so going after the same old types will keep you in the same old pattern.

Think about the characteristics of the partner you want and the characteristics of the partner you want to be. Actively become the partner you want to be. If you don't want to be smoking cigarettes in your wedding dress, then quit now. Think about bae's characteristics. If your dream bae loves to hike - GO HIKE! You're a lot more likely to meet someone who loves hiking on a trail vs. in your DMs or at a bar. Release "your type" - that's an old story. Date your face off in the meantime if you want to, enjoy the interval. Once you're clear about what you want, you'll be less likely to settle for less than the best. DON'T FORGET. You are spiritually contracted to meet your dream bae, you will meet! No way around it. But I'm telling you right now this person will probably not be "your type" - they'll be way, way, way the fuck better.

P.S.

You will be fucking this person for the rest of your life; it's OKAY to let someone go because you don't think they're that hot. The universe isn't gonna set you up with someone you're not physically very attracted to.

Lesson 185:

All I want is peace.

To say these words are one thing, but to mean these words are everything.

Until you realize the value of peace, you'll be chasing all the things you think will bring it to you.

You want the perfect partner because you think it will bring you stability, love, and self-affirmation and you'll finally be able to experience peace.

You want more money so you can buy all the things you want and go to all the places you want and not have to stress out about being broke. You believe that freedom from financial stress will bring you peace.

You want to get that perfect body so you can be free from insecurity and lack and health issues so you can have peace.

You've always been chasing peace; you just don't know it. The approval from your peers and parents, the promotion, the vacation, the divorce or repair of your marriage, the kids sleeping, the president, everything!

Peace is available the moment you ask for it, provided you know where to ask and are WILLING to see peace.

To end suffering, you must stop wanting. To stop wanting, you must have peace. To have peace, you have to have trust. To have trust, you have to believe in what you say you believe in. So, what do you believe in?

Lesson 186:

The world needs me.

Don't let today's lesson scare you, or pressure you. You don't have to change anything or become famous overnight. Understand that the consciousness you develop here is the initial drop that creates the ripple effect that heals the world.

Teaching is being. You don't have to worry about giving love, just be loving any time you can be. Through a state of wordless being and gentle action, you remind everyone that crosses your path of the choices they forgot existed for their life. Peace is an option, and you can show people that better than you could ever teach them. If no one shows you what's possible, you can reside in the illusion that this is all there is much longer than you need to be.

Lesson 187:

Blessing others is blessing me.

At the deepest level, there is no giver, no gift, and no recipient. Just the universe rearranging itself.

Jon Kabat-Zinn

Giving and receiving is the same, this isn't a abstract concept to us. The thing is, you can't give something that you don't have. You can't encourage someone to cut out "rational" self-talk or forgive if you haven't personally implemented those shifts. But a blessing of goodwill towards humanity for what we would like to see more of is a gift you can give for your life, and theirs.

Usually, every time someone or something ruffles our feathers, we react with criticism, ill will ("Drivers like you belong in jail."), or even defensive supremacy ("Thank God I don't have that problem anymore.").

The lovingkindness (Maitri) meditation goes:

May I be loving. May I be loved.

May I be peaceful. May I find peace.

May they be loving. May they be loved.

May they be peaceful. May they find peace.

When we share blessings we are acting as conduits for the flow of abundance not only into others' lives but into our lives as well.

Every time you bless others, you're blessing yourself.

Lesson 188:

My soul shines.

You don't need to wait to finish this book to receive that radiant look that is a peaceful soul; you have it right now. The purest and most contagious form of healing you have is accessible right now for you and for everyone you see. Accessing peace for yourself and subsequently sharing it with the world (it cannot be contained) allows you to see your role as co-creator of your life. It's like fairy dust that you sprinkle everywhere that you go. These small steps, re-framing every situation with peace and clarity, create a wondrous and miraculous world for you to live in if you allow it.

At any point, we can stop and say: "I choose to see peace instead of this."

At any point, we can share this. "I choose to remind this person that peace is A Thing."

Either our panic will catch on, or our peace will. Whichever we choose will encourage and teach others to do the same. One choice will keep them stuck in the same drama they've been stuck in their whole life. The alternative will show them that anything they want is possible.

In the teacher's manual of the Course, they say teachers are obvious to spot. That their faces are relaxed, they are calm in the face of intensity, and they radiate peace.

The next time you're in a trying situation, BE the peace. No need to break up the argument and defend who you think is right; just step back and allow yourself to see the perfection in the unfolding situation exactly as it is. If it is your choice to address the waves in life, may it also be your choice to do so differently.

And so, it is.

Lesson 189:

Love is my natural state.

How would you treat the next person you saw if you loved them?

At times it can be hard to remember that we have an immense capacity to love. We forget that with this, we can access the most important aspects of all people, and if it's hard - we can just imagine what it would look like IF we loved them and do the best to simulate that.

Often a spouse-grade fight can be diffused or prevented if we remember that we love this person. If we're on the same side, we can't fight.

The love you hold alone can save the world, so what would happen if you remembered this and acted on it?

Today pretend you love everyone you see. As you anticipate the interaction, ask yourself, "How would I be if I loved them?" - and move from that place.

Doesn't have to be forever, but if you do it for one day, it'll be a day you will want to repeat over and over again.

Lesson 190:

I choose to see discomfort as an opportunity to grow.

The deeper I get into spiritual teaching, the more comfortable I have to be relaying uncomfortable ideas to people like this one.

Pain is inevitable, but suffering is optional, and this is really true. If big disasters didn't happen in your life, you wouldn't know what you were capable of. Think about it, no matter how hard it's gotten - it hasn't killed you yet. So far, you are the undefeated champion of your own life.

You hopefully know by now that when all the dust has settled, you're able to see the situation in hindsight as being perfect how it was; why not skip to that feeling now? Take the discomfort of the situation, remember the other times in your life you felt this way, and remember how, ultimately, it all worked out in the end. You can go through all the anxiety and then realize it all worked out okay, or you can just cut through it now.

You have the option of seeing pain differently. BDSM participants have been onto this for years. Pain is the contrast that amplifies pleasure. To get just the amrita, the nectar, of a fruit. No pulp, no fiber, no anything else - just the sweetness - it has to be squeezed. Is there a way to enjoy the squeeze?

Let it be beautiful. Let it wash over you. The situation is already perfect if you can allow it to be.

Lesson 191:

I carry Divinity.

One of the hardest fights you'll fight on the spiritual path is wondering if it's okay to think so highly of yourself.

If you could accept now that your desires are Divine and what you want, God wants, all your problems would be solved. If you and God are one, there can be no question of if God likes you or not - the question is only if you like you or not.

You are creating a new identity for yourself. An identity where forgiveness is reflexive, love is a static state, and anything is possible. You're recognizing yourself, and it will be tough sometimes, but that's it on the deepest level.

God, he/she/it, loves you. As you are right now. Because God is you, as you are right now.

Lesson 192:

I have a purpose here.

You came here for a reason. In this world, there is only one of you, and there will only be one of you all of the time. You came here with a great mission that you may or may not be aware of already. Every step of your life has been divinely guided, and you're exactly where you're meant to be, reading this right now.

Everyone is doing the best they can. Every single person is doing their best, even when you think it doesn't look like it. When someone offends you, forgive them. Do it right on the spot. You're going to have to do it eventually anyway if you want any shot at a happy life.

Forgive the world reflexively, not because you're turning the other cheek, but because you're freeing yourself as you do so. If you hold nothing against the world, the world holds nothing against you. This is love. This is freedom. And this is the function your highest self would like a little more airtime with.

Lesson 193:

All things are lessons.

Everyone comes to you with a message, and it's to you to find out that message. When people do things that aggravate you, Spirit asks that you remember this option. Forgive and see this differently.

Forgiveness is the light in lightworking. Like how it can be difficult to see options clearly in the pitch black of judgment, forgiveness makes the same situation look completely different. The setting itself doesn't change, but you see the truth of it.

Until someone I loved died, I was constantly offended by the world. If someone bumped into me on the subway or was short with me during an interaction, I would let it affect me SO much. I would either stew about it or tell my customers about it - either way, it would stick with me for a long time. I hadn't tapped into empathy because I was so defensive. Nothing can penetrate your defenses.

I remember taking the train to Penn Station, about to embark on what would become sixteen months of travel, and someone bashed into me as I walked off the train. Their backpack swung into mine, and I was almost knocked off my feet. I was too empty to care, and all I could think was, "Maybe they just lost someone too."

This was the first time I forgave reflexively, and it changed me. It activated a sense of empathy in me that would only grow as I grew. The pain and offense dissolved on the spot, and what could have been the straw that broke the camel's back was the birth of one of my greatest treasures - the ability to see things differently.

Forgive and see this differently.

Forgive and see this differently.

Forgive and see this differently.

Lesson 194:

I trust God to handle my future.

In this life, we don't get proof that all of this exists. At any point, you can choose to see through a lack-based lens, and all of this goes away.

You don't get a guarantee of the future outside of "If you go with the flow and allow things to come to you, it'll be better than you could have ever dreamed.." The past is gone, yet somehow we let the samskaras of difficulties we once endured tint our perception of the future.

The past is gone. The future isn't here yet. All we have is this moment now. Commit the future into the hands of the Great Mystery. Give it away, hand it over. If you can be HERE now, with gratitude, it's enough.

Your dreams will come true, so make them good dreams. It will be this or something more.

Lesson 195:

Gratitude is a guarantee more is on the way.

Everyone knows you're "supposed" to be grateful but let me incentivize it a little more for you.

Whatever you appreciate, you get more of. If you appreciate nothing, things stay as they are.

The most difficult part of successful manifesting is to stop trying to change the present so much. When you're grateful for the way things are in the present, you make room for more miracles to arrive. Remembering that the Universe responds to feelings and not words or objects, if you're happy - you are on the path to more happiness. If you're disgruntled, you are on the path to more discomfort. Gratitude is the most honest and surefire way to assume the feeling of your wishes fulfilled. When you're grateful for what you have (a device to read this on, eyes to read it with, hands to hold it, a bed to sleep in, food to eat) you signal the Universe you would like more of this feeling.

We get scared about giving thanks when things aren't as they want them because we think by doing so, we cement ourselves into discomfort - and that's not the truth. Gratitude signals "keep the abundance coming." Complaining and focus on lack signals: "keep the disappointment coming."

I'm not saying you have to do what I do; all I'm saying is that my life seriously improved when I started actively appreciating what I had as opposed to what I didn't have.

So, it goes.

Lesson 196:

Judging others makes me insecure.

What makes you insecure? Stop immediately.

You're only concerned that people are judging you when you're actively judging others.

You create a world that requires defenses, and you live a life that's less. You open up a window where you think other people are attacking you, but in reality, you're just attacking yourself.

As you get deeper into your spiritual path, you understand the world as a mirror. Anything you say about others, you're saying about yourself. Your judgments hurt no one but you, and that's a fact.

So, be excellent to each other.

Lesson 197:

It's I who should say thank you when I get the chance to give.

So, many of us only see what's leaving our lives when giving or even paying for something for ourselves. We see the money we spent, not the groceries we got. We see the money we donated leaving our account, not the lives that are improved by it, and the more that's on the way.

When we're nursing a scarcity issue, even our best-intended gifts can be sent on energy that doesn't serve. If we feel like we're giving of our precious and finite resources and that we will feel a great deficit if we let it go, we can't give without it feeling like this enormous act of service. When we feel as if we are giving an enormous sacrifice, and the recipient doesn't give us the thanks we need in the language we want it in, it can feel like a huge smack in the face.

When we find authentic gratitude for the ways we can be of service, things change. Without students, paying or not, I'm not a teacher. I'm just a woman with a lot of spiritual information. Without an opportunity to cater my family reunion, I feel like I don't have a place to shine in my family. What a gift to have an occasion to rise to, to find my niche, to be of service. What better way to acknowledge the endless flow of abundance than by sharing the money I have with those who need it more. What better way to acknowledge the flow of time than to share it?

Without occasions to rise to, we stagnate.

Gratitude is the signal that more is on the way.

Lesson 198:

The only person affected by my judgment is me.

As long as you're judging others, you're creating a hostile universe and forcing yourself to live in it.

When you condemn someone as having "bad energy," you watch their life, looking for signs of punishment. When something bad happens to them (remembering you will always find evidence to support what you believe) you feel an odd sense of gratification at their punishment. A kind of "that's what you get." We think it's a neutral observation on someone's "karma," but it's not.

These condemnations create an Achilles heel for us by being the one little red flag that says, "I believe in a friendly universe unless you piss it off... like that guy did." This superiority complex and sense of duality are what originally emancipated religion from spirituality.

By opening up a portal of punishment, you create a fear that the same thing could happen to you or is happening to you. You're hurting no one but yourself. Make a conscious choice to end this now.

Lesson 199:

I am not my body; I am not even my mind.

I'm always thinking about ways to shortcut into deeper spiritual principles. If you could release the attachment to the body you're so certain is you, you could literally do anything. There would be no suffering because there would be no waiting to be or have more, you would experience no sense of lack because you can jump into any reality at any time.

Attaching to the body you're in would be like petting a leash and ignoring the dog. Attaching to the body is the idea of a leash. When you realize you aren't your body, that you're the spirit that lives within the body, and you can go anywhere and do anything and be anything - this is the end of suffering. This is freedom. This is love.

Lesson 200:

Peace has but one Source.

We think that we'll find peace everywhere BUT where it is. We think that money will bring us peace, that our soulmate will bring us peace, that a new house, a new job, or a new trinket will bring us peace. We think that we'll finally be able to rest in God once we have enough material things to allow us to feel safe enough to trust.

Not the case.

Peace is instantaneous when we ask for it. When we say, "I choose to see peace now." it arrives, no matter what. They say that smooth seas don't make strong sailors, and it's true. You don't learn peace curled up in a bay window cradling a mug of Yogi tea in a white sweater, no ma'am. We learn peace by being in situations that try to derail us, stress us out, and make us lose our cool. Actually, until we learn peace, life will stress us out until we learn we can't control anything and we have to trust.

Remember this mantra from the Kundalini tradition:

SA TA NA MA

Peace begins with me.

Whatever peace you want to see in the world starts with you, and you know how to give it to

yourself now.

And so, it is.

Lesson 201:

Review 181.

I am not the body; I am not even the mind.

181.)   I have no enemies.

We are all in this together, and we are all doing the best we can.

I am not the body; I am not even the mind.

Lesson 202:

Review 182

I am not the body; I am not even the mind.

182.)   I will be still for a minute.

There is a simpler way of doing things.

You'll always get the answer if you remember to ask.

I am not the body; I am not even the mind.

Lesson 203:

Review 183

I am not the body; I am not even the mind.

183.) Ratchet Bible Stories: Moses

I am that I am.

I am not the body; I am not even the mind.

Lesson 204:

Review 184.

I am not the body; I am not even the mind.

184.)   They're not your type, they're your pattern.

I am not the body; I am not even the mind.

Lesson 205:

Review 185.

I am not the body; I am not even the mind.

185.)   All I want is peace.

No matter what you think you want, peace is what you're after.
Peace is what you think every external desire will bring you.

I am not the body; I am not even the mind.

Lesson 206:

Review 186.

I am not the body; I am not even the mind.

186.)   The world needs me.

There's a reason you're here. You're the only one who speaks your students' language.

I am not the body; I am not even the mind.

Lesson 207:

Review 187.

I am not the body; I am not even the mind.

187.)   Blessing others is blessing me.

All that you give is given to you.

I am not the body; I am not even the mind.

Lesson 208:

Review 188

I am not the body; I am not even the mind.

188.)   My soul shines.

I will be still, and let the earth be still along with me.

You can see peace instead of this.

I am not the body; I am not even the mind.

Lesson 209:

Review 189

I am not the body; I am not even the mind.

189.)   Love is my natural state.

Love is who you are.

I am not the body; I am not even the mind.

Lesson 210:

Review 190.

I am not the body; I am not even the mind.

190.) I choose to see discomfort as an opportunity to grow.

I could see this differently. Forgive and see this differently.

I am not the body; I am not even the mind.

Lesson 211:

Review 191.

I am not the body; I am not even the mind.

191.)   I carry Divinity.

You and God want the same thing: you happy.

I am not the body; I am not even the mind.

Lesson 212:

Review 192.

I am not the body; I am not even the mind.

192.)   I have a purpose here.

You are here for a reason.

I am not the body; I am not even the mind

Lesson 213:

Review 193.

I am not the body; I am not even the mind.

193.)   All things are lessons.

Obstacles are detours in the right direction.

I am not the body; I am not even the mind.

Lesson 214:

Review 194.

I am not the body; I am not even the mind.

194.)   I trust God to handle my future.

There is no time but now.

I am not the body; I am not even the mind.

Lesson 215:

Review 195

I am not the body; I am not even the mind.

195.)   Gratitude is a guarantee more is on the way.

Whatever you appreciate, you get more of.

I am not the body; I am not even the mind.

Lesson 216:

Review 196

I am not the body; I am not even the mind.

196.)   Judging others makes me insecure.

Your judgments hurt no one but you.

I am not the body; I am not even the mind.

Lesson 217:

Review 197.

I am not the body; I am not even the mind.

197.)   It can be but the gratitude I earn.

You bless yourself when you bless others.

I am not the body; I am not even the mind.

Lesson 218:

Review 198.

I am not the body; I am not even the mind.

198.)   Only my condemnation injures me.

You're only susceptible to judgments or suspicious of judgments as long as you're judging others.

I am not the body; I am not even the mind.

Lesson 219:

Review 199

I am not the body; I am not even the mind.

199.)   I am not a body, I am free.

You are not your body. You are not your body. You are not your body.

I am not the body; I am not even the mind.

Lesson 220:

Review 200.

I am not the body; I am not even the mind.

200.)   There is no peace but the peace of God.

Peace begins with me.

I am not the body; I am not even the mind.

Lesson 221:

I choose a better thought.

You don't need to get to the origin of every single negative thought you have, recognizing it is a negative thought is enough.

The average person thinks 60-80,000 thoughts every day, and most are negative. If the goal is to create a better reality by choosing better thoughts, you will need to get pretty good at cutting at least 40,000 thoughts day to day. If every single thought that crosses your mind gets a full journal entry and takes about 30 minutes, you will never get ahead.

If there are no neutral thoughts, all thoughts are fear-based or love-based, you have to get pretty good at deciding what thoughts stay and what thoughts go. So, how do we do that? Especially since, most of the time, we're not aware of how much our mind is churning away.

The best way I've found is to recognize when you've started to feel shit. Like your mind has narrowed itself into a tight little corner where it "can't stop thinking about" whatever it is occupied with, and you can't relax until it's gone. In these moments, stop for a second. You don't have to sit down and meditate for 20 minutes or even duck into the bathroom at work. Just stop for a moment, take a nice big sigh with your eyes closed, and relax your mind.

You're already so good at this because you do it every day. When you decide it's time for sleep every night, even if those scraggler thoughts come creeping in asking you to consider lunch for tomorrow or an email you need sent - you tell them, "Tomorrow. It's rest time now" without criticism or analysis. You're doing the same thing here.

After just a couple of breaths, you should feel calmer, and this is where I want you to really focus. As your mind wakes back up, as it always does, decide that the thought you come out of this calm state is helpful. You might need to be very focused here as often your mind wants to pick up and go with the first thought. Use your feelings as a guide. Does the thought make you feel stressed or relaxed, expansive or contracted? Do you feel like you're looking at a panoramic vision or through a tiny little peephole? You can also say quietly to yourself: "Please show me a helpful thought.."

I know that when I stop and seek peace, it is given to me. All I need to do is ask.

My favorite quote from the Bible is, "Be still and know that I am God." Be still is the first step.

One of my favorite lines from the Tao Te Ching is, "Even the muddiest waters clear when still.."

All you need to do to see a different perspective is to get still and ask.

And finally, the Orisha Oshun tells us: "Let it be beautiful.." It's already beautiful if you can ask to see it that way.

Lesson 222:

God is on my side.

If we spent our whole lives just focusing on this one lesson, it would be enough.

We lose the most time in our lives, assuming God is mad at us for wanting to do or doing something that feels fun and good to us. We are inexorable from our God, and the desires we have are put there by God.

Our desires come from God.

We get it into our heads that God has this standard of perfection She is holding us to, and if we're not perfect all the time she's going to be mad at us, and we'll never get to do things we want ever. This could not be further from the truth.

Delight is in the heart of the Almighty, which means God WANTS you to be happy. Wouldn't give you these desires if you weren't meant to have them. You can deny and resist them, or you can ask to be in the best place physically, mentally, emotionally, and spiritually to receive them.

Lesson 223:

God and I are on the same team.

God and I are on the same team. We want the same things, my happiness is God's happiness, and God's happiness is my happiness.

If I'm looking for guidance, I can either ask God what she wants me to do, or I could ask myself what I truly want to do - and I'll get the same answer. That's how on the same team God and I are, and the same goes for you.

What feels like the most fun is usually the best option. What you're most inspired about, or eager to get done is also where you're supposed to be. God uses good feelings, excited, and inspired feelings to guide you to what you're supposed to be doing. God uses shitty feelings to guide us away from what's not serving us. Every great growth in my life has come from me feeling shitty about my situation and becoming determined to change it. I changed it by deciding which projects on my to-do list would get done first based on what I was excited about. This is how I've grown a multiple six-figure business relatively easily, as a co-creation with the Divine.

Here's the main thing that will keep you from using this same trick to your advantage: being convinced that God wants you to be unhappy. It's bullshit, and you'll need to fight it, but you'll win if you do. Every time.

Lesson 224:

Praying to Divine Feminine

This week I'll be teaching you about the two types of prayer and how they differ. For a while, I was combining this with Kundalini yoga for daily practice, but I find that it's my feminine side that usually needs more balancing than the masculine, so I just pray however feels right for me at the moment.

The first style of prayer I'd like you to try is praying to Divine Feminine or the Allmother.

The archetype of the mother (this is particularly useful if you don't feel like you learned entirely good habits from your own mother) is the silent boss. Think about how in a lot of the happy marriages you know, the husband calls the wife "the boss." This is because once you've lived with a woman and seen everything that she handles, and how effortlessly she keeps everything balanced and beautiful, you can't deny that women are cut from some powerful cloth.

I've coached women for many years, and a recurring phrase with dissatisfied women is, "No one appreciates all the little things I do."

This is because A: you have to appreciate yourself because B: no one will ever notice how many little things you are doing and have been doing this whole time. That's just the way of women.

Because a woman, a mother, keeps so many plates spinning, she hates being told what to do. Ladies, you can agree with me on this. Like when your man tells you how to do laundry, or wash dishes, or something else you've done like a million fucking times. Even worse is when someone asks you to do something you were already doing, like closing the kitchen cupboards while you're still cooking.

When we pray to Divine Feminine, we mustn't ever tell her what to do because she's probably already doing it. So, many times we come to prayer and say, "Please tell me why this isn't working and keep me safe and fix my money situation and let me meet my soul mate," as if she hasn't been working on this the whole time already. This style of direct-order praying is suitable for the canine, the solar, and the masculine. But for the feline, the lunar, and the feminine - you need to use a much different approach, and when you do, the results are spectacular.

When we say exactly what we want, we're only ever saying what we think we want. We're taking realms of infinite possibilities, choosing one (usually the most limited one) and saying ONLY THIS ONE I want.

Let me give you examples of this over the coming days.

Lesson 225:

Divine Feminine is like a stylist.

Divine Feminine is like a stylist, and you're the brand-new celebrity with all the talent and tragically pedestrian fashion sense. You come to her with all your requests for Irregular Choice and Betsey Johnson saying, "this is what I have to have in order to be happy!"

Divine Feminine knows every designer, every dress, designs that would make you feel like a completely new person, with the deepest aspects of your personality and all your curves or angles expressed and amplified elegantly - and is dying to show you off to the world - "Look at what happens when you work with Divine Feminine!" But if you are hell-bent on Betsey Johnson, she can't give you her best, and you kind of have to look like a turd for a few years on your own design.

How Divine Feminine works best as your stylist is when you just tell her, " I want to feel fabulous. I want to feel like everyone is in awe of this look. I want to feel empowered and like I belong on this red carpet 100%.." When you bring THIS to Divine Feminine, instead of Betsey Johnson, she can say, "Say no more. I got you.."

You're not bad for wanting Betsey; it's just all you know based on what you've seen.

Lesson 226:

Divine Feminine is like the world's greatest chef.

Divine Feminine is like the world's greatest chef, and you are eating at her restaurant for the first time. She loves to bring you a tasting menu to introduce you to textures and flavors, and combinations that would move you to tears. It's what she does the absolute best, and she can't wait to watch rays of delight creep across your face with every bite.

Yet, you've shown up, and you're demanding she makes a grilled cheese sandwich. It's the only thing you want to eat, and you want it with Wonder Bread, and you want it with American cheese; otherwise, she doesn't love you, and you don't believe she's a good chef if she can't bring you this.

This is so tough on her. It's so much easier when you come in hungry, say, "Surprise me, you've been watching me eat my whole life, and you know what I like." There are no surprises with a grilled cheese sandwich; it's just what you think is the best based on the options you've had so far.

Lesson 227:

Divine Feminine is like a tattoo artist.

Divine Feminine is like a tattoo artist, and you've come in for your first tattoo. She knows what you want, what you're describing, the kind of tattoo look you're actually going for. She's been doing this since the beginning of time, she can give you way more than you thought - yet you're determined to get the crude sketch you've drawn yourself. Yes, it took you 4 tries to get the shading right, and this is the best based on your work in the past, but this is her specialty. She can make it look BETTER than you ever thought it could, and you'll want to get tattooed by her for the rest of your life and recommend all your friends. Yet, she can't do anything for you (except refuse) to keep you from getting your janky ass drawing on you forever.

Lesson 228:

Divine Feminine is like your mother.

Divine Feminine is like your mother, excited to shower you with gifts for your birthday. The problem is you are demanding to know what's in all the boxes. Getting so worked up, even sometimes being so assured that what you want is NOT coming in due time that you'll start outsourcing and making plans for getting what you want yourself.

Imagine how she wants to surprise you, to see your face light up. She knows all the stores, all the things and knows you better than you know you. She knows if you just stop shaking the boxes and freaking out, you'll be beyond delighted with what's in store.

Like a good mom, she's always listening to you. When you drop hints like "I want to feel strong! Protected. Totally aligned, and secure that I'm on the exact right path," she winks at you. "I got you."

Lesson 229:

Divine Feminine Summary

So, now that you see how much we limit ourselves when we try to decide what we want for ourselves, you can see the advantage of praying to Divine Feminine.

Not only that, but it's incredibly potent and free therapy. Getting honest with God instead of trying to pretend like you're not struggling is a whole new level of acceptance. Acceptance, not resistance, is what changes things.

This is a powerful technology, taught by a High Priestess of Ifa. Here are things you have to know when you pray to Divine Feminine:

Do not tell her what to do, tell her all your problems

This prayer frees up all resistance, so expect things to move fast and take every single incident as a sign that your wish and beyond are being fulfilled.

When you pray to Divine Feminine, it's basically saying: "I don't care what you do, just handle it."

Remind me to tell you the roller rink story later ;)

Lesson 230:

Praying to Divine Masculine

We'll go shorter with this one because Masculine loves things short and sweet.

Unlike Divine Feminine that would prefer to just hear your problems and bring a unique solution, men love to be the hero. They love to be told exactly how they can excel and deliver exactly that.

I like to use the analogy of asking your mom for a business loan versus asking your dad for a business loan. Your mom is less likely to ask questions because she wants you to be happy, and she has eyes in the back of her head that have seen everything you do with this money since day one.

Your dad would probably like to see a business plan, some kind of outline for how you plan to spend the money and how you plan to pay it back. Your dad would like to know what you need help with and enjoys hearing what you want with no beating around the bush.

When we know exactly what we need help with, we ask Divine Masculine. When we don't know exactly what we need help with, we just need help - we ask Divine Feminine.

Most of us have been conditioned to pray to Divine Masculine, asking for help and change and guidance. But you only get exactly what you want when it's in alignment with your destiny. For example, if you're praying for a certain person to fall in love with you, and they're not the right person for you, it's not going to happen no matter how much you ask.

There was a time in 2017 when I was praying to Divine Masculine daily for two clients, and it didn't happen for me. I didn't actually want two clients. I wanted the 10k two clients would put in my bank account. The reason I wanted 10k was so I could go to Berlin to chase the guy that wouldn't get on a three-hour flight from LA to Austin to see me. Because I only knew how to pray to Divine Masculine, I thought my prayers weren't being answered.

Had I prayed to Divine Feminine even once, I would have gotten the answer because my prayer would have looked like this:

Spirit, I'm so lonely, and I'm so broke. I'm sick of not being able to share myself authentically with anyone. I'm sick of jerking off and being sober and not having anything to do except for inner work. I feel like such a failure, and even though I feel like two clients would make it better, I don't even want two clients. I just want money without having to work so hard for it. I just want to be in a relationship without having to work so hard for it. Is this all there is for me? Is this the best it's going to get?

From that prayer alone, I would have discovered that I didn't feel like I was myself around this guy, that there was a connection between my love relationships and money relationships, that I didn't want clients, and that there had to be an easier way to make money. I also asked a crucial question "Is this the best it's going to get?" A loaded question like that would get me a loaded answer.

With these tricks under your belt, I'd like you to pray a ton in whatever form is less familiar to you. If you've always asked God for help, pray to Divine Feminine for the next few weeks and see what happens. If you've always vented to God, maybe pray to Divine Masculine for a few weeks and see what you get.

Because there's a suppression of the feminine in the collective unconscious, and most of us only learned to pray to Divine Masculine, most people will need to practice with Divine Feminine. However, pick whichever one works for you and watch what happens.

Lesson 231:

I can call my lifeline.

Salvation, aka your lifeline, is the lifetime warranty you were born with that says you can always be returned to God, no questions asked. Salvation is a guarantee that no matter how chaotic things have gotten, no matter how confusing life seems to be, it will all come back to the truth. When time ends, thoughts end, and the world as you know it ends - something will remain, and that something has always liked you.

The moment you had your first taste of conflict, the antidote to all conflict (peace) appeared. In reality, it was always there, as peace is just the natural state of the ever-expanding Universe. There wasn't a need for the thought of peace before, as there was no pain. But every time we split our mind, Spirit recalibrates to make sure we have the tools to repair it ourselves.

Salvation is an option we haven't seen before. When we're deep in conflict, our ego will try to maneuver us to avoid peace because fear is the only fuel fear has. Salvation is a simple but firm reminder - this conflict isn't "bad," it's just not real. You could see peace instead of this, and all the confusion will dissipate. The clouds will part, and a new way will be shown to you.

For the next few lessons, I will show you some prayers that really helped me out.

Lesson 232:

Duality and Oneness

The most intense-sounding work I have done so far has been exorcisms (in reality, it's just another session for me), which I perform off this principle alone. No chicken sacrifices, tortoise shells, or drumming here - it's a simple conversation based on this concept. Are there dark energies? Sure, maybe. Could there be a nefarious interloper in your auric field causing you to act out in unusual ways? I don't believe in that, but sure, maybe? But if there's dark energy, what is its opposite? Light energy? Let's call light energy Team 1, and on Team 1 we can put God, angels, whatever ascended masters you resonate with, like Jesus, etc. Then because we've created a duality situation, we'll put dark energy, Satan, Baal, demons, etc., all on Team 2. Great.

So, who is stronger, Team 1 or Team 2? And whose side are you on? If you're not on the side you want to be on, what is keeping you there that is stronger than God?

If we remember who we are, there is nothing to fear. We have only to remember who has our back, and there's no excuse for fear ever. It might seem like we're cutting a corner to just head straight to the end of all problems, it might seem like we're missing a spot - but we're not. If you can remember God, there is nothing to fear.

Spirit, help me not to get caught up in the lack and conflict I think I see. Help me to remember that ultimately only what is true exists, and what is true is that you're in control, you love me, and you do all things well. Help me to stop thinking I have to "fix" everything on my own. Help me to see the perfection in this situation, just the way it is. Amen.

Lesson 233:

Stay in my mind, Spirit.

Spirit, stay with me every moment today. Let me not wander for even a second. Let me not feel like I have to handle all this on my own. Every time I check the clock, let me remember that you're with me, that you've never left, and you're taking care of it. Every time a thought or a moment comes up that tries to separate us, let me hear your voice, feel your peace, and sense your presence. Let everything be a reminder I am loved by God.

This is a day without fear. With practice, every day will be a day like today.

Lesson 234:

Spirit, here are the keys - you drive.

Spirit, I turn over all my thoughts to you today. Help me to see as you see. Additionally, I turn over all my plans and expectations for how I think today needs to go, and I give them wholly over to you. Be my hands, my eyes, my feet. Bring you who you would have me serve, and may I be a conduit for the flow of Divine energy at every opportunity. Guide me. I will step back and let you lead the way.

Twenty-four hours with someone else at the wheel won't land you in jail. Give this a whole-hearted shot today. Lean back completely and let the day come to you.

Lesson 235:

I am forgiven.

We'll spend a decent amount of our lives doing some kind of self-prescribed repentance sentence because we assume that the Universe is mad at us. But the Universe has never been mad at us. Ask yourself: "What would my life look like if I knew I was divinely guided? What if I had never made a wrong move?" Forgiving ourselves allows us to operate free of our past and allows us to see that nothing bad really happened. Even the "bad" decisions you made were profound learning experiences, and you made that choice because it seemed like the best option, and that's why you selected it. God has always loved us, everything has always happened for us and not to us, and we don't need to make up for anything because the past is perfect as is.

And so, it is.

Spirit, thank you for always loving me - every day, no matter where I go, what I do, or what I say.

Lesson 236:

God says I'm off the hook.

Here you have it, fam. Straight from the horse's mouth! God says you're all good. It doesn't matter what anyone else says or thinks. Are they smarter than God? Do they know you better than you know you? Is the aspect of yourself that talks shit to yourself as timeless as God? As knowing as God? As loving as God?

No.

The Universe, he/she/it, is telling you right now that it's all good. You don't have to say sorry anymore. All is forgiven; you can go on in peace now.

Spirit, thank you.

Lesson 237:

I am the gatekeeper of my mind, and I must do my job.

You decide what you see. You may not totally realize it, but you absolutely rule 100% of the world that you see, and you can edit it to your preference. If you spot it, you got it. If you don't like what you see externally, you will need to adjust it internally, or you will continue to see various incarnations of the same issue. For example, if you are insecure about your work, you can expect the world to reflect this to you via online comments, local relationships, and articles on how difficult it is for _____ to make it as a _____ in _____ .

Your dominion is your responsibility and only yours. Don't ever forget this!

Spirit, I want to adopt a zero-tolerance policy for negative thoughts. Help me think with your mind.

Lesson 238:

This, in the mirror, is what a masterpiece looks like.

You may now accept your final form. You are a house for God; therefore, God lives in you full time. You can do anything that God can do. You are fucking unstoppable, and there is absolutely nothing that can ever stand in your way except for a little fear that says, God. Go beyond this fear, and you get everything.

I am that I am.

Lesson 239:

The healing of the world begins with me.

When you clean up the inside of you, the outside can fall into place. As the creator of all that you see, when you accept a new reality for yourself, everyone and everything you see must follow. So, yes, the whole world depends on you because nothing exists outside of you.

Every thought is a prayer. Choose wisely.

Spirit, I choose to be an example of the choices others have forgotten existed in their lives. Help me to be the rising tide that lifts all ships. Help me remember that all peace begins with me.

Lesson 240:

I will speak of myself with respect.

Selling yourself short because you're scared of people thinking you're conceited does nothing for anyone. You need not be constantly exalting yourself in order to not talk shit about yourself ever, you can choose to not tolerate negative self-talk. Assuming a false identity (anything less than godlike) is not humility, it's assuming a false identity.

Spirit, thank you for reminding me of the truth about me. Help me to live from a place of truth.

Lesson 241:

There are no rational fears.

F-E-A-R = false evidence appearing real. You can throw 100% of your fears away. Simple, but difficult. The good news is you don't have to fight this battle alone, you can ask Spirit to handle it for you. If a feeling comes up that feels bad, then it's coming from a place of fear, and you can file the entire thing under "G" (for Garbage).

If you figure this out and practice it actively no matter how real external circumstance seems to be - you're good to go for life.

If it feels bad, it's not true. Ask yourself - "Is it true?" "Can everyone make money/be loved unconditionally/run their own business except for me? Is this a fact? Can I prove this?"

Spirit, take this fear from me. I don't even want to deal with it. I'm prepared to live fearlessly, and I need your help. Take this fear from me. Thank you. What is the World?

Our biggest misconception of the world is that it exists outside of us and that our internal state responds to external circumstances e.g., the Maserati (external object) makes me feel successful (internal state). Truth is 180 degrees in the opposite direction; therefore, the exact opposite of this idea is true. The internal state directs external reality. The internal feeling of success will eventually manifest as an external Maserati. This is always true, this is never wrong, it is the law.

Through forgiveness, we come to witness perfection in all things exactly the way that they are. We see the world as a giant mirror, reflecting all the many things we project onto it. When we change the way we look at things, the things we look at change.

So, what is the world? The world reflects you. You can change the world; you can save the world - but it starts with you.

Lesson 242:

Today is my MFN DAY!

Today is cause for celebration! You've learned that if you forgive everyone reflexively, no one can hurt you and no one and nothing has any dirt on you that can keep you from getting everything you want! Congratulations! You did it. You found the key to this wild, weird, world!

Also want to add the two caveats for forgiveness here:

1. Forgiveness is accepting that people don't change, so if someone's always been a dick to you, don't "forgive" them by inviting them back into that place where they can be a dick to you. Put them somewhere in your life where what they do doesn't matter.

2. You can't forgive someone if you haven't been honest about how deeply they hurt you. So, if you're mad at a hostess because she sat another table before y'all, you can probably see the full impact of her actions right there in the restaurant, and you can forgive her on the spot. It's not this speedy with like a parent or a long-term friend, someone that has a big history of hurting you. In these situations, you have to, have to, have to make a list or a graph detailing all the big things you need to forgive them for. If not, you will not make any progress. An added bonus of this is when you evaluate the full scope of the relationship, you'll see that people don't change, and it's easier to accept them when you realize this.

I realize that we are all connected, that as I forgive others, I forgive myself. That everything I give to others, I give to myself. I figured this out! I'm free.

Lesson 243:

I let God lead today.

I will not try to figure today out on my own, instead, I will remember that I can ask for directions every step of the way. I can be God-like today with every thought, action, and deed. If I forget, how I can ask to remember?

Spirit I come to you with an empty cup.

Where would you have me go?

What would you have me do?

What would you have me say?

And to whom?

Lesson 244:

Today I judge nothing.

Today I will do my best to see the perfection in things as is. I won't let myself fall into the age-old trap of thinking there is something going wrong in this picture. I don't know the whole story. I don't know what motivated someone to rob a store, wear a sarong, or flip me off after THEY failed to turn a blinker on - therefore, I can't judge them, and I don't want to. Today, I take a day off from letting the world get to me.

Spirit, I am willing to see the perfection in things just the way they are. I will sit back and let you show me the divine way everything unfolds. Even if I can't see the end result, I will lean back and trust that every step is divinely placed. Thank you.

Lesson 245:

I am safe wherever I am.

There is nowhere I can go where Spirit is not with me. There is nothing that could happen where I would be left unprotected. The Universe never takes days off; there is nothing to fear in any place at any time.

We lean into the peace this statement offers. There are no blind spots. You are safe. You are protected. You are home.

Lesson 246:

I am peaceful wherever I go.

Anywhere I go, you are with me. Your peace radiates outwards to everyone I see. There is not one soul not touched by this peace. Today I ask: "Bring me who you would have me serve," bring me exactly who needs this energy the most.

And this is how we roll. To every single person that bumps into us, cuts us in line, recognizes us from kindergarten, we bring this peace. And to the ones we love, a stressed spouse, a frustrated coworker, and a screaming child. Peace is contagious, and we act accordingly.

Lesson 247:

Respecting myself is respecting God's handiwork.

To love God is to love myself because I am a vehicle for God. My life tried to teach me that even to hint at this was sacrilegious, but I am willing to see things differently. Let me not praise the Creator for all the beauty in the world and then scrutinize myself and my body in the mirror. Let me recognize my sense of self and remember that I am as my Creator. Divine, all-knowing, all-seeing love.

I choose to totally accept myself as I am at this moment right now. I choose to stop setting milestones of lovability for myself that I am constantly trying to reach. Let me accept my own perfection today and judge myself no longer. Thank you.

Lesson 248:

If I'm not forgiving, I do not see the truth.

When I see someone doing something, and I determine it is "wrong," I am judging. As long as I am judging others, I will think others are judging me. As long as this is the reality I am creating for myself, my life will suffer. But if I forgive reflexively (a key form of non-resistance), then nothing can hurt me. I don't take things personally, and I am in a state of peace with the world and everyone in it.

Spirit, let me remember that everyone is doing the best they can and that even though I might think someone could do better - I don't know their life. Help me to accept this and take nothing personally and be a beacon of peace to everyone that comes my way.

Lesson 249:

If it feels bad, it's ego talking.

Your soul will never make you feel like shit. Your soul will never tell you that you've fucked up, and you'll never be able to fix it. Won't tell you don't have enough time or resources to do what you must. Won't tell you there's something wrong with who you are or how you are. When you hear voices like this, it's not your intuition. You can always tell your intuition because it feels good. It feels doable, even if it's scary.

Spirit, I remember who I am today. I am made just like you. I am as I was created. Divine.

Help me remember this all day today, and let it be the last thing in my mind as I go to sleep.

Thank you.

Lesson 250:

Forgiveness makes things easy.

Forgiveness allows you to see the absolute perfection in things exactly as they were, are, and always will be. When you stop wanting to change anything about the past, you're freed of anxiety for the future. This allows you to live in the only moment we can be certain exists - this moment right here. Buddhism 101 leads you to "Life is suffering.," but beyond that, there is more. You can end suffering, by ending wanting. Forgiveness allows you to stop wanting things to be so different because forgiveness is acceptance..

Spirit, help me to see the perfection in all things just the way they are. Instead of dreading certain outcomes in agony, being devastated when they unfold or embarrassed when they don't, before finally, in hindsight, seeing it all worked out for the best - help me cut to that now. Help me to rest assured that everything that happens to me is the best possible thing that can happen to me. Amen.

Lesson 251:

Let me see without limits.

Your external circumstance is at the moment catching up to your visualizations. What you're seeing now is the ripple effect of your conscious and unconscious thoughts. As you develop an unconditional perspective, you can visualize with no limits. Nothing holding you back, keeping you small, and telling you it's impossible. You are not bound by your body, your bank account, or any other external circumstance. Today we ask to see ourselves, unlimited.

Let me remember that I am whole, that anything is possible, and that the entire Universe is rooting for me.

Lesson 252:

I will tell the truth.

The best way to end worry is to tell the truth. Out loud, to someone, preferably.

What's the truth? You are God. God loves you and wants you to be happy more than anything else. Why? Because God IS you, and you can really believe this is true if you double down on trying to see God in everyone, and every situation. Everything is unfolding for your greatest benefit, and there is nothing to fear.

Spirit, thank you for this truth I can put all illusion to rest in. Help me to remember it first thing in the morning, all throughout the day, and be the first thing on my mind as I am heading to bed. Thank you.

Lesson 253:

Truth is my name.

I have given myself many identities to live under in my life. I have called myself a friend, brother, daughter, employee, and Scorpio, and I have thought these titles were who I am, but those are just details. The only Identity I have that is true is that I am loved by God. Loved as a parent loves their child, x1000. This is who I am, and this is why I walk in such peace.

Spirit, let everything I see today be proof of your love for me. Thank you.

Lesson 254:
Nothing exists outside of me.

Everything that I see on the outside is coming from a Source inside. Every thought is a prayer, and peace begins with me.

Additionally, everything is unfolding in a way that will bring me to my greatest joy and for the highest good of all concerned. Even when something happens that I think I didn't want, it's rerouting me onto the path of what will truly make me happy - for life. For example, when the guy I want isn't calling me no matter what I try to do to make him love me, it's not because I DO want him- it's because he wouldn't really make me happy. I know I want to be with someone who truly makes me happy since this guy doesn't - I don't want him. Therefore, he's not the one for me, someone else is - and the guy I'm stuck on would actually make someone else truly happy. When I let go of attachments and trust that Spirit is guiding me towards my truest happiness, everyone else gets closer to their truest happiness as well.

Spirit, let me remember that my thoughts create my reality. Help me to dream BIGGER today, knowing that my desires are divinely placed. Help me see every single occurrence as a sign I am on the right path and all is coming.

Lesson 255:

I only want to hear one voice talking today, and that's God's.

The voice of God is still and small; it's heard in silence. It's the voice of the heart. Our heads will give us words and words and words, pros and cons, details and details and details. But our hearts will give us a nudge. Stay. Go. Be still. Yes. No. Wait. Sometimes it'll show us a picture or give us a feeling, and if it's a critical junction in your life, you might get three words like the "One more day" message I got 24 hours before my fiancé died. Let's be clear, though, the words and words aren't coming from God. It's coming from your intellectual center.

We can save a lot of time if we go straight to the heart, and it will never steer us wrong. A way I love to make this distinction during a decision-making process is by asking, "What does my head say?" and then asking, "What does my heart say?"

Try it now!

Lesson 256:

Today I will be peaceful.

Some days it doesn't feel like we have the option to choose peace. The day has barely started and already it feels out of our hands. The kids are maniacal, the phone hasn't stopped ringing, and you're moving houses, to boot. Is peace a possibility?

Yes! Peace is always an option we can see through. It's like having a pair of glasses on your person at all times that changes what you're seeing from chaos to perfection.

Yes. The essence of God is peace, and we are like our creator, which means we have pieces of this DNA in our system at all times. Any time we request peace, it is granted - instantly. Choose peace today.

Spirit, let me remember today that peace is the option, and it begins with me, always.

Lesson 257:

Let me remember my one job today.

There's only one lesson - forgiveness. With every discomfort, we can ask, "what needs to be forgiven for this to disappear?" and it will be so. We have reiterated : "Forgiveness is my function. It is what I am here to do.," and here we do it again. In any moment of difficulty, we could forgive and see it differently. There will be many options besides forgiveness, always. It is our job to make forgiveness reflexive. I assure you, when you truly understand no-one is trying to hurt you, everyone is just doing the best they can, nothing can hurt you.

Spirit, let forgiveness be a neon sign in front of my eyes today. Every time there is an opportunity to get frustrated or lash out, let me remember forgiveness. Thank you.

Lesson 258:

Let me remember that my goal is to think as God thinks.

If you remember that God is on your side, there is no problem. Ever. Full stop.

Every issue we ever face in the physical, mental, or spiritual realm is rooted in an idea that we are separate and in it alone. Think of any issue you've ever had. Were you tapped into Divinity? Were you asking for Divine help? We forgot we were one, but now we remember, we remember, we remember.

Sometimes my only spiritual practice is looking up at the massive sky above me and realizing that I am a speck, an absolute speck in existence. I'm the tiniest black dot on the palest blue dot and the smallest happening in the cosmos. Yet here is this force, this EVERYTHING. All of the observable Universe, and the unobservable as well, and it likes me. It loves me. And it helps me with anything any time I ask. My jaw drops as I think about how vast these realms are, how far they reach, and here I am. This one little person getting the MOST from life because God helps me any time I ask.

Without even meaning to, I find myself praying:

I am nothing, you are everything, and you love me. Thank you. Thank you. Thank you.

To date, I think these 30 seconds every few months are the most heartfelt and powerful prayers I ever pray.

Lesson 259:

Let me remember I can't make a wrong turn.

This should be a total relief for you! You can't mess up the flow of love, and neither can anyone else. You can't make a wrong turn! The learned (not natural) concept of sinning is the pulpit we stand on when we want to judge people, aka the most self-destructive practice available.

What if you had never made a wrong turn? If you want to really believe this for your life and bask in all the peace that comes along with it - you must make it a truth for everyone else in the world. Only one person will get hurt by making an exception to this rule of "can't fuck it up!" - you!

Spirit, thank you for reminding me that everything is as it should be. Help me remember that everyone is exactly as you created them, and we have all been divinely guided into this moment together.

Lesson 260:

Let me remember my natural state is Godly.

No matter how bad you think you may have fucked things up in your life or how deep into fear you get, your original state will always be as Source created you, which means you can always return to it.

No matter what you look like, where you go, what you choose what to or what not to do - you are as Source created you. You are perfect, you are worthy, and you are loved exactly as you are right now.

Spirit, I have had so many impostor identities in my life. Thank you for reminding me that when all is said and done, I am yours, created in your image, with your powers. Thank you.

Lesson 261:

What is the body?

So, many of our limitations are based on our bodies. Our sense of location, vitality, the time we have, universal support, and what is possible is all anchored in our body being the end-all-be-all with who we are in this world. Sure, our body is super important, and taking care of it is key - but it is a home for Spirit, and that's it.

The Course describes the body as the fence we build to keep ourselves finite and separate. Sometimes our body is working in our favor, and it seems like this emphasis we've placed on it is beneficial - but so quickly it can turn to fear. A little sickness, a little aging, an unexpected pregnancy - and suddenly, we are separated from Source. In these vulnerable moments, we believe that even though Spirit has been driving the car the whole time, it has now kicked us to the curb at the hospital, bank, or gym - and we're left to fend for ourselves. Our fear of aging has us believing that time is finite and that once this body ends, we're done-zo. Our whole lives become a defense for the body and its endless limitations, and it's not that it's bad - it's just inconvenient.

You ARE Spirit. That is what you are. The body is just a vehicle for this Spirit on this tiny blue dot, suspended in infinitely expanding abundance, time, and space.

You will identify with whatever you think will keep you safe, so choose well. Place your faith in something that never runs out, ever.

Lesson 262:

Miracles lay beyond the senses.

The five senses are the body's greatest pleasure and it's the greatest limitation.

Miracles lay beyond the realm of the senses.

Miracles are making what is impossible possible. It's very real and very achievable, but this power lays BEYOND the realm of the senses.

We incarnate into human bodies to have the pleasure of crushed velvet, LSD, that one Tame Impala album, and oysters. The downside is that we use our senses as the barometer for what is real and what isn't. A miracle cannot be filtered through the senses. If you're looking for "real" evidence it kills the miracle. It's not that it will be unexplainable, just unexplainable to the senses. To heal illnesses or transcend time and space - you have to defy your senses and see the miracle.

Not everything you see is real. Not everything you feel is real.

Lesson 263:

I place my trust in God.

I've placed my trust in money, partners, houses, my body, jobs, and so much more - and they have all let me down. I counted on these for my sense of security, something to turn to when things got rough, and I've been let down every time. Today I place my trust in what has never changed, never ended. What keeps the stars in the sky, water on the earth and birds singing is my refuge and my strength. What could I possibly fear?

Spirit, I place my future in your hands today. I turn over all my fears to you. Every time I feel like I am alone, help me remember to turn my eyes upwards and remember that I am loved and protected by the greatest force in the Universe. You're in control, you love me, and you do all things well.

Lesson 264:

Let me see us all as equal today.

If anyone sits still long enough, they'll all come to the same conclusion: we are all equal, and we are all in this together. We love to categorize, separate, and isolate ourselves from others. We do this not only by putting ourselves above others (feeling superior to say, a heroin addict) but also by putting others above us (idolizing our mentors and feeling as if we'll never be at that level). Not that either of these is wrong, just unnecessary. We're all equal. There's not one person above you, and because there is no one above you, you cannot be above anyone. This is good news! You are your heroes, and you are your villains.

Spirit, let me see the one truth that binds us all together. Let me not see myself as different. Help me to treat all people as an extension of my own Self and to give the world the service I would most want to receive. Thank you.

Lesson 265:

Let me see the beauty of what is.

Through the lens of compassion, all things are perfect. Even situations that seem to demand the most rectification, the most interference on your end - there is a way to see that exactly as it stands, is perfect. Once you see this way, this Tao, you're a lot more likely to feel okay with handing the keys over to the Divine because you have daily visual proof you can trust this force to capitalize on your best interests.

Spirit, thank you for this gift of vision. Allow me to see the perfection in all things and feel the freedom of stepping back and allowing you to keep unfolding this story for me.

Lesson 266:

I am surrounded by love.

All is full of love. Everywhere you turn, everyone you see, everything you know is suspended in the energy of love. It is above you, below you, and all around you. Hard to believe in love? Don't worry! Let's look at it from the perspective of dark matter.

Here we have energy that comprises 22% of the observable universe. We don't know what it is, where it comes from. We only know it exists because we've seen other things fall into it. Whatever this force is it allows us to have gravity, oxygen, water, and all the other necessities for life. We don't know what it is, but it keeps us alive. Why? Maybe it's because dark matter is benevolent. It might love us. Either way, Einstein says this question (is this force friendly or hostile?) is the most important question we must answer in this life.

Spirit, help me to see all things today as proof of this love all around me. Thank you.

Lesson 267:

It's safe to slow down and appreciate what is.

The urgency is over, rush hour has ended. I used to see the world as a place that needed to be fixed because it reflected the way I thought I was broken and needed to be fixed. As I realize more and more that God created me and She makes no mistakes, I realize I was never broken at all, and neither is the world. Everything that I look at is a reminder of the easeful way that the Universe rearranges herself.

I accept the option for peace in all things today. I am in no rush because I know I am exactly where I am meant to be. And so, it is.

Lesson 268:

God resides in me full time, I want to reside in her full time as well.

As much as God as in you, you are in God, and the whole world that you see reflects this connection. This means that every single person you see is here for a reason, reflecting an aspect of you/God you didn't know existed. They say every person comes to you with a message, and it's up to you to discover this message. This is true. Step lightly, speak softly, love always, and the message will be clear.

Spirit, teach me to soften, to open myself up completely to the world so I can see the purpose each person and interaction is here for. I know my purpose, let me see every event as an opportunity to create more love in this world. Thank you.

Lesson 269:

My life today reflects the peace I have found.

I live in an infinite Universe where nothing ever runs out. There is always plenty of time, there is always plenty of money, there are endless health and vitality, there is love. I never wonder if this heartbeat will be my last. I never wonder if when I exhale, there will not be another breath behind it. These rhythms continue, on their own, no matter what wrongs I think I've done, no matter how bad of a mood I'm in. Every heartbeat is a reminder I am protected. Every breath is a reminder I am love.

Spirit, I will stop everything and listen to the sound of my heart, the waves of my breath.

Thank you for this life. This is peace. This is bliss.

Lesson 270:

I will let all things be exactly as they are.

There is perfection in all things exactly the way they are. Every situation has been entered into in agreement with the higher selves of all concerned. Everything is unfolding in the exact way it should, with each person getting exactly what they need and the Earth receiving exactly what she needs as well. Let us not interfere today or try to fix what isn't broken. Lean into the perfection of this unfolding life exactly as it is and into the perfection of yourself, exactly as you are. Once you see it, you can't unsee it, and nothing will ever be the same.

Spirit, today I end my prayers of what I think is right for me and instead ask for the highest good for all concerned. Thank you for bringing me what I need and protecting me from what I think I want.

Lesson 271:

I see deeper.

Today we bypass all judgments of what we think others are showing us and see the truth of things - we are all one. All people, all places, all things are an extension of your own Self, of your own mind. How can you be sure? Well, when YOU die, all these people and things cease to exist for you. They only exist within the constructs of your reality, which is your perception, which is your mind. You can't be sure that any of this will be here after you die. Even religious deities only existed in this lifetime for you once you put faith in them. You created God - not the other way around. When you treat every single person as an extension of your own Self, everything changes. The Course explains this as seeing the face of Christ in all people, which can also work - but it is all coming from one source. You. You decide in your mind who your friends are and who your foes are, but each time you see foes, you create a whole world of judgment and defense. It's not that this is wrong, it's just inconvenient.

Today I pray the ancient Sanskrit "Namaste" to everyone I see. The light in me recognizes and honors the light in you. We are all in this together, Amen.

Lesson 272:

I will use my higher vision today.

Our body's eyes translate everything through the lens of the past, and this is not vision. When we choose to see with our mind's eye, a.k.a. third eye, a.k.a, the mind of God, we see things exactly as they are in the present moment. We see people free of judgments, grudges, and misconceptions from the past. We see the world as abundant and teeming with possibility because there is no illusion from the past telling us that everything is finite and hostile. When you see with the mind's eye, you're seeing things and possibilities that fill you with joy, options that weren't there when you only saw with the body's eyes. I will give you a disclaimer about this vision no one else will - other people will think you're crazy because they SEE no reason to be as happy as you are. I will also assure you that it's beyond worth it.

Spirit, open my eyes. Help me to see as you see. Let me see the truth of things as they are. Let me see no reason NOT to be overjoyed every day. Thank you.

Lesson 273:

I choose what I see.

I choose what I see. Many times in my life, I have forgotten this, and I've felt forced to observe piece after piece of evidence that I am alone in the world. I looked upon myself, my fellow humans, and this Earth as lacking over and over again. Now I know, I can choose to stop seeing this. Even when I do see things that seem to challenge me, I can see them for what they really are. Growth opportunities.

Spirit, thank you! I will allow my vision to be restored to what it's always been capable of. I will see.

Lesson 274:

I will not settle for illusion.

Today we are pushing past the illusion of lack and into the truth of our existence. Lack does not exist unless we put it there. A good resource on this is my YouTube video "Scarcity Mindset: Deleting the Illusion of Lack.

When we see a world that's lacking, we are literally settling for nothing. We are seeing the world at a deficit! We're not even breaking even in our mindset and seeing things as neutral, we are taking the reality of abundance and diluting into nothingness. The problem is, we're comfortable here - it's what we think we've always known. You MUST stop tolerating illusions. Don't let your satisfaction end here. You deserve more.

Spirit, I claim my power over the world I see! I am sick of seeing a world that feels so inadequate. I know there is more, I choose to see proof of this everywhere I go.

Lesson 275:

Today I choose peace.

Today I believe we are ready for a day of undisturbed peace. This doesn't mean that things won't come up that try to ruffle your feathers - that will probably happen today, as a matter of fact. But here's where you see the magic of claiming peace. When something comes up that wants to stress you out, use it as a doorway to peace. Close your eyes, breathe deeply, and say this prayer:

Spirit, you have clearly said that all I have to do is request peace, and it is granted. As surely as an illusion of terror can enter my mind, I can end it with peace. I choose it again. I choose a different thought. I chose to make peace in my default setting. I choose to see peace instead of this. Help me see the truth of this. Thank you.

Lesson 276:

Today I will be fearless.

Dedicate today to fearlessness. That doesn't mean that things won't come up that cause you to feel fear and anxiety - but go beyond it. Life is beautiful if you can allow it to be. Let it be beautiful.

Spirit, I allow things to be as you created them and created me - perfect. I won't edit my vision with fearful interpretations and personal attacks. I will replace this clouded vision with the clarity of truth. I am exactly where I'm meant to be, and I'm not there alone.

Lesson 277:

I will be still and know that God is in charge.

When you're still, you can hear the voice of God. It sounds like your voice, which can make things confusing. You wonder if you're really hearing God or if you're telling yourself things that make you feel good. There's nothing wrong with you for thinking that but trusting in God is trusting in yourself. To listen well, though, you need two things. Stillness and silence.

Make space today to be still and know that you and God are the same. Do this as many times as you can, asking for guidance at every possible interval. "Where would you have me go? What would you have me do? What would you have me say? And to whom?"

Lesson 278:

There is nothing wrong with me.

Today God has a message for you. What is it?

"You are pure and holy just like me because I made you that way.."

What does this mean? It means there's nothing wrong with you. You're not broken. That you haven't done anything wrong, and there is no reason you can't have anything you want. There is no limit to what is possible, and nothing holding you back.

This is your gift today, a direct message from Source. You are all good, and you are loved.

Spirit, thank you for this reminder. Help me to remember it all through the day and be the last thought in my mind before I drift off to sleep.

Lesson 279:

Let me drop my obsession with limits for once today.

You are limitless. Limitless. You can achieve anything you desire, and this will never not be true about you. You place so many restrictions on yourself; you sell yourself so short, settle for less, and entertain the failures of things you haven't even tried yet. These are all the ways you bind yourself to the body, limit yourself, and play small. Let today be different. What would you do if you could do anything? What would you see as possible if you saw no limits?

Spirit, today I unleash myself! Help me see a world with no limits. Let this day be filled with a clarity I can never forget again.

And so, it is.

Lesson 280:

Limits I place on me are limits I place on God.

There's no point in believing in a God or thinking in any kind of quantum way if you think that you're going to say "it's impossible" to yourself all the time. On any spiritual road, you will hit the bit about you and God being the same or at least roommates in the same house. So, if you're not capable of greatness, then everyone in the world, and also whatever you think created and sustains the world, is not capable either. Know that whatever limits you place on yourself are limits you place on God. Remove the word "can't" from your vocabulary. You can do ANYTHING.

There are no unreasonable goals, only unreasonable timelines.

Spirit, I open to greatness. I will not place limitations on myself, my brothers, or the cosmos. I have had so many conflicting thoughts about who I am and what I'm capable of, and they all are illusions. I choose to return to the truth. You and I are one.

Lesson 281:

Where are the Gods?

Rainer is in a phase where he wants to know everyone's name. He'll stomp up to me and say, "Mommy, aquí now. What's your name?" It's the same every time.

"My name is Onami. It means 'Great Wave.' What's your name?"

"My name is Rainer."

"That's a beautiful name, what does it mean?"

Even though I always tell him it means "warrior of the Gods" he usually forgets. I realized today he doesn't say things he doesn't understand, unlike adults.

I needed to explain warrior, and also the Gods to him before he knew what his name meant.

I said, "A warrior is like a strong and brave ninja who is fearless and powerful, and because he's of the Gods, nobody can beat him. The Gods are the same protection that kept the icicle from falling on your head when you were a baby and keeps your feet steady when you run fast in the woods."

"But I can't see them, I don't know where the Gods are."

"Well, when Daddy farts, you can't see it, but it's definitely there, right?" His eyes say he gets it.

I said, "The Gods are something you feel, and it's what you feel when you look at something beautiful or when you are getting love."

"BUT WHERE ARE THEY??" he demanded.

I gave him a few examples, but he was losing interest, and I made him a deal. "From now on Daddy and I will let you know when we're in the presence of the Gods. "

My kid gave me the homework of remembering to close my eyes and make a wish when the desert wind whips the oak trees, the presence of Oya. To say Aho Mitakuye Oyasin when the density of the forest shifts, and you feel your feet on sacred land. To stop everything and sit in the cathedral windows when the monsoons roll in so we can see a full bolt of lightning crack across the dome of desert sky. I cannot tell him where to find the Gods, all I can do is point out the texture of the moments where the Gods have found us.

Attention is the beginning of devotion.

Lesson 282:

If God be for us, who can be against us?

For real, think about this: If you are loved and protected by God and have all the powers of God at your disposal: what's the problem? In the Bible, it says, "If God be for us, who can be against us?"

I'll add a personal disclaimer here as someone who has directly experienced the frustration of Advaita Vedanta or Oneness teachings. Yes, you're God, so technically, there's no problem, but when you're struggling (and in life, we will struggle - technically unnecessarily), this little you-are-God-so-quit-feeling-shit is the most emotionally useless scrap of information you'll get.

If this is you right now, I'll tell you it was in these moments I learned how to ask for help. Instead of trying to suck it up, find solutions, and power our way through it - we come to prayer in surrender. We imagine telling our Great Mother all of our problems. We don't worry about how we sound or if we're being "negative" or not - we just get honest about how bad we feel, how much we need help, and trust that just like a good Mom, she'll elegantly pull the right strings with the right people.

Let your prayer practice be different, try hitting your knees and sparing no detail as to how you are unsatisfied, lonely, or whatever. Spill your guts, see how you feel, and lean back and trust that Pachamama's got your back.

If it is your choice to do so, may it also be your choice to do so differently.

Lesson 283:

The Four Aims of Hinduism

A key concept in Hinduism is the Purusharthas, the four aims of life. I will teach you three and a half of these.

1. **Dharma**

    What are you here to do? What are your gifts? I can help you to re-cognize your gifts, and share them.

    When you do this, you connect with your purpose and direction in life. Everything in nature, from streams to monarch butterflies, know where they're going. When you have a direction, everything flows to you.

    I teach this in my workshop: How to Start a Business From Scratch

2. **Artha**

    Getting paid for these gifts.

    Yes, learning to speak money with the universe is a multifaceted life lesson you will revisit and refine for the rest of your life. You can't get to the third aim without mastering money first.

    I teach this at:

    Level One: Breaking Broke

    Level Two: Empress Academy

3. **Kama - Desire**

    When you've done the work on receiving, which is the essence of money mastery, you learn that your desire can never be satiated by achievements or material wealth.

We enter the world of desire, how our whole life hangs in the balance of fulfilled and unfulfilled desire. If a desire is met, we could sing for joy! If a desire is unfulfilled, we want to kill ourselves. We are slaves to desire, yet we've never asked ourselves WHAT makes us crave croissants, choose a black dress over a white one, leave a marriage, or pursue greatness. When we utilize the supreme function of desire, it's as if we finally get off the congested highway where we've been stuck in bumper-to-bumper traffic for our whole lives, onto a beautiful clear open highway into the sunset - your joy and destiny. Things you want come to you before you can manifest them! Outrageous heights of success and fulfillment! To achieve this requires a lot of specialized education, available in The School of Unified Spiritual Laws. I also must tell you that if you try to nail this without a teacher it's really hard because all the teachings are paradoxical, so you need someone that can show you how to be both/and right now instead of either/or right now.

You can study this with me in The School of Unified Spiritual Laws

4. **Moksha - Liberation**

Consider steps 1-3 as if you were climbing a tall ladder to a high diving board this whole time.

Going forward, your body will keep revisiting the same lessons over and over, but you're not your body. You're something else. Limitless. Desireless. This force keeps you and everyone alive, never asking for anything in return except that you come to say hi sometime. I can show you how to do this, accompany you all the way to the end of the diving board, but I can't jump for you. That my love is all on you :)

Lesson 284:

Life doesn't hurt. My thoughts do.

Your thoughts are the most powerful thing you have. Imagine there are only two categories: fear and love.

You can choose your thoughts and subsequently choose your feelings and reactions. Many times, we forget that we have this option.

Every thought is a prayer, and every prayer is answered.

The surge of thoughts we have during a situation can escalate an event from unusual to uncomfortable. Thoughts of shame can tell us that having an overdue phone bill makes us a bad person. Guilt can tell us that enjoying a piece of chocolate or skipping a workout means no one will ever love us. These are not true facts; they're just thoughts.

Mantra:

I can be hurt by nothing but my thoughts. I am not my thoughts.

Lesson 285:

Love is my secret weapon today.

The only thing missing from any situation is love. You can end every single conflict with love. So, how can we be afraid of love? Well, it's easy. Think about how flustered you can get in a situation before sitting down to take some deep breaths. Think about the times when you knew if you took a little more time to decide before jumping to a conclusion, you could have had a more pleasant outcome. Think of the times you could have ended an argument (or prevented one from ever occurring) if you could accept an apology or resist the urge to add one more thing. Think of all the times you knew you needed to drink more water.

We always know the answer, but so many times, we will resist asking, pausing, or choosing the loving approach. This is how we keep ourselves in the dark, away from Love, away from others. Not today!

Mantra:

Today I choose to do it lovingly, or not at all. I will take as many breaths as I need to in order to remember the loving way.

Lesson 286:

The Identity Game.

This is one of the most powerful coaching tools, and when I did 1:1 still, every client would get this at some point. I call this the Identity Game.

We have so many stories about who we think we are. We have an outer self we manicure and curate and present to the world (just look at social media), and often it conflicts with the inner self we show to no one. The excess of the outer story, e.g. "I'm enormously successful," and the pressure of maintaining it can cause the inner self to create a self-story that is at a major deficit, e.g. "I'm a complete failure.." Neither the story of being a success nor a failure is true. The inner self and the outer self are not aligned, this is the substance of an identity crisis.

Please do this exercise with a pen and paper. Don't just think it, please do it. I cannot possibly stress the potency of it.

List the aspects of your outer personality. The side of you present to the world, for example, brave, successful, calm, hopeful

Next to it, please make another list, this time the aspects of your inner personality. You may notice some opposites arise, for example: worried, discouraged, frantic. More importantly, you will notice some consistencies, for example, Outer Self - brave, Inner Self - brave.

Now please go through the list, and cross off every single aspect that is not a match on both sides. If it's not a match between the inner self and the outer self, it is not really you. They are just excess details that result in confusion, striving, and identity crisis. Toss all these ideas of self into the garbage.

The ones that remain that are congruent with the inner and outer self; live from these aspects. If there are congruent aspects on both sides that you aren't happy with, e.g. worried, make those a priority for healing.

The rest, write down and put somewhere you can see them every day. Live your life from these aspects. Identify with these aspects. Be proud of them. By ridding ourselves of what we are not, we can relax into the nature of who we are. An added bonus is you never have to worry about maintaining what you're presenting. You can finally just be.

Mantra:

I am not my personality.

Lesson 287:

I can choose better thoughts.

So, only your thoughts can hurt you, right? Your thoughts can take a situation from unusual to uncomfortable, allowing you to create a much bigger story ("He doesn't want me, and no one will want me. I'm unlovable") off of a very small incident, (He's not responding to my texts). We also have complete autonomy for selecting our thoughts, we forget that we can choose a better thought. Apply The Work of Byron Katie. Ask:

Is this thought true?

Can I absolutely know that it is true?

Who am I with this thought?

Who would I be without the thought?

Finally, turn the thought around.

Mantra:

I am not this thought. I choose again.

Lesson 288:

I won't let my plan stand in the way of God's plan anymore.

To be sure you're in line with Spirit, surrender. It's the ONLY way you can make sure that your plan isn't blocking God's plan.

No matter how hard you fight, or whether you accept it or not, God's plan is the plan that's gonna go down. Period. You are not a Great Big Happening on the pale blue dot in the unfathomable universe. God's plan holds everything together, and you have basically no control.

Imagine you're in a lake, the water is choppy, and you're not sure what's the right direction to row in. Water always returns to its Source. Surrender. Stop paddling. Be still, know that God is God. and allow yourself to be floated to where you're supposed to go. The flow (Tao) will never steer you wrong.

Mantra:

You're in control, You love me, and You do all things well.

Lesson 289:

I choose to let the world off the hook today.

Forgiveness allows others to show up differently. It's an incredible, tangible energetic shift that occurs when you allow someone to show up free from the stories that have been plaguing them for so long.

Think about when you've gotten into a fight with someone very close to you, like a sibling or lover. You argued, and then you apologized. Even though the fight is now over, the atmosphere is still tense. You feel as if you're walking on eggshells like you can't make any mistakes or you'll be right back to the argument. This black cloud of regret - wondering if you've really been forgiven or they're still holding it against you - is exactly how people we've not forgiven feel around us.

You don't have to call anyone and tell them you've forgiven them, all you have to do is say in your mind " _____, from now on, I send you love."

If you see them again (cause forgiveness sometimes means not seeing someone again), see them only as they are in the present moment. Let their past stories go. That person is never coming back. When you do it for others, you'll know others will do it for you and all the heinous things you've done in your life too.

Try it.

Mantra:

From now on, I send you love.

Lesson 290:

The past is the past.

I pray you quit overthinking, feeding self-doubt, replaying failed scenarios, and seeing the good in everyone but yourself.

You deserve more. - Unknown Prayer

The only moment we can do anything about is the one we're in right now. The past is gone; it's never coming back. Our focus on the past frequently manifests as anxiety about the future. We're so scared of our horrible history repeating itself that we are either stuck in a rerun of our failures or future-tripping about what's in store. Both of these moments are a waste of time because one's never coming back, and one will likely not ever happen.

The only way to change the past is through forgiveness. It will not change the incident, but how you feel about how it went down. Forgiveness is also called "letting go." It's also accepting this shit went down, was hard on you, was painful, and positively shaped you.

Choose a story from your past. Right now. Pick one scenario specifically that has hounded your mind and choose to let it go right here. That story is never coming back. You have to let it go.

Mantra:

The only moment I know is real is this one. I choose to leave this past story behind and be here now.

Lesson 291:

I will stop and savor the present moment at least once today!

There is a reason "Be here now." is such a cliche. That reason is: it works. You could focus only on being completely present and reaching enlightenment. No deities, no inner child, no vision boards, no meditation. If you live each moment focusing only on the here and now, you are living in a state of enlightenment.

The only moment we can be sure of our impact is the present moment. Any time we are in a state of discomfort, it is because we are focused on an incident from the past or fear about the future. Even in something like childbirth, the discomfort of the current moment can be amplified by a fear that either a story you've heard from the past is unfolding right now, or that in the future the pain will never end.

Today, zoom out of where you think you need to be and understand that simply existing is a miracle. Let your breath expand into your body. Contemplate the intricate network of cells that make up your physical form. Ask yourself who watches your thoughts. This is presence. This is bliss.

Mantra:

Be still and know that I am God.

Lesson 292:

Today, I will chill.

At any time in our lives, stillness of the mind and peace in the body are choices we can make. When you're taking peace days regularly, you're less likely to respond to unusual situations in the habitual, stressful way. Let today be another one of those days. Take 3-5 breaths and scan through your body, rating your internal pace on a scale of one to five, five being the fastest. Try to use these breaths to calm the sympathetic nervous system to lower the pace down to a one or two. Feel what the state of calm feels like in your body, and rate the relaxation and clarity of mind. When you feel the internal pace rising, take three to five breaths again to calm it down. Remember: smooth seas don't make strong sailors. We don't learn peace from oversized cowl-neck sweaters, Yogi tea, and sleeping in. We learn peace by refusing to see obstacles as adversities, and when we are in the face of intensity - choosing grace.

Prayer:

May I remain still enough to see all my options clearly.

Lesson 293:

Joy is my journey; Joy is my destination.

We panic about letting go of our plan and surrendering because, on some level we believe that if we don't damage control, some terrible outcome will unfold. This returns to Einstein's great question: Do you believe in a friendly Universe or a hostile Universe?

Surrendering involves acknowledging you can't control this, and if you aren't in control, it means something or someone else is. Now the real question: do you believe this force will guide you into reward or punishment?

I want to be clear here: God (He/She/It) wants you to be happy. God has always wanted you to be happy and will always want you to be happy. This is because God and you are on the same side. What makes you happy makes God happy. The only time you will not receive what makes you happy is when what you are asking for is a temporary desire (a date with so-and-so) that will obstruct you from receiving what would truly make you happy in the long run (a lasting partnership with your soul mate).

Even when it seems like things are blowing up in your face, stop. Breathe. Understand this is all happening for you, not to you. In time you will look back on this situation with gratitude it did not unfold the way you had designed. You'll see that this experience rerouted you onto the correct path and that you learned valuable lessons on the way. If you know that you'll be grateful for it one day - just cut to that feeling now! You can, and you will be happy you did.

The pain might be inevitable, but the suffering is optional.

Prayer:

Allow me to see this obstacle for what it is: a detour in the right direction.

Lesson 294:

All fear is rooted in the past.

All fear of failure comes from a moment that is gone because, in the present, there is nothing to fear. Your story of who you think you are is gone because you have freed others from their story of who you think they are. You and everyone else are free to show up as is. Without needing yourself or anyone else to drag around the ball and chain of their past failures, we show up in the present moment liberated, innocent, and pure. From a presence like this, we aren't worried about the future because we see it only as an extension of the present bliss.

Prayer:

May I be loving; may I be loved. May I be peaceful, may I find peace.

May _____ be loving, may they be loved. May _____ be peaceful, may they find peace.

Lesson 295:

My body is the vehicle for the Real Me.

Most issues we face in this life are due to our getting so attached to our body, confusing it with who we are. Our body is only a vehicle for our Spirit's expansion. It's incredible the amount of time we lose and the degree to which we hold ourselves back because we're either focused on what we think we need to change about our body or the limitations (age, sickness, location) that our body is bound by. Our bodies are neutral vehicles, and it works just like any other vehicle. Yes, it's very useful to have one. Yes, it's important to maintain it by keeping it clean and filling it with quality fuel. Yes, it's best to operate it soberly and avoid speeding. But without the power of you behind the wheel, it's just a neutral, stationary object. Without the power of you operating it, it's just a piece of metal we've assigned so much value to.

Understand that you are the driver, and the body is the vehicle. Nothing more, nothing less.

Spirit, help me to see my body with gratitude for what it truly is, a vehicle for my spirit. Heal my thoughts. Let me release the pattern of judging it as good, bad, more than or less than. Let me experience the freedom and infinite time that is made available to me when I stop obsessing over my body and its limitations and recognize the truth of what has always been. I am not a body, I am free. I am still as God created me.

Lesson 296:

Spirit runs the show today.

Seeing as the body is just a vehicle for our Spirit, our body does not recognize and processes each experience, it's our Spirit.

The eyes look, but the Spirit sees.

The ears hear, but Spirit listens.

The mouth talks, but the Spirit says.

We can get stuck in the untrained mind's desire to judge, quantify, and classify, and in doing such, override our inner intelligence - but that's a choice we make. We can just as easily choose to let our Higher Self show us how to see, how to listen, and how to say.

Spirit, show me how you would have me see this. Where would you have me go? What would you have me do? What would you have me say? And to whom?

Lesson 297:

I will be impeccable with my word.

It's possible that your voice could be used for truth and love only. It's possible that your speech could be the rising tide that lifts all ships around you. It's possible that you would never say something you wish you could take back again. Every word you say can hurt or heal. Let today be an experiment for you on what is possible when you release the head's need to over-clarify, defend, or broadcast what you think others want to hear. Instead, try speaking from the heart. Before you open your mouth, stop, and check in with your Inner Guidance system with this prayer.

Spirit, what would you have me say here? Guide my words and give me exactly what I need to make this experience a loving experience for all those concerned.

Lesson 298:

Forgiveness is my gift today.

The prayer has already been answered. The only reason the things you've been manifesting haven't materialized for you yet is that you aren't open to receiving them. Why?

Because, on some level you don't think you deserve it.

Why?

Because you have guilt or shame about something from the past that needs to be released, aka forgiven. Some things you'll be aware of (conscious blocks), some things you won't be (unconscious blocks).

So, how do I get rid of these blocks if I don't even know I have them?

You forgive others reflexively and as frequently as you can for every possible offense. If everything you give others is given unto you, and the slate is wiped clean every time you forgive - forgiving others will allow you to believe that your slate has been wiped clean of every possible offense. If you believe consciously and subconsciously that there is no reason that you cannot have everything your heart desires, then there will be no reason you cannot have everything your heart desires.

Spirit, help me remember this truth: whenever I'm in a state of discomfort I can ask: "What needs to be forgiven for all this pain to go away? I know that the answer is always available if I remember to ask, so please help me remember to ask.

Lesson 299:

As is, I'm enough.

God can only love you as much as you love yourself. It is the same. You cannot expect to feel loved, held, supported, and protected by the cosmos if you do not feel worthy of love, honor, support, and protection. You alone are responsible for creating your capacity for love so it can be filled to overflowing by the world and everyone in it, and the cosmos and everything/everyone in it. Everywhere that you criticize yourself is a block to love. If you don't love yourself because you think your belly is too pudgy to be loved, you'll convince yourself that no partner will ever love you as you are and that God doesn't love you as you are. To receive more, you must be willing to go into the areas where you think you're most unlovable and love them to death.

Spirit, help me to release all the ways I have held myself back from fully loving myself. Help me to understand that what I consider my greatest flaws are actually my most lovable aspects. Help me remember that my relationship with myself directly mirrors my relationship with you. Today I open myself to love. Please show me the way.

P.S.

If you really struggle with self-love, I believe my video:

How to Love Yourself (When You Hate Yourself) will be of great service to you.

Lesson 300:

I am good.

You have within you an intelligence, a light, a magic that cannot be stolen, duplicated, lost, or turned off. All it can be is forgotten. As surely as you exist, it exists. It's not up to you to determine its quality, how it got there, or how it compares to anyone else. It's not up to you to decide if it's good or not or wonder how others will receive it. Your only job is to **remember** as often as you can and trust it is enough.

Channeling Martha Graham in that last paragraph, but I've read it probably fifteen times, and every word is true, I really mean it, and I can't say it in fewer words. Bottom line is this: You're super fucking strong and super fucking talented. You have gifts literally no one else on Earth has. No matter how flawed or incapable you think you are.

Place your hand over your heart, close your eyes, and breathe deeply. Imagine the most radiant, beautiful, and elegant version of yourself smiling right back at you. Breathe into your heart, into this version of yourself. Smile.

Write down the qualities of your ultimate role model?

Did you know that you ALREADY possess these qualities, they're just waiting to show themselves more? It's a spiritual fact. If your ideal role model is fearless, ask yourself with every decision, "What would I do if I were fearless? What would I say if I was fearless?"

I don't recommend any practices I haven't done, I'm telling you. It works.

Lesson 301:

This, too, will pass, and you'll be grateful for it.

Acceptance allows us to feel authentic gratitude for the painful events in our lives. We see them as the lessons we needed to teach what we are here to teach. We came here for our souls to expand and that smooth seas don't make strong sailors. When times are hard (and times will be hard - it's not in the nature of the ocean to be still), can you remember that down the road you will be grateful for the way this all went down? Grateful because it was necessary for this to happen exactly the way it did to get you to your future, joyous self. If you can know this and remember it in the face of intensity, you can let the difficulties wash over you. You can cut to the gratitude. These moments only last an instant in the scheme of things, and through gratitude, you can allow them to carry you. This is the education that creates trust.

The pain may be inevitable, but the suffering is optional.

Spirit, please help me to remember that I've never made a wrong turn because I've been divinely guided every day of my life. Help me to see my obstacles as opportunities and not as adversities telling me I've fallen off my path. I surrender my need to know how everything will work out and instead trust it will work out as it always has. Help me transform my expectations into appreciation and let me view them with gratitude.

Lesson 302:

Practice: Daily Wins

This practice is one of my favorites, and on the Slack for my mastermind, The Bruja Report we have a whole thread devoted to it.

For the longest time, I would go to bed at night reviewing all the things I needed to do tomorrow and all the things I DIDN'T accomplish today. I'm a Capricorn which means ambition feeds me, and I love scheduling, so it seemed pleasurable to have this nightly "How can I do better?" ritual.

Once I had a kid, and my precious plans were chronically sabotaged, I felt like I didn't have enough time to complete anything, and I felt this way as a lifestyle. I would usually go to bed with a sigh, like "Guess it's never going to happen.," and it was usually because I had failed to complete a New York Times Bestseller that day. Writing a book takes time, like everything else, so there will ALWAYS be something undone that you can hang over your head at the end of the day. Because this was where I was regularly focusing, this was the attitude I met new ideas and goals with. "Nice idea, let's see if it actually gets done."

Ideas are gifts from the Gods, like we discuss in the Ajna module of Wheels: Reinvented. If you're not greeting new, sane, and insane ideas with "YES! THANK YOU! MORE PLEASE," you'll stop getting them. When you stop getting creative ideas, you become depressed. Your fire goes out.

Patrick, whose Divine Masculine advice I took for once, told me, "Your to-do list is never going to be over. That's how to-do lists work.." When he said that, something clicked. If my to-do list will never be completed, then why am I focusing on what's NOT been done at the end of the day, as opposed to what I DID accomplish today?

That night (I was still on Instagram), I posted on my stories: Today's daily wins. I took inventory not only of the "productive" moments I had or sales I had made but also the subtle moments like not losing my shit when Rainer was being an asshole, not beating myself up for things out of my control or avoiding an anxiety trap. I intended to get as many down as possible, and I went to bed for the first time in weeks feeling SO good about myself. The next day, I saw a few other people had been inspired to post their own wins, and over the next few weeks, it started to gel into a tradition for myself and my followers. Now, in my mastermind, we have a thread always going for these wins, and it's one of my favorites.

When you're focusing on what you've aced and not where you fell short, your self-concept changes. When new ideas come to you, you have a solid track record with yourself of succeeding, doing hard things, and taking care of business. You're aware that it is true, the Tao does nothing and leaves nothing undone. That sometimes the most productive days come out of nowhere, and that emotional victories are as real and important as the financial/business/body victories we've been so conditioned to see as the "real" ones.

When you genuinely feel like the type of person who is capable of accomplishing great things, and this is the main benefit of this practice, you are the perfect host for new ideas, and they come to you abundantly. You also just feel good, which I believe is reason enough to make it a habit.

Here's how you do this:

You can do it mentally, but I guarantee you won't get as many down. It's easy to get distracted so close to bed, but mentally is better than not at all, so don't beat yourself up.

The BEST way you could do this would be to share it with an audience, either on social media or on a group chat or in Bruja Report (obviously). When you get a witness on something, it's twice as strong. I also can type faster than I can write, and with a baby on the boob, that phone comes in real handy!

Start with a goal of ten wins. I say this because initially you'll be used to focusing on what didn't get done, so it'll seem like you had only three wins today. Learning how to take a bath instead of forcing yourself to meet an unreasonable deadline is a win. Catching a fear before it became a full-day anxiety trip is a win. Good sleep is a win. Good food is a win. Grieving is a win.

When you see yourself as a winner, you meet new challenges like a winner. With faith.

Try it tonight, and hopefully, you'll get addicted and never second-guess yourself again.

Lesson 303:

There is no rejection, just options you didn't know you wanted.

With a grateful mindset (and a lot of dedicated practice), you can view all obstacles or rejections as crucial detours in the right direction. Think about an event from the past that did not go at all how you wanted it, for example - a boyfriend or girlfriend you thought you really wanted but who lived far away and wasn't giving you what you wanted. Maybe you were also devastated by a lack of finances because if you had some money, you could fly to go deal with their trifling ass in person. So, you were praying for money and praying for this person to love you, and it simply was not working, and you were rightly disappointed. It took a while, but you ended up finding a job you loved and, later on, a true love. Had your prayers for money and the wrong partner been answered, you would have been halfway across the world, doing a job that wasn't right for you, trying to make it work with someone who wasn't right for you either. The disappointment is transformed into appreciation. The appreciation you didn't get what you prayed for so you could be on the path for what would truly bring you happiness. Obstacles are detours in the RIGHT direction, so when faced with an obstacle or disappointment - how can you practice appreciation? If you know that down the road you'll be grateful for it all, can you cut to the appreciation and gratitude right away? I know you can, with practice. So, start this practice today!

Lesson 304:

I can tap into power at any point.

I hear people refer to kundalini energy all the time as a sleeping serpent at the base of the spine, implying this energy is dormant and needs to be activated. This couldn't be further from the truth. As my teacher, Rod Stryker, put it: "the kundalini isn't asleep, you are."

You have inside of you the answer to any question you could ever ask. The only reason you feel like you're not tapped into it is that you either: A.) aren't asking.

or

B.) aren't trusting in what you hear.

Integrate with this thought. Every question you could ever have, you contain the answer to - if you can remember to ask. With this truth, the need for all astrology, Tarot cards or psychics goes right out the window. You don't need them because you already know the answer.

Intuition is a muscle; the more you work it, the stronger it gets. The more you remember to ask, the clearer the messages, the quicker you can hear it, and the more likely you are to trust and apply what you hear.

Today, remember to ask. As often as you can. You have a wealth of support and information at your disposal, and you're using a fraction of it. If you knew your life was divinely guided, that there was an all-knowing guide with you when you were lost, would you continue to wander, or would you ask for directions?

You are Divinely guided. Use it.

Lesson 305:

Let me not lose the plot.

Today you might have a small opportunity to reframe your perspective on obstacles, or you may have a large one. It could be related to family drama, money, work, or bae - regardless, we will take what we learned over the last couple of days and apply it to any issue that comes up.

Every obstacle is happening for you, and not to you. Additionally, we came here to expand, and we can only do that when we're faced with an obstacle. So, obstacles are going to happen for life, on every topic. If we can accept this, knowing that shit will go down in life no matter how hard we try to avoid it because that's what we came here for - how can we change the way we react to it? How can we NOT take obstacles personally? How can we accept the discomfort with gratitude instead of creating any unnecessary discomfort?

Take this mantra out into the world with you today: "How can I grow?" With any

opportunity for discomfort - big or small - ask: "How can I grow."

Lesson 306:

Peace begins with me.

The last few lessons showed us how we can use gratitude and appreciation to end the suffering we feel when we're faced with an obstacle in our own life. But what about everyone else's problems? What about political issues? The Middle East?

We can get so consumed with what's going on outside of us we forget there is always a solution inside of us.

You are the creator of your own reality, so if there's no peace inside of you, you will not see peace outside of you. Even though it seems backward, to create the change outside - it needs to start inside.

Lesson 307:
My pleasure is my power.

A GREAT morning practice is to ask yourself the first thing in the morning: "What would I like to do today?"

By creating a pleasure-based intention when you're still sleepy, before the world and your ambitious to-do list have caught up with you - you get on the path to more pleasure, more inspiration, more joy, real fast. This is also a great tool for productivity. A woman in her pleasure is a woman in her power. I worked with a terrific business coach named Chela Davison, and the best takeaway I got from it was taking the "random" result of "When I prioritize my pleasure, everything else gets done easily" and making it a principle of my business. After spending a couple of days praying, "How can I make sure I remember my pleasure??" (because it's really, really easy to forget), I was able to condense it down to JUST asking myself this question in the morning. Not "what do I have to do?" but "what do I WANT to do?"

The fear that will keep you from trying is telling yourself you will wake up every day saying you want to go to Turks and Caicos, never work again, or gift yourself a $2800 ring. This is not the case. You're not going to wake up in diva mode, and you'll be surprised at how reasonable your requests are. Mine are usually things I want to eat, projects I want to work on, the amount of time I want to spend outdoors, etc. If you really hate your job, you will probably wake up every day saying, "I DON'T WANT TO GO TO WORK!" This is not the practice. No one cares what you DON'T want to do, and the Universe can't do anything with that anyway. I will say this, though: if you hate your job, and you work 40 hours a week and you're usually up for 14 hours a day or 98 hours a week, that's 40% of your life that you don't like, and you need to do something to change that. My workshop, How to Start a Business From Scratch (with no time, no money, and no business plan) would be a good place to start with that. As long as someone else is cutting your check, you don't control your finances, and you have a job you could lose. If you hate your job, you're also not connected to your purpose, which means you haven't taken the first step towards enlightenment (Recognizing your unique gifts and sharing them, as per lesson 283).

What DO you want to do, and how can you make this happen today? That's the practice. I wouldn't be recommending it if I hadn't done it and loved the results. That's true of everything I'll recommend for you in this book.

After a couple of days of this, your relationship to your life will change. When you feel like you're regularly getting what you want out of life, more things seem possible for the future, but you're also experiencing the present. It's easier to be present when you're enjoying what's going on.

Can you slap a post-it next to your bed? "What do I WANT to do today?" or maybe on your bathroom mirror? Where should it go so you don't forget?

Lesson 308:

I trust in the sequence of my unfolding life.

If obstacles are detours in the right direction, inevitably sometimes, we are guided away from what we thought we wanted. The disappointment of this can be painful alone, but when we convince ourselves that that was what we needed to be happy, and without it, we won't be happy - the experience can be downright excruciating.

Your Eternal Self will never allow your Temporal Self an instant gratification that would block you from perpetual bliss. It is "this or something more.." If you are being blocked from the "this," it is because there is something far, far more awaiting you. Your life is not a countdown to a miserable fate, but rather you are getting closer and closer to destiny every single day.

The lesson of "I don't know what I truly want" is one of the toughest to master, but if you can trust that when you don't get what you want, it's because you don't want it. You only think you do based on the X number of years you've been hanging around on Earth, and you're not allowed to have it because it would be settling for less, and your Higher Self just ain't gonna do that to you.

How can you trust in the unfolding of your life today? It's this or something more. Always.

Always. Always.

Lesson 309:

This moment is the only moment there is.

The only time we can be certain exists is this moment right now. The past is gone, the future has not happened, and depending on our perspective the memory of the past or the prediction of the future can look different. 99% of our thoughts attempt to drag us out of the present and into either the past or the future. We also know that when we meditate, we push away thoughts, focus on our breath, and thus arrive fully into the present moment. The more we become present, the more we see is possible. When you're 100% present, that's enlightenment.

Here are two ways we can use what we've learned to get present:

1.) Forgiveness brings presence by allowing us to erase the past we hold against ourselves or others. When we free ourselves and others from the weight of our past, we stop worrying that the "past will repeat itself". When this happens, we are in a moment of truth. We are present.

2.) Releasing the need to control situations and doing our best to find the beauty in them just the way they are (use the question portal "How is this great?") brings presence because when we stop trying to change the way things are, we can appreciate the world exactly as it is. This brings us to the full experience of the present moment.

The past is gone, and the future is an extension of the present moment. If you can make the most of the present moment without trying to change it, you can ride this high until the end of time.

Like the late, great Wayne Dyer said:

"There is no way to happiness, happiness IS the way."

Use either practice today to bring you into the present moment. It's the only time that matters. It's the only time there is.

Lesson 310:

Today, it starts with me.

One of the great granfalloons (as Vonnegut would call it) of life is this idea that when we need an answer for something we need to outsource for it instead of getting still and turning within.

We're trying to get to Mars and get a deeper understanding of outer space, yet we have no idea what's at the depths of our own oceans or understand the inner space of our minds.

To understand outer space, we must understand inner space.

Entertain this as true, immense of a responsibility that it is:

Everything you see outside of you reflects what is going on inside of you. You'll stop seeing it on the outside when you stop believing it on the inside.

It takes a brave soul to see something outside of you that drives you crazy and take it into your heart. To ask: "What is this teaching me? What false belief of mine is this incident or person reinforcing? What needs to be forgiven for this to go away? What needs to be healed inside of me for this story to change?"

Today, accept full responsibility for your experience of this life. Accept that it all starts and ends with you. Take every incident, beautiful and terrifying, into your heart - and let it expand you.

Sat Nam

Lesson 311:

It's only fear.

The war for your whole life will be the love vs. fear war. It's easy to get confused by the varying expressions of the battles, but it's only fear that makes you feel bad. Fear feels bad because it isn't ever true. So, when these feelings come up, and we feel constricted, worried, alone, and afraid - it's because the thought isn't true, and our bodies and mind are feeling poisoned by it and reacting. It's like if you ate rotten food. You would feel off before you showed symptoms of food poisoning. It is the natural response of your body rejecting what doesn't belong.

All the bad feelings you have when you believe a fear-based thought are your body and mind begging you to release it and remember that you are unlimited, unstoppable, and are guaranteed to come out on top.

No fear is greater than another. It's all just F-E-A-R : False Evidence Appearing Real. No matter how great or how original a bad feeling seems - it's only fear, and you've already overcome fear thousands of times to be the person you are today. You've already won.

Today, go beyond fear. See it for what it is and walk on by.

Lesson 312:

All judgment is a two-way street.

Every time we pass a judgment on someone or something, we create an in-road of susceptibility back to us.

For example, I decide someone is "bad energy" and cut them off from my life. When mutual friends ask after so-and-so, I'll say, "I'm not hanging out with her, she's bad energy." I believe this judgment is a one-way street, but it's not. So, when someone isn't returning my calls in the future, I'll wonder if they've randomly cut me off. Even if I did nothing, I'll believe they could simply not like my energy. Not only that, but I'll have a worry window that they're talking shit about me to our mutuals as well. I'll get paranoid. Did she stop following me? Who else is involved?

Passing any judgment on anyone reinforces God the Punisher, who is the protagonist of Principles of a Hostile Universe. When we decide that something or someone is "bad," we'll watch the ebbs and flows of their life like a bad telenovela. Every time something goes wrong, we'll see it as "karma," serving them right for behaving badly. Our judgment creates the crime, and our judgment creates the punishment. Everyone's life will have ups and downs, but if you try to make it about justice and punishment, you'll believe that punishment is coming for you. When life sucks, as it sometimes does, you'll be trying to find what you've done wrong to deserve it, and you can chase your tail here for a long, long time. It's either a Universe that is 100% friendly or 100% hostile. It cannot be hostile towards some and friendly towards others, and every thought you think reinforces one of these worlds. If you believe in punishment because you're addicted to judgment, you believe in a dual Universe - heaven and hell. Two gods warring over your mind. If you cut out judgment and pray to see the perfection in all things as they are, you awaken to the world of Oneness.

Why would you want to do this?

Because if everything is on the same side, nothing can be against you.

If nothing is against you, you never lose. You never even fight.

Lesson 313:

I decide what I see.

If I'm not judging any situation as good/bad, right/wrong, or fair/unfair - I'm able to see the perfection of all things exactly as they are. If I release my need to be the rescuer, victim, or judge of the situation and instead accept that all parties are getting exactly what they signed up for and that the situation has been presented to me as an opportunity to grow - I can stop worrying about all the happenings in the world and my social circles and see peace where everyone else sees chaos.

By choosing not to judge a situation, I decide what I see. I free myself from societal pressure because I decide what society says. I free myself from the sense of political oppression because I see perfection in what is happening here today. I release my need to be right or decide who is right and relax into the bliss of knowing there is, was, and will always be a bigger picture into which all these little bumps in the road fit perfectly.

Lesson 314:

I choose to see peace.

I will apply what I've learned. I release my need to judge a situation as good/bad, right/wrong, fair/unfair. I can choose how I perceive things. I decide what I see based on my perception, and I choose to see peace.

Am I being negligent? Spiritually bypassing? Shirking my responsibilities as an upstanding member of society? You could believe that if you wanted to, but does getting involved, worrying, or stressing out bring you peace? Does it make you feel good?

The only control we have in this life is controlling our reaction to the world because things are not in our control, and never will be in our control. There is perfection in all things exactly the way they are if we can see it as such.

I choose to see peace.

Lesson 315:

I accept a new future for myself.

Forgiveness allows us to release the past and see all events "good" and "bad" as crucial and beneficial for our growth. As we recognize this in our own history, we apply it to the world. We free up the present moment because we understand that things are going exactly as they're meant to, and even if we're a little (or a lot) uncomfortable now, we'll be grateful that things went down as they did and we cut to that gratitude now.

Our fear from the past used to cast a shadow on our vision of the future. We would be constantly pulled mentally between reflecting on the past or worrying about the future. Both of which are not here, therefore, it's not real. You can do nothing about the past, you can do nothing about the future, but when we are present - anything is possible.

The future is simply an extension of the present moment. By creating peace in the present moment, an internal peace that abides even within the most chaotic circumstances, we give ourselves a visa for our future. I may not know what the future brings, but I know the end of the road is joy. I don't know what's going to happen, but I know that whatever it is, I can be peaceful.

Today we leave behind the fear that our awful history will repeat itself. We release our obsession with future-tripping, and instead relax into the knowing that what we want also wants us, and we can't make a wrong turn in getting there.

Welcome to your life.

Lesson 316:

Their success is my success.

Here's a great way to get out of the jealousy and comparison trap. Many times, we can see another's success and feel fear, thinking that they have taken all the success, and there is none less for us. We'll see people at the top of the industry we are in or wish to be in and feel despair and dismay, thinking that they have taken our opportunity, instead of remembering that there is plenty of room at the top. We'll see others with one-of-a-kind jobs and get discouraged, thinking we'll never be able to achieve or have what they have or achieved.

You're either WHOLEHEARTEDLY rooting for someone, or you're jealous.

There are only fear-based thoughts or love-based thoughts, no neutral. When we send someone fear-based thoughts, we wish it on ourselves because our life reflects what we're putting in the world. There's a woman I knew indirectly and followed on social for several years who was always, frankly, a bitch to me. But because she symbolizes NYC success (old model for me) a part of me is still jealous, and still wants her approval.

Like everyone else, she has problems, and I recently heard a hefty slice of gossip about her new marriage. I wanted to check even more! My illusion is that somehow I'll be lifted up as "right" if she's tanking as "wrong" and that's just not true. The transit from six figures to seven figures is a strong mental game, and in it, there's no room for little judgments because there ARE no little judgments. So, now I ask myself: when I survey your Instagram, am I wholeheartedly rooting for you? Am I rooting for your success? Am I rooting for your marriage to work, your proposals to be accepted, and your income to double? Am I wishing fertility, abundance, creative surges, and all your dreams coming true with all of my heart, as if it were for my own life?

If not, just unfollow. The only person you're hurting is yourself. If you still go for a looksie without following it'll give you extra time to set that intention of "I'm gonna go bless the tits off of you, sister. VERBALLY! In the comments."

Let's raise our women supporting women game up substantially. Will we? Let's move away from the conditional feminism we hold other women to, into unconditional feminism. All women. All the time. If you'd like to dig into the topics of jealousy and comparison more, you've GOT to do my mini-workshop, Jelly. It's a game changer!

Lesson 317:

All that I give is given to me.

So, many of the great texts reiterate this idea of it being better to give than to receive and that when we give, we are blessed a hundred times over, but let's make it easy to understand today.

One of the most difficult levels in this video game we call Life is the concept of scarcity or things running out. This illusion of there not being enough time, money, love, or whatever other resources you need to live free is just that, an illusion, and it will keep us straitjacketed in resistance for as long as we keep this illusion alive. This illusion leads us to believe that there is barely enough for us, let alone enough to share. When we buy things, all we can think about is the money we spent on it we don't have anymore, which sometimes creates a big enough guilt trip we don't even enjoy it. We're focused on the money leaving, not the purchase coming.

Releasing the scarcity mindset is fucking hard, especially if you grew up broke or with unavailable parents (or both!). The best way to carve out a new neural pathway is to give freely, as if you had infinite resources, knowing there is always more where that came from. Does this mean you should ride a spiritual high and empty your bank account and give to everyone you can see when you're unemployed? No! I've tried it, and that was definitely self-sabotage, but give whatever you can, whenever you can while still feeding yourself.

Give with a full heart, with no sense of "you owe me" to the receiver or the Universe. Give because every time you give, you're erasing this idea of scarcity, and once you're past scarcity, you remember that the power of the entire Universe is at your disposal, and you can have anything you want. That's why giving is living.

Every time you give or spend today, say this mantra out loud. Freak the cashier out, it's okay. "There's plenty more where that came from."

You're doing this, and it's working.

Lesson 318:

I have an appointment with destiny.

"Fate is what happens when you do not consciously engage with your life, and destiny is what happens when you do." - Guru Jagat

The idea of cause followed by effect is a byproduct of the illusion of linear time. When texts talk about the end of time, they don't mean Armageddon. They're talking about the collective consciousness fully accepting that the fourth dimension, time, does not exist. Everything happens at once. Spacetime.

I felt like most of my life was shit, and because I was stuck in the order of cause/effect, I was wondering what I did in my past to cause (a.k.a deserve) such shitty effects. Little did I know my cause was in the future. I had an appointment with destiny I needed to make. Now, at 30, I'm just catching up to my cause. To be here on this day, all those things had to happen, and I've never been more grateful. Every tear, every ounce of frustration was so, so worth it.

At this stage in the story, you are catching up to your cause. You are coming to understand that you have never made a wrong turn, that every tear and every triumph was integral to getting you where you are today, and my dear, you are getting started.

Lesson 319:

I complete me.

Enlightenment isn't about fixing yourself; it's about remembering that there is nothing that needs to be fixed. You relax the layers of personality you've kept up front for so long that you've believed they are you. You release the "I can't" and "what will people think?" and allow your joy to guide you to higher heights. As you accept more accountability for your experience of this life and do the work (like you've been doing for the past year), you become your own source of joy, stability, security, and wisdom.

The idea and necessity of "the other" fade into the background. All the voices you needed to tell you, "You're enough. You're enough," and never did, lose their hold on you. You've affirmed to yourself, "I'm enough. I'm enough," and now you believe it.

Could it be this whole time the only love you needed was your own? The only validation you needed was your own? The only forgiveness you needed was your own? That all it took was for you to stop beating yourself up, replaying past failures, and seeing the good in everyone but yourself? Could it be this whole time, you were waiting for someone to come to see you as the diamond in your own rough, but all you needed was to see it for yourself, and suddenly it all made sense?

It's true. That's how it works. God can only love you as much as you love you because you create the bandwidth for how much love you can receive. Doesn't matter how much someone loves you, cares for you, roots for you. If you only have the capacity for 500 grams of love, all you'll be able to receive is 500 grams and everything else will be sent away.

Repeat after me.

"I complete me."

and again

"I Complete Me."

and again!

"I COMPLETE ME!'

Smile.

Lesson 320:

Healing begins with me.

When you die, your story about the world will end. All the characters, settings, stories and everything you know as you know it will cease to exist because nothing exists outside of you. What if it were all a video game designed by you, with everyone and everything representing an aspect of your own consciousness and beliefs? What if everything you saw on the outside was malleable, able to be manipulated and transformed with an increasingly shortened buffer time if you simply adjusted what you believed on the inside?

With the people near us, like our family, we can want to heal them the most. As we wake up spiritually, the pain of others starts to stick out. We want to share what we know has healed us with the people near and dear to us still struggling, yet somehow we can't seem to reach them. They don't want to be taught, they don't want to learn, and it kills us. This is where today's lesson comes in so handy.

Don't try to change them, heal them, or help them. You have only to focus on your own healing. Keep doing the work for you because it's all you can do. By simply being different than the person you used to be, they will see it. One day, and only when the time is perfect, they'll ask you how they can do the same.

Lesson 321:

I have the power.

You have the sole responsibility for everything you see in this world. While it can feel intimidating when you think about all the stuff you don't like representing internal work you still need to do, think about it this way: you have the power to change anything you don't like! You don't have to ask anyone's permission, wait for someone to say sorry, lose the last five pounds first, or anything else. All you have to do is decide that you want to see it differently, and it will be so.

Like the late, great Wayne Dyer says: "When you change the way you look at things, the things you look at change."

My favorite question to ask myself to help me see a different perspective is, "Why do I think this shouldn't be happening?" When I open my mind up to this question, I see various ways this situation is perfect, just the way it is.

Lesson 322:

With this thought, I am free.

Trauma is only a misunderstanding. We observed something that we didn't understand, it wasn't explained to us, and so we explained it to ourselves. Problem is, we were children when we did this. Things were abstract, bigger and scarier, and we couldn't adequately comprehend what was going on. Something as simple as our mom slamming the refrigerator door could be deciphered by us as: "She's mad at me because I'm laughing in my highchair. Laughing is bad. What makes me happy is wrong, there must be something wrong with me." and we end up with the origin of shame. With every entry in our book of facts about life, we forgot our true nature a little more. As we accumulated more stories based on misunderstandings, we believed these "facts" were true. We confused our true identity with misunderstandings. We lost ourselves. Instead of remembering we are God, and possess the powers of the cosmos, we came to believe we were a series of shortcomings, for which the Universe would be out to get us.

You - Trauma = God

The ultimate truth? You are God. As such, nothing can stop you, defy you, or block you from claiming all that you desire. As God, you planned out this life in the way that would result in your greatest joy. As long as you stay in a state of trust and surrender because you know you are on your path, vs. panic and resistance because you're certain you're not, and are thus trying to avoid an inevitable punishment from an outside God - then there is no problem.

If you can absorb this thought, and relax into the truth of it, then you are free for life.

I am God.

Lesson 323:

All I want is what's in front of me.

"To think that you need something you don't have is insanity." - Byron Katie

A grand percentage of the sadness and disappointment we feel in our lives is connected to a sense of wanting something that is not here right now. We feel like we're waiting endlessly and that what we want is so far away. Our state is one of expectation as opposed to appreciation.

In the present moment, we have everything that we need - and more! If we are focused on what we lack in the present moment, there will be more lack to see. Lack is something we create, and it's subjective. For example, you may feel an intense lack around your love life or your financial state, and because you've made yourself aware of this lack, you're very upset about it, and you remind yourself of it almost daily. When you see happy couples, or a celebrity buying a $20k purse, it reminds you of how much is missing from your life versus seeing it as a sign that what you want is also on the way. But at this moment, you are also missing a yellow velvet beret (unless, by some freak chance, you actually have a yellow velvet beret). You were never upset by this until you assigned the state of lack to it by remembering you don't have it. Even though you were fine in your life without a yellow velvet beret, now we've put attention on it, and the desire is activated. If you have not decided that a yellow velvet beret is hard to get (like we typically decide about love or money), you'll have no resistance around it. You might see yellow hats everywhere, then yellow berets, and then finally a yellow velvet beret, and maybe even something more than you could have designed. Each time you see an indicator, you are filled with joy because you know it means your desire is on the way. But if you are convinced that a yellow velvet beret will be hard to get because you've assigned lack to it, every time you see an indicator, you'll take it as an affirmation of what you don't have, and it will upset you. The more resistance you create to your desire manifesting, the less able it is to manifest. You could be walking right by your beret, bae, or bankroll every day, unable to see it because you are determined to see its lack.

Today transform your expectations for the future into the appreciation of the present. You have everything you need right now to enjoy this moment right here, and you'll miss it if you're focusing on what you don't have. You think if you could have this thing or that thing, THEN you could appreciate the present, but that's not true. As long as you see lack there will always be something missing, able to drag you out of the present. You must learn to appreciate the present moment if you want more in life to appreciate. So, today, appreciate it all, starting with the richness of your breath.

Whatever you appreciate, you'll get more of. I promise.

Lesson 324:

It's (still) only fear.

Any discomfort, any worry, any feeling of disease is still only fear. You're not afraid of snakes, you're afraid of death, and it's only fear. You're not afraid of falling in love, you're afraid of losing what you love, and it's only fear. You're not afraid of going broke and being evicted, you're afraid of being abandoned and destitute, and that's still only fear.

It's always going to be some incarnation of fear, and there are no rational fears. If it's not in this exact moment right now, it's not real. If it's not in this moment right now and you're focusing on it you're asking for it to happen. Each thought is a prayer, a request. Fear-based thoughts are prayers for the worst-case scenario to unfold.

You don't have to journal out all the fears and try to talk yourself off the ledge, you can just throw the entire thing away. Deactivate the toxic thought by choosing a different thought, choose again! Choose the opposite of that thought.

Use this prayer:

Spirit, I know this thought isn't serving me. Please help me. Heal my mind. Flood it with thoughts that uplift and serve me, that make me feel safe and abundant. Help me to remember the protection that has walked with me every day of my life, leading me to today. I choose again, I choose to forget this fear, and remember my power.

P.S.

If it's a painful and recurring fear such as "Everyone I love will leave me." I strongly recommend getting The Work by Byron Katie app. I've used it dozens of times, it's free and it's fantastic.

Lesson 325:

I relax and allow myself to be drawn towards destiny.

Those assured of the outcome can wait without anxiety. - *A Course in Miracles*

Our biggest fear for letting go of our plans and letting Spirit take the wheel is that we won't get what makes us happy, and that simply isn't true. Because of childhood misunderstandings, we have lower chakra issues like guilt and shame lying to us telling us that we've either done something wrong or are something wrong, and impending punishment is all that can be expected. This is also simply not true.

The things you want also want you. Your desires are attracting you like you are attracting them. You and your desires are two magnets, pulling each towards the other.

Imagine that you are in a canoe in a lake. It is windy, and you cannot tell which direction the natural flow is going. You are vigorously paddling, but the lake is wide, and you want to be sure you're going in the right direction. From your current vantage point, you can't see which way is the right way. This is like when you're pushing your agenda, heavily exerting yourself, and striving towards what you think you want. In this situation, you want to lift up your oars and allow yourself to be carried. You cannot feel what the natural flow is when you are in a state of effort. The low AUM of Source energy cannot be heard when you've got the mic. The only way to be certain that you're on the right path and in line with Source is to be in a state of surrender. Surrendering your plan can be scary if you think you will be carried to an awful fate instead of a blissful destiny, but that fear is only a fear. You won't feel the joy of being caught if you refuse to leap.

What plan are you attached to? Why are you afraid to give it up? What do you think would happen if you stopped trying with it? Is that fear talking or love?

Lesson 326:

I see only what I believe to be true.

One of our biggest confusions in life is believing that what we see on the outside determines what we will believe on the inside and this is the opposite of the truth. The world we see is a neutral mirror, reflecting whatever it is that we choose to believe onto it. If you smile into the mirror, your reflection smiles back. It doesn't get mad at you or ask if you're really smiling or fake smiling, it only reflects what you've put onto it. When determined to keep believing what we have chosen to believe, our perception is skewed because we will always find evidence to support whatever it is we are believing.

Forgiveness allows us to instantly change our perception, adjusting the lens through which we are viewing our life and offering an opportunity to transform a belief that tears us down into one that lifts us up. As our beliefs change, the world we see reflects something different.

For example, I used to have a belief that men could not be trusted and that loving relationships were fake. When I would see a man walking down the streets of New York holding flowers, I would assume that he was covering his tracks after cheating on his girlfriend or attempting to salvage the relationship after a big fight. I did not believe healthy relationships were possible, and so I remained captive to abusive relationships, reinforcing my belief daily.

What needed to be forgiven for that lens to go away? I needed to forgive my Dad. Once I did, my perception changed. I would see the same exact event in a different light. I saw men buying flowers for the women in their lives they worshipped, even after all these years.

Through forgiveness, my perception changed instantly, my belief changed gradually, and my world responded. Now I'm in a healthy marriage. My husband doesn't buy me flowers, but he buys me candles because he knows I prefer them.

Pick one (or all) of these topics. Love, Money, Health, Career, Friendships

What do I see as true about _____? For example: "I see men cheating on their

girlfriends."

What internal belief does this observance correspond with?

Is that belief true?

What is the opposite of that belief?

List three instances when you have witnessed the opposite of this belief to be true?

1.) _____

_____

2.) _____

___

3.) _____

___

Write this new belief somewhere you can see it all the time. Affirm it to yourself daily and watch how the world you see starts to change.

Lesson 327:

Love doesn't have a bad side.

It is impossible to ever be on Spirit's bad side because there isn't a bad side to be on. The energy of Spirit, God, Love, the Universe is always the same. Infinitely expanding, peaceful and loving. There isn't anything that you could ever do to make it mad at you because it IS you. What makes you happy makes Spirit happy. If you can keep digging to find what makes you happy, you can freely move towards that, trusting that Spirit has your back.

If you have a hard time trusting this, the work becomes locating the reasons you think you don't deserve to be happy. Why do you think that others' happiness should come before your own? Why do you think you shouldn't be happy?

There's a big difference between thinking a question, asking a question, and answering a question. Every prayer we pray is answered the moment we request it, the only reason we don't see it is that we have a list of reasons we think we don't deserve it. No matter how insignificant these reasons may seem, they can block us from receiving what is rightfully ours. Conversely, no matter how significant these reasons may be, it is still impossible for you to be on the Universe's bad side because there isn't a bad side to be on. Getting them down on paper is so difficult because the ego knows once we say it we'll realize how ridiculous it is. As long as these lies go unchecked in the shadows, they can grow bigger and scarier, like an urban legend told and retold. All that's needed to debunk it is a solid fact check, but we can avoid that for a lifetime.

If you're feeling 100% supported and in full awareness that God's got your back, carry on. But if you do not feel that 100%, let today be the day you clear the slate. When you first ask yourself, "Why do I think the Universe doesn't like me?" you might brush it off with an "I don't know." I encourage you to keep gently pushing yourself with "If I did know, what would the answer be..." until you reach a "Maybe it's because..." Face these fears head-on and forgive yourself. It's only fear.

So, if you're digging today - why do you think the Universe is mad at you? Free write.

Lesson 328:

All I have to do is ask.

Inside the vehicle of your physical body is your soul. The consciousness that is much older, much wiser, and much more experienced than your current physical incarnation. It has lived many long lives, and all of the wisdom garnered in these lives is at your disposal. Any question you could have, it has the answer to - all you have to do is ask.

Spirit, your higher Self, and your guides, aka your soul's BFFs can only intervene on your behalf if you ask for help. It would violate your free will if they offered unsolicited help. So, you have to ask, and when you get an answer, you need to trust it. How can you be sure it's your intuition when you're still getting started? How does the answer make you feel? Expansive? Relaxed? Prepared? Peaceful? Natural? That's a sign it's your intuition. Does it make you feel stressed, anxious, or like there's not enough time or money to make it happen - that's just fear talking.

Today, open your day by asking these questions from *A Course in Miracles*. If they resonate with you, you can make it a part of your daily routine. It's been a part of my morning routine for a long time.

Where would you have me go?

What would you have me do?

What would you have me say?

And to whom?

The answers will unfold as the day goes on because you remembered to ask.

Lesson 329:

I choose oneness over separation.

I performed an exorcism one time after assisting an elaborate exorcism rooted in the Ifa tradition. I went because I was scared shitless of demons after growing up in a cult that frequently ranted about the gravity of spiritual warfare, aka God and Satan battling furiously over control of my mind. I figured if I faced this fear head-on, it would have no power over me anymore. The exorcism I attended lasted about three hours, involved a chicken sacrifice and about $200 worth of strange ingredients, like Barbados rhum, bay leaves, palm oil, and dried fish. The second I got there, I understood what was going on - it's only fear. The subject stood outside afterward in a sopping-wet turban and a necklace soaked in chicken's blood, and I asked him how he was feeling. He looked upset. "It's still here," he said. This was his sixth exorcism, and exorcisms don't run cheap. My priestess friend asked me in Spanish to reason with him, that the issue was mental and there was no way this demon was still here. The spirit had gone into the chicken, and the chicken was now dead, killed bladelessly in the honest-to-God most humane way I had ever seen, under the priestess' foot. I told him and his associate: "My friend, listen to me. The demon is gone, if it's here, it's because you're keeping it here for some reason. Can you think of why you like its presence here?" He couldn't, so with the blessing of the priestess, I instructed him and his friend to sit with this question, and if he really couldn't figure it out, to call me, and I would take care of it. Three weeks later, I had my first exorcism appointment booked for 10 AM, and so it was. I tell you this story because it was the most extreme client I had ever had, one that involved me addressing my own deepest fears, and principles of oneness were how we resolved it. I met my husband earlier on that day, and in flirting with him missed my opportunity to meditate, which was the only thing I felt I needed to do to prepare.

He arrived at my house ten minutes early, and I started the recording, so he could replay the conversation in times of distress. I asked him to assign names to the two sides at war over his mind. Team A became God's team, and Team B was Satan's team. I asked him: "Which side is stronger, Team A or Team B?"

"Team A", he responded.

"Which side is on your side?" I asked.

"Team A", he responded, a smile creeping onto his aged face.

"So, what's the problem?" I asked "There isn't one", he said.

I stopped the clock. One minute, forty-two seconds.

We spent the next 40 minutes driving that point home until he knew it to be true, he went home laughing. I invite you to do the same. Even in the illusory world of duality, there is a clear conqueror. If you take the Bible literally, you get the story of God created Satan and would one day return to defeat him. He created evil and has always had the power to destroy it. We also know that God's forgiveness is absolute, and we can never be abandoned because God doesn't have a bad side (even though the Bible would try to convince us otherwise). Even in an illusion of dualism, oneness is the truth. God created Satan And so, it is a part of him.

Getting the story straight about your God not having a weak side is crucial if you will be outsourcing for your salvation. You don't want a God who can be defeated. You want to trust in God's adequacy as God, otherwise, you will have to worry about yourself AND God. To believe in an undefeatable God, he/she/it, negates the "evil" because as they say in Romans 8:13 "If God be for us, who can be against us?" If you release the need to separate yourself from the world by making yourself better or worse than humanity and release to separate the "them" from "us" by making "us" better or worse and adopt the idea that we're all one, and all God - then there cannot ever be anything that is against you. If nothing is against you, there is nothing to fear. If there is nothing to fear, anything is possible.

If there is nothing to fear, anything is possible.

Lesson 330:

I want what my Eternal Self wants for me.

The things you want also want you. Desires are foreshadowing. It is your Eternal Self, the part of you that sees your past, present, and future, whispering through time at you. It tells you via desire that this wish has already been granted and is in your future. By sending you a desire, it beckons at you to move towards it. Desire asks you to take the available steps so you can be a match to it when it manifests. For example, if you have a desire to be with someone in excellent physical shape, this isn't wrong, and it doesn't make you shallow. Desire is good! To be a match to this, you may have to train yourself. Why? Because if you don't understand what it's like to take excellent care of your body when the bae you've been manifesting wants to leave first thing in the morning to go hit the gym, you will bitch and moan about it. If they leave anyway, you'll be bummed, and if they don't, you'll sabotage your own dream of having a partner in excellent physical shape by encouraging them to stay in bed instead of training. Desire gives you an opportunity to start making yourself a match to what you want to manifest now, so you can receive it when it does.

What should you clear up to trust that the things you want also want you? And if the things you want aren't showing up and seem to be pulled away from you, how can you trust you might not want these things? That if you had them, you would block yourself from something that would make you happy in the long term. That you don't know what you want?

This is our work.

Lesson 331:

I choose again.

No matter how far we've gone with a fear-based, lack-based, or judgment-based thought - we always have the opportunity to choose again. When we notice that we're ragging on someone else (or ourselves!), stressing about what we think is missing from our lives, replaying past failures, or worrying about the future - we can always choose a different thought.

Human beings are the only species in the world who can change their biology with a thought. When we believe the untrue thoughts in our head, our whole body responds. We stop breathing with integrity and switch into the sympathetic nervous system - fight or flight mode. Blood rushes to our appendages, adrenaline pumps, and we feel reactive, stressed, anxious. As simply, when we choose a peaceful thought to believe, our whole body responds. Our breath becomes rich and spacious, our heart rate slows, our countenance softens, we relax into the parasympathetic nervous system. Our energy centers itself, and hormones like dopamine and oxytocin are released. We feel calm, peaceful, safe.

This works in the opposite direction too, if our body is relaxed, our mind will also relax.

One of the main ways we lose force (the essential energy our soul needs to direct us well) is by being in a state of physical tension. Stop right now and scan through your body. Are your shoulders soft or tense? Is your face frozen in a weird expression? Is one of your hands doing a weird grippy thing? Is your foot tapping?

The most relaxed person in the room has the most power. Additionally, the best directive for meditation is to JUST RELAX for a few minutes. If your body is in a relaxed state, stressed out, angry responses will not come out of your mouth.

The next time you get upset about something, or maybe you're embroiled in a difficult negotiation or conversation, notice how your body feels and do your best to relax it. You'll be astounded how the mind follows suit, and new options surface.

Today, when you catch yourself in a thought not serving you (remember, there are no neutral thoughts), stop yourself. Say out loud, "I choose again!," and select a thought that serves you better. It's never too late to choose again.

And again, if you catch yourself in a state of physical tension, no need to be upset! Just do your best to relax and see how things flow after that.

Lesson 332:

What my ego wants is not what I want.

Our ego is a mask of sorts, built during our lives. It is pretending to be us, and until recently we believed it. Incidents unfold in our lives, and we make up meaningful stories about these incidents we come to believe. A relationship that ended abruptly gets the storyline of "I'm commitment-phobic.." A friend who ultimately wasn't much of a friend in middle school humiliated you because of her own insecurities, the story becomes "I can't trust women.," maybe even "I can't trust anyone.," maybe even "She's right, and I'm worthless." These unchecked stories accumulate. Over time we get so used to our own false narrative we believe this ego identity is really us. Our unchecked identity has high demands which tint our prayers and desires without us even knowing it. From the ego perspective of the commitment-phobe, we pray for short-term gratification, perhaps attention from someone so unavailable it would be impossible to reach any commitment with them, thus perpetuating our false belief we cannot commit. We're convinced this story we wrote about ourselves is true, and we're attempting to use it as a foundation for manifesting.

Meanwhile, your heart of hearts, the Real You, knows that you aren't afraid of commitment and that your soul is crying out for a sacred relationship. Your manifesting of a zero-commitment relationship is not working, even though you can try to force it and end up exhausted and disappointed.

Your false identity has no birthright, no sound current, no manifesting ability because it's a fake avatar of you. This includes the negative identities you beat yourself up with aka "I'm such a failure," as well as the "spiritual" or "more lovable" identities you might conjure to be the face of your social media or coaching business, aka "I'm such a success!" The only you that can manifest, is the REAL you.

Today, and whenever you can remember, use this prayer to check yourself: "Thank you for bringing me what I need and protecting me from what I think I want."

In doing so you'll free up all the resistance towards what you want, and what your true Self needs to vibrate at your highest possible frequency can flow to you freely.

Lesson 333:
There are no justified resentments.

I used to believe resentments felt good. Especially group resentments, a bunch of us pissed at the same person. But it's a major block, I'm learning. The more you resent the more frequently the memories come up because you're focusing on it. I think it makes me happy, but I like nice things, and I want more of it. Resentments block me from receiving more nice things, and here's how:

Resentments are painful loops of memories from the past. Revisiting a resentment is focusing on the past. Miracles are only possible when you are present (appreciation being the fastest route there). As long as you have resentment, you cannot accurately manifest. Don't let your attachment to someone who already pissed you off be what blocks you from manifesting what's rightly yours.

When resentment comes up today, force yourself to drop it. Say either "I'm willing to see their innocence," "From now on I send you love." or "SPIRIT, help me!" Shift your attitude to appreciation by making mental gratitude lists. You're not letting them off the hook, you're letting you off the hook

Lesson 334:

We can't fight if we're on the same side.

It's amazing the stories of conflict we can cook up in our heads when we're on the defense. This isn't limited to people bumping into you on the subway, either. Oftentimes it will be the people nearest and dearest to us that can make a simple comment and we can twist the entire thing around and come back raging.

For example, my husband telling me that our son's head has gone wonky while he's napping on me. My shame kicks in, distorting the message. It hisses: "He's saying you're a bad mom. You are." I can't stand to hear anything shame ever has to say, it's never true and always horrible. But if I'm on the defense, I can find every reason to lash back. My thoughts are going haywire, looking for the right opportunity to catch him being an "awful parent," which just doesn't exist with him. I'm nitpicking out of defense. And what am I defending? A shame story that was never true. True stories need no defending because they will always be what they are - true. Doesn't matter how much you fight over it; the truth is the truth.

What's the truth in this situation? My partner loves our kid as much as I do, and like me, he wants to make sure he always has the best we can give. Just because my baby's head can be supported more, doesn't mean that I'm a bad mom. We are on the same side about the most important character in our lives. By defending myself against an attack he never made, I'm creating a conflict where there isn't one. When I remember we're on the same side, I have such peace knowing that there's an extra set of eyes on him. Good for me, for my husband, and for our son. If I make it a conflict through defense, it's bad for me, my husband, and our son.

Everyone in the entire world is struggling under the weight of their emotional pains and is doing the best they can. We all want the same things, to be loved (accepted)for exactly who we are. If you can use empathy to tap into the Universal suffering, you don't see society as something you must defend yourself against. If you know all anyone needs is love, that replaces any weapon of defense you thought you needed. When we're all on the same side, nothing can be against you.

Lesson 335:

I'm doing this for ME.

Why forgive?

Because until you forgive, you're focusing on the negative pattern the person habitually plays out for you. If you're focused on it, it must repeat because wherever awareness goes, energy flows. They are bound to hurt you again until you forgive them (even though fear says that if we forgive them, they'll just do it again). You're doing it for you. Also, if there's a pattern around you it's coming from within you. You can break it! You're doing it for you.

Focusing on someone's failures is obsessing about the past. You can't transcend time if you're only seeing the past. Miracles occur when you transcend time by living fully in the present. Don't let them keep you stuck! You're doing it for you.

If you're holding the past against someone else, you create a world where someone can hold it against you. Imagine on your wedding day when they ask if anyone has any objections, and the one person you cheated on in the 8th Grade jumps up and shouts: "I OBJECT! They're a cheater! Once a cheater, always a cheater!", and everyone believes them. It's the same thing. The recent past and the distant past are both as out of reach. Let it go. You're doing it for you.

Forgiveness lets you see the perfection in your history. You learned something. You met someone better. You became a better mom. You got rerouted. If you aren't holding onto a "terrible" past, you can trust your future will be just as beautiful. You're doing it for you.

No need to call them up, no need to wait for them to say, "I'm sorry." just so you can say, "I forgive you." - just cut to that! Plus, many people who hurt you will never apologize. Some are dead. Just because you don't get an explanation or apology doesn't mean you have to live with pain around that person. And it's condescending to ever tell anyone you've forgiven them. So, don't! You're doing it for you.

Lesson 336:

I am willing to see their innocence.

There have been resentments I've thought I loved hanging onto. Some are newer, from the last year. Some I thought I forgave already, but with renewed honesty came renewed anger. I can tell I'm holding onto it when the person crosses my mind, and after indulging in the wtf-ness about whatever I feel they did me so dirty with, I'll huff and puff and try to put them out of my head.

This doesn't make them go away. This "writing-off" process is not forgiveness. These black hole resentments that seem unsalvageable are the areas of life where we're resistant to forgiving.

We must ask: "Why do I want to be mad? Why does it feel better to hold a grudge than forgive? Why am I "not ready" to be free of this resentment if I know I'll feel transformed the second I do? What is the value of this grudge? What have I done that I consider unforgivable?"

This mantra is tough for me. Kind of like a naloxone shot will force all the opiates out of your system - this mantra will force resentment out of your system. That Pulp Fiction-style injection can save your life when you've overdosed, but the downside is that it's extremely, extremely uncomfortable. By affirming that you're willing to see the perpetrator's potential innocence in the situation, you will be shown - but that means your resentment won't have a pot to piss in anymore.

Naloxone, aka Narcan, is the Pulp Fiction style injection you give to someone overdosing on heroin. It's pretty uncomfortable for the person but better than dying. The discomfort comes from the naloxone pushing the heroin out of your body. It's an instant forced withdrawal. I call this mantra "spiritual naloxone" because when you use it, it's very uncomfortable, and it will push the resentment right out of your body.

Pick someone right now that you've felt so justified in resenting. Replay the scenario where you feel they did you the dirtiest. Look at that story and say to Spirit: "I am willing to see their innocence in this story. Please show me the story of their innocence."

You don't have to know the new story, being willing to see is enough.

Lesson 337:

We're all in this together.

A person free of defenses becomes aware of a world free of attack. Everyone to your left, and everyone to your right, in the buildings above you and in the tunnels beneath you and the whole entire cosmos are all on your side.

So, if this is true, what's up with the people you feel are attacking you? Briefly, you asked them to be here, on these terms, doing whatever they're doing, to alert you to what you most need to heal or most need to change to get the expansion you need to receive the gifts you most want. Sometimes this hurts a lot. We take it so personally and let the actions of one person act as a Universal message of hostility and spite, but it's not.

Through the most heavily disguised messengers and uncomfortable situations, I've learned crucial lessons in record time around boundaries, control, not knowing what I want, and more. In some cases, it took me years to see that it was happening for me, and not to me, because, ultimately, this whole show is about me - just like your whole life is about you. And the recognition of these instances as miracles were only made possible by, you guessed it! Forgiveness.

One day at a time is how we do this, all day, every day. <3

Lesson 338:

I never made a wrong turn.

Like obstacles are detours in the right direction, what you consider the wrong turns in your life were actually key steps towards your destiny.

I've learned way more by learning things my way, a.k.a. The Hard Way, than any book could have taught me. Sometimes I've had to learn in ways absolutely cringe-worthy, but I literally never made that mistake again.

So, today, extend all the gifts of your own forgiveness towards yourself. All that gunk you feel so bad about, things you've said and done, things you've not said and not done -release yourself from the cringe, the guilt, and the shame because that serves no one. The past is never coming back, and it wasn't "bad" if it brought you here.

Repeat after me:

I accept my own love and let myself off the hook. Today, and every day, I wake up with a clean slate, a little wiser, a little slower to react, and a little less likely to put up with your bullshit.

Lesson 339:

I am not my thoughts.

The choice of a thought can change our entire circumstance. Imagine you're walking through a forest. The sun is shining, the birds are chirping, the wind whispers through the trees, and you are in a state of complete peace, feeling safe and in unity with your surroundings. Then, out of nowhere, a thought flashes across your mind "This is mountain lion country. I'm not safe.." Suddenly, the woods don't seem so peaceful anymore. The bliss of solitude quickly boils into "if something happened, I'm helpless out here." Every sound you hear makes you jumpy. As you believe this thought more and more, your mind rushes to find evidence to support it. Every FOX News and urban legend connected to any wildcat attack on the planet come rushing to the forefront of your memory. Your heart races, you're on edge. You can't get home and under the covers fast enough. Now, nothing in the woods has changed, all that's happened is a fear-based thought came up, and you believed it. This one thought had the ability to change how you perceived everything.

You only have to think a thought for seventeen seconds for like-minded thought to join it. Going down the wormhole of one fear-based thought can quickly spin out into a tornado of anxiety.

But you're NOT your thoughts. They come and go, like clouds in the sky. Selecting a fear-based thought and attaching to it so fiercely that you can't see around it can keep you imprisoned in your own illusions. Instead of falling into the hole of the thought, can you step outside of yourself and observe it for what it is, just a thought?

No matter how deep in the fear you are, you can always choose a better thought. Always.

Lesson 340:

May I see all my choices.

This is the only prayer I pray, ever.

I used to think I knew what I wanted until I regularly started getting what I asked for, and it was not what I wanted at all. I'd pray for the strength to get through events I thought I needed to attend, and sure enough, I got the strength - but upon leaving, I realized I didn't need to be there, and in being there, had missed an event I would rather have been at. I prayed to get a spot on a podcast I really wanted to be a part of, and then I got it, and it was a disaster. When it was over, I wished I hadn't done it. Because I couldn't trust I was divinely guided to an event that would bring me the most joy and satisfaction, I would attempt to plan and control where I thought my life should go.

This prayer has now been extended to the whole world. I don't know someone "shouldn't" be sick right now, maybe it's what they need to learn how to slow down. I don't know someone "should" get a certain job, maybe it's not where they're meant to be right now. I don't know that two people engaged in a vicious and inebriated fistfight aren't getting exactly what they need. I don't know what I want or what anyone else needs, plus - whatever is meant to go down will. I don't need to attempt to control it.

I used to think I had no choice until I realized every thought was a choice. My suffering, shame, anxiety, and guilt - those were all choices. The need for approval, jealous thoughts, criticism of my own creativity - all of those were choices too. Even my opinion I was hated by the cosmos - that was a choice too. I don't want to pray a decision in for someone, and I don't want to control my own life anymore now that I know what it's like to let Spirit surprise me. All I want for myself or anyone else is to see all my options clearly so I can make the choice that feels best.

Lesson 341:

I release the need to suffer today.

Every day you have the choice to be free, but today you will take advantage of it!

When we zoom out of the shame, emotions, and story we assign to a regular old bump in the road - it's not that bad. Seeing it minus the drama allows us to get right to the core of the issue and strategize a solution way faster than if we allow ourselves to be put out by it. What's more, if we can see the issue for what it is - a crucial detour in the right direction, instead of feeling poorly at all, we can cut straight to an experience of gratitude. At first, it might take deep breaths and some creative optimism, but with time it will become reflexive, and that, my friend, is some serious fucking power to wield in your life.

Lesson 342:

I will not attack what keeps me safe.

Understanding you and God are one, or at least on the same side, is enough to protect you no matter how deeply embroiled in the issue you think you are. What's stronger than God? And God's on your side? What could there be to fear? Knowing that you're on God's team keeps you safe no matter what's going on. So, stop attacking yourself with self-deprecating thoughts. Drop the story. Whatever it is. Every time you say, "I am," you're invoking your own God powers, and whatever follows those two words, goes. If you say, "I am healthy. I am supported. I am enough. I am beautiful," so it will be. You're uplifting your true identity and keeping yourself safe. If you say, "I am a failure. I am not worthy. I am never enough. I am sick," so it will be.

When we put it into terms like "attacking our own safety," it seems so backward and futile, we would never agree to do it, but thoughts are sneaky. It can be so tempting to be hard on ourselves, wear ourselves down, and beat ourselves up. Why? Most of the time, we would never, ever treat others or speak to others the way we speak to and treat ourselves. It's time for that to change.

Write in eyeliner on your mirror, "Not one more nasty thing." You're permanently forbidding yourself to say one more nasty thing to yourself about who you are or how you are. Drop it, now. Remember who you really are, God.

Lesson 343:

The more I forgive, the more I know I'm forgiven.

If you're holding grudges against others for the big horrendous shit they've pulled in your life, you won't think forgiveness is possible for the big horrendous shit you've pulled in your life. As long as you do not forgive others, you're not forgiving yourself, and vice versa. You cannot extend forgiveness to others if you haven't experienced it for yourself.

If you haven't forgiven yourself for the horrendous shit you've pulled in your life, every time you hit an obstacle (and this will always happen in life), you'll interpret it as something going wrong. If you believe it shouldn't be happening, but it is, you'll look for what you did to deserve it on the list of things you haven't resolved with yourself. You can chase your tail here for decades, trying endlessly to get in the Universe's good graces again by any means necessary when you had never fallen from grace, to begin with.

You must forgive yourself. For all of it. And if you're struggling to forgive something you feel so awful about, forgive someone else for something huge. Make it a reality for yourself that huge things can be forgiven. By doing this, you'll erase your list of why you don't deserve it, and when that happens, you can finally receive all the blessings the Universe has been waiting to give you.

What is something awful someone else has done that you think is unforgivable?

Are you willing to see their innocence?

What is something awful you've done that you think is unforgivable?

Are you willing to see your innocence?

Lesson 344:

It's not a sacrifice if I don't want it.

Giving up alcohol was one of the hardest things for me until I realized I didn't want it. Scarcity increases value, and by telling myself there would be no more of it because I had to be sober as a spiritual teacher, I had created major scarcity around it. Through this lens of "it's coming to an end," I saw a distorted impression of value. It wasn't just "alcohol" I was giving up, it became "freedom, laissez-faire, independence, individuality, relaxation, sexiness, reward, being easygoing, delight," which seemed like a LOT to give up. That's why you can't shame yourself into sobriety or try to pretend like there will never be a substance in your path again. There always will be. If you've said, "I'm not allowed to have it.," it will be a battle every time it comes your way. If you say, "I don't want it.," it will be as easy as declining Auntie Barb's double-mayo macaroni salad.

I thought that alcohol was a major sacrifice I was making, and I wanted God to prove that it was worth it, that what I would get for my massive sacrifice would vale la pena, be worth the price. But God's not testing you, and you can't test God because you're playing yourself. You don't get a paycheck and a piñata for not doing what you know you shouldn't be doing, at least not right away. It's more subtle than that. You have to do it for you.

I quit drinking by applying the same rules as an elimination diet, a process I learned in nutrition school for identifying and removing undiagnosed food allergies. You remove what you know you shouldn't be eating, kind of like going cold turkey with alcohol, but you don't go into this detox saying you'll never have these foods again. Once you know what it's like to not eat trigger foods, you add them back in. In AA they would call this a relapse, which is why I don't AA anymore. As you add each of the trigger foods back in, you stay diagnostic about it. You keep a food journal, answering questions like "How does this make me feel?" "What symptoms do I feel?" "How do I feel the night of, the next day, after a week?. Without any shame whatsoever you identify if this is a food that you thought made you feel good, but once you really got down to it you found that it didn't make you feel good. If you like to feel good, and a habit consistently makes you feel bad, it becomes much easier to turn something down because you don't like the way it makes you feel. With alcohol, I thought each drink would send me into something comparable to a first-time molly experience, where I'd be tossing my hair and dancing with wild abandon with my best friends. Alcohol had never been like that, and it actually made me feel kind of tired and bummed out. I had been trying to quit for years, assuming it would be a sacrifice, and when I finally gave it up, it wasn't difficult, and I've been sober ever since.

What habit are you resistant to sacrificing? Is it a relationship that's been lukewarm for years? Weed? Attacking blackheads? How does the idea of cold turkey quitting make you feel like it's a huge thing to give up? How can you analyze how you feel about it? What truly makes you happy?

Lesson 345:

Freely I forgive, freely I receive forgiveness.

I met a friend at a restaurant once, one of those seafood places where you order at the counter and bring the number to your table. There were several unappealingly located two-tops and a large six-top in the middle. I spent over a decade in the service industry, so I understand how it works, but if you haven't had restaurant experience, it's difficult to see that every table is not fair game. The restaurant was not particularly busy, so my friend went ahead of me to stake the table and chose the six-top. He hadn't been seated more than a few moments when a runner came up to him and informed him he needed to move tables, as this larger table was reserved for larger parties. My friend pointed out that several other tables could be moved together and that the sign said: "Sit Anywhere." The runner held his ground, and after reminding the runner how frequently he attended this restaurant, my friend begrudgingly moved tables right as I was returning from the restroom.

I sat down, and my friend was at an 8. He had selected the restaurant and wanted me to like it, as we talked about food frequently. He hated the new table, as it was dangerously close to live children and away from the window. He was upset because he didn't recognize the runner and felt like he was being singled out and treated unfairly, given his attendance record and the money he had spent there over his visits. A single emissary for a party of five arrived and sat at the larger table, which pushed my friend over the edge. He signaled the runner over and demanded to know why someone else could sit where he had been forbidden.

By the time his food arrived, he was too mad to enjoy it. He attempted to order a beer from the runner, who informed him he would have to get back in the queue and order from the front. At this point, my friend was ready to leave and never come back. My friend said, "This always happens to me!" He was really the only person hurting in this situation; the runner probably says this 20 times a day and even seemed amused with how bent out of shape my poor friend had gotten.

What needs to be forgiven for all of this to go away?

If my friend could freely forgive the runner, on contact, without trying to get to the bottom of if it was "right" or "wrong," "fair" or "unfair," so much suffering could have been avoided. What started as an environmental issue (the state of the restaurant), quickly became personal (him vs. the runner), and escalated to Universal ("This always happens to me, everyone is out to get me, and it doesn't matter how "good" I am"). By resisting an opportunity to freely forgive someone, he kept himself under attack. If this thought pattern ended in "everyone is out to get me, there must be something wrong with me that forgiveness can't remedy." Psychologically this is turmoil, and it all can be avoided if you stop trying to determine if someone is worthy of forgiveness or not and fucking forgive them as soon as you notice you're upset. Be willing to see their innocence.

With a broadened perspective, you can often find out you were incorrect about something you were certain was right. So, maybe lose the idea that you know what's right or wrong, and attempt forgiveness every time you feel warranted to react. The beneficiary is you.

Lesson 346:

I forgive for me.

Are you convinced yet? How can you put this into action? Pick a person to forgive who you've been resistant to letting off the hook out of fear that they'll repeat the hurtful deed again.

Try to condense the action that they did into a statement, for example, I was treated unfairly by the runner at a restaurant, or she was spreading rumors about me that weren't true.

When you believe this thought, what false belief do you get escorted to? Some examples might be I never get what I want, It's not safe to be me, I should have been born a boy/girl, There's not enough time/love/money.

Scan your mind for a time in your life when you perpetrated the same hurtful deed to someone else. Be open to this. Have you ever talked about someone behind their back? Have you ever treated someone unfairly, even unintentionally?

Take your offenses and stack them next to the other's offense. Recognize that when you forgive them, you're forgiving you, and vice versa. Additionally, you're weakening a fear-based-and-false belief keeping you from progressing in your life.

You have nothing to lose, and everything to gain.

Let it go.

Lesson 347:

Be love.

Today I would like you to decide that every action you take will be an action that heals everyone it touches, no matter how hurt and broken they seem.

Everyone is doing the best they can with the information they have. Everyone is trying to cope with the emotional pain, childhood trauma, false beliefs, and the illusion of societal pressure and it's a wonder we all haven't offed ourselves yet.

Be gentle with the world. Release the need to be right, or first, or credited. Recognize that everyone just needs love and if that's all anyone needs be that for them.

Ask yourself with each person you come into contact with: How would I treat this person if I loved them? What would I say to them if I loved them?

Everything you give to the world will be given back to you, so give love away - because whether you know it or not, that's all you want, too.

Lesson 348:

I now allow the world to show up differently.

As long as you're determined to see people through the lens of "They did me wrong," they'll be obligated to do you wrong. Like the analogy we used at the beginning about me telling you my dinner date is on LSD. As long as you're attached to the backstory, you will only be able to see my dinner date as frying on LSD. Everything he does will seem suspicious and psychedelic- even if I tell you I was kidding. You will treat him differently, and the more you feed into the backstory, the more likely you are to be escorted to a deep false belief, for example, my dinner party is ruined, I never get to have nice things.

Let me make this clearer: until you forgive someone, they will be obligated to keep doing you wrong. If you forgive them, they can show up differently. Even if nothing changes about them, they were an asshole pre-forgiveness and are an asshole post-forgiveness - you can accept that about them. Instead of losing sleep, hoping they'll suddenly defy all odds and morph into an avatar of Mother Teresa and being racked with disappointment when they fail to; you can simply carry on with your life free of resentment. They've always been an asshole, so maybe they're not my date for the next wedding I attend. They can be an asshole, but it doesn't have to hurt me. They can be an asshole, and in a world constantly changing, I like that I can rely on them to be this way. Maybe once or twice a year, I can even find a way where their particular quirk can help me out? Or I can appreciate it because they're one of the only people I know that operate this way, and it's like watching a bad comedy.

The perfection of the world will never cease to impress you. This is how it's always been before you felt you had to change it to protect yourself. The time of protecting yourself is over. It may have served you in the past, but now you're safe. Now you're free.

Lesson 349:

There are no rational fears.

F-E-A-R = false evidence appearing real. You can throw 100% of your fears away. Simple, but difficult. We get so attached to feeling bad we want to believe certain fears are good and are keeping us safe. This is not the truth, and I guarantee you the only time you're looking at in this mindset is in the past, and that's a habit you want to get out of.

The good news is you don't have to fight this battle alone, you can ask Spirit to handle it for you. You don't have to journal it out or do trauma work on it, you can ask Spirit for help. I do this all day long! If you think it's bad with all the fears regarding you and your life, wait until you have a kid! My prayers look like, "Help me. Thank you. Help me. Thank you." All damn day.

If a feeling comes up that feels bad, then I assure you, it's coming from a place of fear, and you can file the entire thing under "G" (for Garbage).

If you figure this out and practice it actively, no matter how real external circumstance seems to be - you're good to go for life.

If it feels bad, it's not true. The bad feeling is your body rejecting what does not belong. Test it right now. Isolate your fear into a statement and ask yourself - "Is this true?"

It's only fear. You've got this.

Lesson 350:

I remove myself from the triangle.

The analogy of the triangle describes the three roles we feel compelled to fill when something is bothering us. I find this particularly true around family drama. The three roles are The Rescuer, The Victim, and The Judge.

For every discomfort, we habitually (not naturally) select which role fits us best, and then we toil under the weight of it. The goal is not to pick a better role, it's to step out of the triangle altogether. When we do this, we achieve COMPASSION. We are seeing as God sees.

Imagine if you were able to lovingly walk away from a conflict instead of getting involved and trying to figure out who's "right." You could do this small scale, i.e. with two co-workers, or you could do it on a large scale, i.e. with politics. What happens when you find out who's right? You get to walk away and sleep at night? Why don't you do that now?

Your natural state is unconditional love with yourself and others, so none of these roles will come naturally. They're just habits, and habits are the opposite of consciousness.

Lesson 351:

I choose to see miracles.

You will always, always, always be able to explain away a miracle if that's something you want to do. You can boil it down to "coincidence," "freaks of nature," or a "random" act of kindness. 11:11 is just a number. Money on the ground "could happen to anyone" and the clocks could be wrong when you arrive on time even though you were twenty minutes late in getting out of the door.

But if you want to prove every miracle isn't a miracle, that's the world you'll live in. When things get tough, and it looks like whatever the solution is, will have to be a miracle - you won't be able to rest with the statement, "I believe in miracles.." You'll be stressed out, and all you'll have to go on is a lukewarm memory of a few "random" things working out "by chance" in your past.

If you believe in miracles as a natural aspect of a friendly Universe, you can be in a bind and see 2:22 on a clock and be able to relax. Is it just a number? Sure, but you've given it meaning. You've made it a sign. So, when you see it, even if it "just so happens" to be that time, you can relax, knowing that it will all work out.

You'll never get proof of a miracle. I know someone whose mom beat cancer through powerful faith, and her kids roll their eyes and say that it was an incorrect diagnosis in the first place.

If you're determined to see miracles, you always will. If you're determined to see no miracles, you never will.

Lesson 352:

All judgment is a two-way street.

Every time you judge someone, you create an inroad of judgment right back to yourself. Remember I talked about that exorcism a few lessons back?

That person "got" a demon because someone he decided was bad energy passed it onto him. I asked what made him believe this person had a demon, and he described the hedonistic activities he had witnessed this man engaging in (on Facebook), the fact that he had been divorced multiple times, and his steady stream of girlfriends that showed up in his pictures. Because this man had judged his Facebook friend as being possessed as punishment for this lifestyle, he forced himself to believe in a world where divorce, dessert, and sex were punishable offenses.

Because everything we say about others, we could always say about ourselves, and it would be true one hundred percent of the time. The man now suffering from the contracted "demon" admitted to being divorced twice, indulging frequently enough, and enjoying a thriving sex life with his current girlfriend. He judged someone for the sins he was certain they were committing, and felt judged for the same choices he had also made. He was punishing himself, and no amount of exorcisms could make him stop.

In reality, none of this stuff was ever "wrong" in the first place. Had our friend stuck to a "live and let live" mentality, he would never have a vulnerability to this idea of punishment.

You only believe you're being judged when you're judging others, and you're the only person who will get bit by it - so quit that! Today.

Lesson 353:

As long as you're trying to "fix" them, you're not loving them.

I try not to use the word "love" all that much because I spent a long time trying to love myself and others based on what I had read and seen "love" portrayed as. I felt like I loved myself and the world, "in spite of" all the shortcomings I saw in myself and others. I assumed I had mastered a lesson when I hadn't even scratched the surface yet.

Loving yourself "even though" you're heavier than you've ever been isn't loving yourself. Why? Because it's loving yourself "even though" you have something you've decided is unlovable about yourself. It sends a subconscious message to your heart of hearts: "Well, at least you love yourself, cause no one else is going to with that belly of yours."

Loving a family member "even though" they're such a fuckup also isn't loving them. It's the same message, just slightly different. "Well, at least I love you because no one else would love all that crazy."

Love is acceptance as-is. Nothing more, nothing less. Accept that your pudgy belly could never change, and that's okay. There's nothing wrong with it, there's nothing wrong with you. Accept that you may have a family member who always has been and always will be a loose cannon, and in a world always changing, you can somewhat rely on them to be a loose cannon - and that's okay. Accepting someone as-is and accepting yourself as-is, that's love.

As long as you're trying to get someone to pick up a self-help book because you're determined to fix them, you do not love them, no matter how much you think you are. And as long as you're trying to change aspects of yourself into something you're convinced is more lovable - you do not love yourself.

What if it ain't broke? What if it's exactly how it's supposed to be?

Does this mean you're going to just give up and eat like shit and never get off the couch? Absolutely not. When you stop being so hard on yourself you'll actually want to do nourishing things for yourself out of love, not guilt. And when you stop trying to fix everyone around you, they'll have an opportunity to show up as-is, and it will be enough.

P.S.

Accepting where you are does not mean you'll be stuck there. It means you're releasing all the resistance towards your current state, and that resistance is what's actually kept you stuck there.

Lesson 354:

I see peace, I speak peace, I am peace.

The eyes are hardware but seeing is software - and software is programmable. If you are determined to see peace, you will. Today, judge nothing that occurs. Commit to vision today. "I choose to see peace instead of this."

The mouth is hardware, but how you use your voice is the software. It's possible to only use your voice for communicating peace. You could decide today that you will never start a fight again, ever. From this day on, you could never waste a word. Instead, every word you spoke could radiate peace.

Your body is the vehicle, but your consciousness is the driver, and the natural state of your consciousness is total and complete peace. You can BE peace, and your presence alone could instantly calm others without you saying a word. Your choice to be peaceful no matter what the external circumstances seem to warrant will silently teach everyone you come into contact with. By being calm in the face of adversity for yourself, you remind people of a choice they forgot existed in their life.

Sa Ta Na Ma - peace begins with me.

Lesson 355:

Love never fails.

A Course in Miracles says:

All communication is a cry for help or a loving response.

Underneath every outburst, every meltdown, every fit of rage is sadness. Sadness can be healed with one thing, love, which, as I've defined before, is just accepting someone no matter how crazy they're being. No matter how voluminous the explosion is, underneath it is a simple sadness, a sense of separation. No matter how upset they are, love can heal it.

Hurt people hurt people, and it can be the toughest thing to love someone when they've hurt you deeply. It takes a lot of courage to open yourself up to their side of the story. The side of them that has been used and abused so many times that all it knows now is a series of defense mechanisms, ready to be fired at anyone close enough.

If you can empathize with their pain and love them instead of demanding that they get over it and treat people better - then they have a chance of healing. It's always the solution; it always works.

This is particularly true with our parents. Often we're too busy focusing on the way we feel they let us down to ask them about their own upbringing. It only takes a few minutes of listening to your parents' stories to find out that a hurt cycle in place didn't just start with you. They were hurt by their parents, and their parents by their parents, and so on and so forth. Because we can't seem to trace where this original hurt came from, we must love them all, and the whole world, too, while we're at it. We're a bunch of hurt children doing our best, and we all need love.

Lesson 356:

I am unlimited.

Everything you see reflects your own beliefs. If you don't like what you see, change your beliefs. There are no limits to what you can create if you are determined to see and take as many steps as you can into creating and reinforcing new, supportive beliefs.

Anything is possible, and whatever you focus on will solidify into reality, so make sure you're focusing on the best-case scenarios and not the worst.

There are no limits, so see no limits when you dream for your life. Don't tell yourself why something wouldn't work or reasons it couldn't happen - there are no limits. If you convince yourself there are, you'll settle for sub-par experiences when you could have it all. No need to explain to the Universe how it could or could not work. It's always going to surprise you, so dream bigger than big and see no limits in your brave new world.

See no limits.

Lesson 357:

I choose to remember my wholeness.

It's funny the way we fall in love with the idea of being broken. We become totally comfortable in a state of discomfort. Because we cling to our stories and are desperate to belong to someone or something, we identify with illness instead of risking being the only person we know who says: "There is nothing wrong with me, I am perfectly whole."

In verse 71 of the Tao Te Ching, Lao Tzu states: "If one is sick of sickness, one is not sick."

Are you sick of being sick, or have you gotten used to it?

Here's a true statement that pisses off 99% of the people who hear it: "The only reason you're stuck where you are is that on some level, you're comfortable there."

What don't you have to try if you are broken? What story gets to stay alive? Here are a few examples:

"I'm not lovable as I am, something has to change first." "_____ is possible for everyone, but me." "I should have been born a boy/girl."

"I'm not supposed/allowed to be healthy/wealthy/loved."

You decide what stays and what goes in this world, and with practice, you make it manifest faster and faster. I thought I was sick of living off under $20 a week, but not sick enough of it to get sober and get out of my comfort zone by reading some damn business books instead of smoking weed and hoping that manifesting clients would be enough. I thought I was sick of not getting what I wanted in relationships, but not sick enough of it to say outright - "I'm not tolerating less than the best. Not from myself and not from others. I am good."

As long as the "No matter what I do, I'll always be broke." story stayed alive, I didn't have to push myself to the next level. I could stay indoors rolling blunts and crying about nothing working out in my life. As long as "No one will ever love me." was alive I didn't have to learn how to accept myself, or dump anyone. I could live off emotional scraps and feel jealous of everyone else who ordered whatever they wanted off the menu and sent back what wasn't up to snuff. Can you get clear about where it is you feel like you're stuck, and be willing to answer why you feel comfortable there? Can you find what the value of the discomfort is? Can you get sick of being sick?

It's deep-diving work, but if you can do it, the next level is waiting for you.

Lesson 358:

We'll all meet up at the truth.

Only something that isn't true needs defending. You only need to vent or have something validated when you did something you know was out of integrity, and you'd rather pull someone else in for a second opinion than being integrity to it.

It doesn't matter how you or anyone else feels about the truth, the truth is the truth, and everything eventually will boil down to the truth. The truth needs no defending because no matter how hard you try to defend it or who you get to back you up, a lie will never be true. And when the dust settles, we'll all meet up at the truth.

Cross your t's and dot your i's for life by committing to never tell a lie. To speak truthfully from this moment onwards, free of embellishments or elaborations - just the truth.

Recognize that the only person whose motives you can be sure of are your own, so you cannot rest assured that you're speaking the truth if you're talking about someone else, especially if they're not present in the conversation. You would only be talking about your assumptions, which might not be true.

If any story of yours is obscuring the truth, you won't be able to step away when drama is going down in the workplace, in your relationships, or at home because you'll feel like there are a couple of floors you built that will have to crash down before inevitably landing at The Truth. Conversely, if you only speak the truth, when drama is going down you can easily step away without giving it any life. You'll know that you've already gotten to the bottom of the situation and that eventually, everyone will meet you there. It's such an amazing tool, especially if you feel like drama chases you.

Honesty is the best policy, trust me.

Lesson 359:

I am guaranteed an answer if I remember to ask.

One of the greatest granfalloons (to quote Vonnegut, again) is this idea that we "don't have time to ask.."

So, we do have time to throw shit to the wall all day long hoping something sticks and that we're on the right path, but not to take a few minutes to get precise direction?

We have time to go against what feels right because we think it's what we're "supposed" to be doing for months, maybe years on end, but we don't have time to stop for one second and listen to our heart?

We have time to get all worked up from swimming against the tide because we don't know which way the flow is going and therefore cannot go with it, but we don't have time to take a couple of breaths and align ourselves with the energy of the day?

You will never NOT get an answer if you be still and ask. It may not come within five minutes, but it will come to you as the day progresses if, and only if, you remember to ask.

You're almost done with this book, so I encourage you to take this practice with you for the rest of your life.

Before you do anything in the morning, pause and take a couple of breaths. Ask these questions from *A Course in Miracles*:

Where would you have me go?

What would you have me do?

What would you have me say?

And to whom?

An old Buddhist saying is: "Meditate for ten minutes a day unless you don't have time. Then you must meditate for twenty minutes."

You can make everything so much simpler if you remember to ask.

Lesson 360:

Peace is all I want.

Bottom line: Peace is the best.

You want a sacred relationship so that you can finally know that you're loved and you can experience peace.

You want more money so you never have to worry about paying bills again and can experience peace.

You want to be healed of every ailment, mental and physical, so that when you go to bed and wake up in the morning, you have peace of mind.

Whatever it is you think you want, it's leading you to peace, and you can CHOOSE to experience peace now without needing to change anything outside of you at all.

The second you ask to see peace, it is granted. With just three minutes of controlled breathing, you can actually change your biology, and release hormones that make you feel genuine peace.

Here's a little extra meditation for you, from the Kundalini Yoga practice. It's one of my favorite ways to shift a mood fast and is a great set up for bedtime.

Inhale in four sniffs, to the mental rhythm of SA TA NA MA

Then hold for sixteen counts, mentally chanting four repetitions of SA TA NA MA

Then exhale all the air in two sharp exhales out of the mouth, to the mental sound of WAHE GURU

Sa Ta Na Ma means "Peace begins with me." and Wahe Guru means something like "Wow, God!"

Do this until you feel your energy shift, for a timed duration of three, seven, or eleven minutes, or until you fall asleep :)

Lesson 361:

I give peace freely; I receive peace freely.

Have you ever met someone with really good energy that made you feel really good just by being around them? That person was radiating peace, and you can do it too!

Having spent the last year studying what it's like to trust that the Universe is conspiring on your behalf and that everything that happens to you is the best thing that can happen to you, can you now put that into action and share it with anyone that comes to you?

When everyone else is panicking, can you stay calm, face smooth, eyes lit? When everyone else is hustling and bustling at rush hour, can you step lightly, appreciating the buzz of the city and the stories that unfold in every moment? Can you allow others to cut ahead of you in long lines, knowing that in every moment, you are exactly where you're supposed to be?

Can you double the dosage of peace in your life by giving the gift of peaceful presence to everyone in your path? The peace of the Universe works like a bartender that loves you, and every time you offer someone a sip of your peace, your glass is topped off anew and even runs over.

I promise you, people will be magnetized by your grace. You will be the one that people say, "You have such good energy" too. People will cross streets to talk to you. Children will gaze and smile at you, recognizing a fellow peacemaker. You'll hear "Wow" a lot.

If we've already established peace is the best, by radiating the peace that began with you, you will have that intangible je nais sais quois about you, and everyone will want a bit. Lucky for you, every time you share it, you get double back, and you have all the tools now to teach others how to do the same.

Enjoy it.

Lesson 362:

I surrender to the bigger picture.

Surrendering means releasing your need to control how things go. Releasing means you are letting go completely. You're either holding on or letting go, and if you're holding on just a little bit, you're holding on all the way.

This takes an enormous amount of trust, I know. If you let go of the rope of control, you're sure you'll fall, and you have no proof that something will catch you. It's a veritable leap of faith, and it's scary the first few times you do it, but you will not know what it's like to be caught, supported, and loved by the cosmos until you do.

A life without knowing how much the Universe has your back is no life at all.

Everything you think you want for the future is based on the options you can see right now, and you cannot see the whole picture no matter how much you think you can. There are things that will bring you so much joy you have not even seen yet, you can't even fathom them for yourself. You haven't seen all your options yet, and some of the things you're absolutely convinced you need to be happy are so wrong for you and getting them would block you from what would make you truly happy. This is especially true with big commitments, like a relationship, mortgage on a house, or job.

Can you surrender to an idea of yourself and your life that is bigger than you can see right now? Can you let go of your expectations and say, "Surprise me?" Can you release the fear that if you're not controlling everything, you'll end up disappointed and lacking in your life?

Letting go of certain things you're sure you need to have can be very hard, and I know this. Accepting that people were wrong for me, jobs I interviewed hard for were not the right fit for me, or that certain living situations were just not going to work out brought me to tears many a time; but the life I have now is beyond anything I ever thought I deserved or could have. I never thought I could be this fortunate in my life, but Spirit knew it, and I'm so profoundly grateful that I didn't get all those things I was sure I wanted.

When God shuts a door, she opens a window. It's habitual for us to see a shut door and be so upset. We'll demand to know where the window is and how it compares to the door before we're grateful for it. That's not how it works. Gratitude is the window. If you can be grateful for the shut door, as soon as possible, you get through the window. I know you want to walk through a door like a "normal" person sometimes, but the door opens to the street, and the window opens to the sky. The bigger picture. Trust me; you want the sky.

Ask:

What am I convinced I need to be happy right now?

_____

_____

_____

_____

_____

_____

What am I afraid will happen if I let go of my need to have this?

_____

_____

_____

_____

_____

_____

Is this feeling based on love or fear?

_____

_____

_____

_____

_____

_____

Do you want to stay afraid?

Lesson 363:

I visualize success for everyone I see.

Every thought you have about anyone (including yourself) creates the world you want to see. Because we're now exposed to more people than ever through social media, we have the opportunity to judge and make assumptions even more.

You can imagine a model as having an eating disorder, and a world where you must hurt yourself to be slim will become more real for you.

You could see someone who was a train wreck in high school talking about spirituality and imagine that they're faking it, and a world where you cannot turn your life around in one holy instant will become more true for you.

You could worry about a friend or family member living alternatively and imagine that they're with the wrong person, recklessly making choices they'll regret, and maybe "losing it," and a world that will not allow you to step outside of your box freely will become more true for you.

You could judge a celebrity's spending choices as being overindulgent, selfish, or just plain stupid, and a world where you cannot be rich without being an asshole will become more true for you. This one is dicey because you'll be cornering yourself into believing you must choose between being "a good person" or rich.

Can you bless every person you see by assuming that everything in their life is perfect because everything in the world is perfectly placed? Can you use your energetic velocity for a positive mindset versus praying for a hostile world where people have hidden agendas, selfish intentions and are in danger?

Anything you wish for others, you wish for yourself, and, like my husband always says:

"Every thought is a prayer."

Pray wisely.

Lesson 364:

God knows who I am.

And God loves you. God knows you'll eat bread even though you swore you would never touch it again, and God loves you. God knows what you looked like at your smallest and your largest, and God sees no difference, God just loves you. God knows you were a little asshole when you were younger, and God loves you.

God knows everything you've tried to hide and everything you think is so unlovable, and God loves you. There is nothing stronger anywhere than God and this force, he/she/it, dark matter, the Universe, whatever you want to call it - this power is on your side, and it loves you more than you could ever imagine you loving anyone.

I'd like you to please set a timer for three minutes on your phone and sit down with your left hand over your sternum and your right hand on top. I would like you to breathe deeply and feel your breath at your heart center, right under your hands. While you breathe here, I would like you to allow yourself to think of all the times in your life you have felt love. This might be very emotional for you because sometimes we have loved and we have lost, and it hurt so much it made us never want to love again. You may have many instances, and you may struggle to find any at all - but whatever it is, keep that little flame alive for these three minutes and let it get bigger and bigger. With each breath, imagine a white orb under your hands growing bigger and bigger with each inhale. When the timer goes off, visualize yourself throwing this orb up into the starriest night sky, where it lands and becomes a twinkling star. That little star you threw into the sky is all the love you know, and all the stars that you can see in the sky and beyond is how much the Universe loves you back.

This might be an overwhelming idea for you, but let it change the way you see the night sky. Every single star is looking back at you and saying: "You are a masterpiece, and we are all rooting for you.."

It's true. I promise.

Lesson 365:

Serve with love.

You've learned so much over the last year, and now as you go forward, you have the chance to change lives without saying a word.

Life is art, and you have the opportunity to make every interaction a work of art.

Everything will go out of style except kindness.

You can take an ordinary experience like getting your morning coffee and elevate it to the most memorable time of someone's life.

Maya Angelou says, "No one will remember what you say, they'll only remember how you made them feel," and the most memorable feeling anyone can experience is unconditional love.

You don't have to go around handing out free hugs or dialing random numbers saying, "Hi, I love you, pass it on," although you could if you wanted to.

Or you could simply take a couple of breaths before you get out of bed to remember that everyone in the world is doing the best they can, and like you, they're trying their best with the cards they've been dealt today. Empathize with the Universal suffering because you know what it's like to suffer, you know what it's like to feel alone. Fill your heart with love and then say to the Universe, "Bring me who you would have me serve.." I even made a post-it that said that and put it on my door, so I would read it every day on the way out.

The bottom of every person's discomfort is rooted in a sense of aloneness, and that can be cured with love. By being slow to react, gentle, generous, and kind to everyone that crosses your path, you will radiate love in all directions. You will heal the suffering people didn't know they had, and this will make every interaction you have indelible. Magical. Art.

Go Forth and Conquer: So, be it.

Every prayer is answered the second we pray it, and in some pagan traditions, you end prayer with "So, be it."

This statement affirms that what you say goes. I believe it is a double entendre because your world is a manifestation of what you are and what your beliefs are. Whatever it is that you want to see changed in the world must begin with you.

As above, so below. As within, so without.

Would you like to see world peace?

So, be it.

Would you like to see the end to poverty mindset and a world flush with abundance? So, be it.

Would you like to see a world free of jealousy, judgment, comparison, and bullying? So, be it.

Would you like to see a world where everyone, everywhere is accepted and loved exactly as they are?

So, be it.

You've learned a lot here, and it's been an honor to teach you. Thank you for being willing to see choices you forgot existed and having the courage to question what you always assumed was true.

Love created you loving, and kindness created you kind.

So, be it.

Bonuses:

I wanted to make sure you had as many resources as possible to help you complete this book. If you go to mamionami.com/365bookbonus , you'll see multiple treasures with your name on them.

First of all, access to this book in my app, where you'll be able to continue your studies when you're traveling without having to tote a book around. All of the lessons are there for you.

We also have a virtual book club, with live calls you can access, and a chat room where you can meet other people waking up on your same timeline. It's also a great place to start to flex your spiritual muscles privately. You master things when you talk about them, but it can be really hard to start talking about this kind of stuff in a friend circle that has only ever known you as a Muggle.

I made this especially for you, and all of these little bonuses are here to make your experience easier and more fun. I hope you enjoy it.